Angels and ~~Demons~~
that Play

A Musical Memoir

Paul Sears

Angels and Demons that Play: A Musical Memoir

Print ISBN 978-1-949267-18-1
ebook ISBN 978-1-949267-19-8

Front Cover and Cartoon Illustrations by Nick Prol
Cover Design by Guy D. Corp
www.GrafixCorp.com

Rear cover photograph by Laurence Lynn
Front matter photograph by Cat Brown

STAIRWAY PRESS—APACHE JUNCTION

STAIRWAY≡PRESS

www.StairwayPress.com
1000 West Apache Trail, Suite 126
Apache Junction, AZ 85120 USA

Dedication

For Deb, Rowan, Adrian, Vicki and Niall

Introduction

THIS IS A book about my musical experiences, influences, and opinions. It is for entertainment purposes and is not presented as an absolutely factual or fully accurate history.

It is my best effort from memory.

It is not an autobiography. Except for the music stuff, a lot of stuff in my life would be a boring, depressing read. Instead, I offer a mostly chronological narrative about my life in music—with the occasional foray elsewhere. Some of it is jumbled date-wise because of the many connections from different times. Think of it as a low-rent version of Frank Zappa's Conceptual Continuity. It is written entirely from my incomplete (oldmanititus has set in) memory and includes comments from many friends and collaborators.

Among the contributors are four actual journalists and published writers; Jamil Guellal, John Paige, Ted White aka Doctor Progresso and Michael Layne Heath. Additionally, Jamil, Ted, and John were all DJs at one time on WGTB-FM in Washington, DC during the 1970s.

The title is a nod of respect to, and a variation of the title of the great 1960s record entitled "Angels and Demons at Play" by

Sun Ra and his Myth Science Arkestra.

Special thanks go to Nick Prol, who provided the wonderful cover art and great cartoons. Thanks go to Guy Corp (www.GrafixCorp.com) for the CD artwork.

Thanks also to my very supportive wife Deb. There's no way would I be where I am in life without her.

I have been thinking of doing this book project for years, but it was Chad Hutchinson, a friend and co-founder of the popular NEARfest progressive rock festival in Pennsylvania who sealed the deal—he got tired of hearing my wacky stories a few years back, and said, "Just write a book, willya?"

So I did.

I treated this book project as kind of a casual "I'll do it someday DIY project" until an actual publisher dropped on my lap a couple of years ago and expressed real interest in doing it all good and proper.

Towering thanks are owed to Ken Coffman and Stairway Press for support and encouragement.[1]

Credits and Cadre of Contributors

Proofing: Judy (MacNiven) Prantl

Contributors:
Steven Feigenbaum
Jamil Guellal
Tom Scott
Michael Layne Heath
Ted White aka Doctor Progresso

---

[1] Publisher's Note: And cash. Giant wads of cash.

John Paige
Jon Brayton aka Mystr Treefrog
Judy (MacNiven) Prantl
Russ Strahan
Jon Gibson
Bob Siegel
Bruce Hellington
Adrian Bronson aka Cosmos Organon
John Hage
E. Doctor Smith aka Eric Smith

The views expressed herein by all the contributors are solely theirs.

Also, thanks are due to some fine folks that have been a help to me over the years: Susan Webb, Kara Jensen, Steve and Joyce Feigenbaum, Shawn and Lynn Pruitt, Sandra Galejs, Ken Newman, Mike Bloom, Mike Ostrich, Guy Segers, George Daoust (RIP), Keyes Elliott, The Bees family, the Progday, NEARfest, and RIO France festivals, Geoff Wright, Doug Mendelson, Bruce Oliver, Mark Klieger, Caroline Forsyth, The Muffins, Michel and Rosine Bessett, Joe Downs, Mike Potter, Katina (Bovis) Conn, Ken Rick, Roy and Julie Amador, Heather Hanford, Colin Thomure, John Logan, Steve and Shirley Holmquist, WGTB-FM, Rich Mueller, Lynnette Shelley, Archie Patterson, (Eurock), the Bethel and Preusser families, John and Jesse Davidson, Bruce Hellington, Bruce Gallanter, Glenn Max, Judy (MacNiven) Prantl, Jamil Guellal and wife Momo, Danny McClure (RIP) and Giorgio Gomelsky (RIP).

About Paul Sears

BORN IN WASHINGTON, DC in 1953 and currently living in Superior, Arizona, Paul is the son of Lawrence Sears (1925-1983), a prominent music critic, organist, pipe organ consultant and teacher in Washington, DC from the late 1950s until the 1980s, and Doris Sears (1925-1991), an amateur vocalist and pianist.

Both parents hail from Coatesville, Pennsylvania. Paul started by playing the trumpet and autoharp and during the early 1960s, experimented with guitar and bass, before settling on the drums during 1967. Influenced by all the music he grew up with and the burgeoning Washington, DC local rock music scene, he began to play in rock bands in 1968 and bands that wrote and arranged all their own material by 1972.

Since then he has played/and or recorded with The Muffins, and other well-known musos including Andy West, Don Preston, Bunk Gardner, Fred Frith, John Greaves, Peter Blegvad, Daevid Allen, Jerry Goodman, T.S. Henry Webb, Al Bouchard, Judy Dyble, Steve Hillage, Karda Estra, Pepe Gonzalez, Thee Maximalists, Cyndee Lee Rule, 9353, Bernie Wandel, Henry Kaiser, David Byers, Bill Laswell, Yochk'o Seffer, Present, Cyrille Verdeaux's Clearlight, Marshall Allen and Knoel Scott, Mike Keneally, Harvey Bainbridge, Morglbl, The Red Masque and many others.

He continues to record in his Arizona studio, Garage Mahal, and plays out both in the U.S. and occasionally abroad. He is also a broadcaster since 2014, weekly presenting The Paul Sears Radio Hour as part of the popular Prog Rock Diner cable and Internet progressive rock show on Radio Fairfax in Virginia. He has also appeared on KOTO-FM, in Telluride CO.

Paul Sears photograph credit: Cat Brown

1955-1967—Setting the Stage

SOME OF MY earliest memories are from my parent's apartment near Fort Belvoir, Virginia, and include music being played all the time, and a large acoustic guitar lying around that belonged to a friend. Of course it looked big; I was freaking crawling—I was around two-years-old. Both of my parents were from Coatesville, in eastern Pennsylvania. They were raised there, and attended Coatesville High school. I found out much later that the famous true crime writer Ann Rule went to that school with my parents in the 1940s.

After my folks were married, they moved to Virginia to seek work in DC where my dad had job leads. From 1952-1955, they lived in an apartment near Fort Belvoir close to Alexandria, VA. I was born in 1953 in Washington, DC. My godfather was Mario Segreti, who sang sometimes in my dad's men's choir, and later owned Mario's Carryout on River Road in Bethesda, MD. I was *really surprised* to find out this year, 2018, that there is a "Mario's Carryout on River Road" page on Facebook with 300 members. I joined, of course. That guy was my godfather.

From when I was VERY little I can recall music being in the house, and my parents had an upright piano which they both played. But, back to the guitar—my parents had a friend who played acoustic guitar. The friend would lay this thing down on the floor on its back so I could crawl over to it and fiddle with the strings. This really fascinated me; the noises I could make. I was avant-garde even at two.

In 1955, we moved to a house on Military Road in Washington, DC. My parents nearly always had something playing on the Magnavox or would be playing a piano and singing the popular tunes of the day, liturgical music. German and Italian operas, organ music, even some Edith Piaf, and later, stuff like *Sound of Music*, Leonard Bernstein and Gershwin were popular in our home.

My dad secured employment in the mid-1950s as the organist and choirmaster at The Shrine of The Most Blessed Sacrament Church, a Catholic church with an associated school next to Chevy Chase Circle, about eight blocks from our new house—a twenty minute walk, tops. He remained in their part time employ until he became too ill to work in the 1980s. He was also a music critic for the Evening Star aka Washington Star-News, a Washington, DC newspaper. Blessed Sacrament School next to the shrine provided a large choirboy pool.

During August of 1957, my little sister Marianne arrived. My sister and I attended Blessed Sacrament School, the Catholic school connected to the church my dad worked for. I didn't know it at the time of course, but this school was private and full of kids from mostly very well-off families. My sister and I would not have been able to attend this (still) expensive school if our dad did not work there. Unlike public and most other schools of the day it had one attribute I did not appreciate until later: *The sons and daughters of diplomats from many countries attended this school, and so, many countries and cultures were represented there.*

I got used to hanging around with kids of all colors from many countries and cultures from kindergarten on up through 6th grade. I thought everyone grew up with Technicolor friends—kids from Saudi Arabia, all over Europe, Guatemala, Venezuela, Soviet Union, and African and Asian countries.

Many kids were connected to, or were from, embassy families. It was a WASPy and very white Catholic demographic. Some of these families were large, with many children. Families with seven or more kids were common in our neighborhood of

Chevy Chase, DC. Two doors down from us, there was a family with nine kids and one with seven girls three doors in the other direction. That, I thought, was okay. One family in the hood had fifteen kids. With just my sister and myself, we were an anomaly.

It was here at this Catholic school, when I was in 3rd or 4th grade, that my father decided it might be a good idea—and make him look better—to put me on display at the church and school as some kind of musician.

His first plan did not work.

He encouraged me to study music, and tried beat the piano and organ into me. (I did end up taking tap dance lessons and earnestly tried the trumpet by the 4th grade.) My dad had a nasty temper and even less patience than me, so the first endeavor to force-feed me the piano was unsuccessful and dreadful. I also HAD to join the boy's choir, which I loathed because…

(a) I did not care for too much of the music, and…

(b) …the other kids razzed me incessantly because my old man was the choirmaster.

(c) I have never been much of a singer.

I felt bad for some of the kids in the choir, as my dad would get pissed off enough to actually throw hymnals at them once in awhile. He could be the Buddy Rich of school choirmasters. Buddy was well known for verbally eviscerating his bands. "Whaddya sing? CLAMS?" Look up the famous Buddy Rich rants on the web.

It was a bad situation for a kid trying to find peace and individuality. Add that this school was staffed and run by a convent full of fire-breathing nuns.

For example, Sister Mildred, 4th grade I think, got so pissed off that she put her fist through a windowpane while yelling at some poor sap. Mind you, these windows were the old thick non-safety glass (which had not been invented yet) with *chicken wire* embedded within the panes. Hard core.

Oh, yeah, in kindergarten or first grade I nearly qualified for an exorcism by writing with my LEFT hand. I was made to learn with my right, enforced by having my knuckles whacked with a ruler. This was 1958 or 1959.

This forced distortion of perspective MAY be a reason why, when I started to play the drums, I played—and still play—the ride cymbal with my left hand and have the drums going to the right; I don't know. It just seemed natural to put the ride cymbal right next to the hi hat and use the left hand for both.

More on drums later.

I ended up not hanging out with Blessed Sacrament kids too much—many of these large Catholic families had kids that were into sports, Boy Scouts and were from legal, Government and/or military oriented families, and so we had little in common. They had a Boy Scout troop based near there, and my parents knew these same kids were the very same ones spray painting the school and involved in all sorts of Halloweenish minor vandalism and other rapscallionry.

Some of the homes in our area were rented to guvvy types and we would get new neighbors every time the administration changed. My parents kept me at home listening to music and going to operas and theatre events such as *The Play of Daniel*, organ concerts, symphonies, ballets and so on. I must have seen the *Play of Daniel* five or six times.

Concerts at various waterfronts by the Potomac River were common back then. When my dad had his music critic helmet on, he would take me along to whatever the concert was, then sometimes over to the Star offices and write the review, which he would have me proofread. Sometimes we were there long enough to watch the huge presses generate the next day's paper.

Pretty cool.

I thought this practice of keeping me off the streets was a little weird when I was a kid, but in hindsight was a wonderful way to keep me out of trouble and inculcate my young brain with good stuff.

It worked.

By my late teens I had been exposed to a ton of different music and today, I am very thankful for my parents keeping me away from kids with mostly mundane habits. Other than riding bikes or playing ball and Frisbee in the numerous alleys around there, I did not hang out with them too much, but Go-karts and mini-bikes did occur. There is a great network of alleys in those neighborhoods. I still don't think they have been mapped. I can remember going most of the way from Chevy Chase, DC to Tenleytown and beyond without using streets other than crossing them.

Knowledge of these alleys came in very handy when the cops were on the tail of your mini-bike or go-kart.

Our music teacher was Sister Louise Cecile, who by about 5th grade was in my court and told me NOT TO listen to my parents or anyone else, and TO play autoharp, trombone, drums, trumpet, or join a damned circus and train tigers and do what I wanted—which I thought was really pretty cool.

She had a great sense of humor, a big heart, and would have been great in a Harry Potter-type movie or even a sci-fi flick. I used to go back and visit her later in life until the convent was either cut back or she retired, I forget. She was a sweet human being, and was in her 60s around 1965, I would go to the convent door during the early 1970s, dressed in leathers, long hair, earring, etc. and ask for her, and they would go "WHAAAAT in god's name...?" and she would come out, hug me and we would talk for a few minutes and get caught up. She was the one and only free-spirited sort of rebel nun I ever met. The students loved her. Getting ahead of myself here...I left BS—as we called it—just after 6th grade.

Blessed Sacrament Church also had a summer camp for the boy's choir. For several years starting about 1961, the whole choir, maybe twenty grade school kids would pile into a mid-sized school bus and several cars and caravan with parents and counselors to Camp Read—which was near Dares Beach, Maryland—for a week or two every summer.

Great.

Now I was cooped up with my parents AND the choir with mandatory choir practice every day and no escape. By then I had met some kid musicians. Because my dad was THE BOSS, our family got the only real house there, and the rest of the entourage stayed in a large bunkhouse a little ways up the dirt road on the property, which at the time, I think, was owned by our local diocese. I have many pleasant memories of Dares and other nearby beaches on the Chesapeake Bay.

The church owned a reel-to reel tape deck, which may have been a Roberts or Grundig. It had seven-inch reels and had an internal tube amp and fold-out speakers. This thing ran hot enough to heat a room. We got the el-cheapo Shamrock tape in the green boxes from the local Drug Fair on Connecticut Ave, and Scotch in the red plaid boxes. In those days these would be either in five-inch or seven-inch reels.

Angels and Demons that Play

What did we know about tape?

In those days, the local barber shop in the "Arcade" on Connecticut Ave even had, get this, a vacuum tube tester. As teens we actually used this thing for testing 6L6, 12AX7, and other tubes from our Fender, Silvertone and Ampeg guitar and bass amps. Anyone from the old hood will remember. My first exposure to recording was choral recitals and choir practice. This deck also had two decent dynamic microphones, and I remember it being very heavy when it was folded up like a suitcase.

At around twelve-years-old in 1965, my dad started letting me peruse his record collection—what a treasure trove. I spent months, hell, years listening to Wagner, Stravinsky, Bartok, Poulenc, Donald Erb, Karlheinz Stockhausen, Edgar Varese, J. S. Bach, and (later PDQ Bach, ha-ha) Carl Orff, Oliver Messiaen, Yma Sumac, Mozart, Martin Denny, Florence Foster Jenkins, Buddy Rich, Louie Bellson, Dorseys, Artie Shaw, Miles Davis, Andres Segovia, Delius and later many obscure records on the Nonesuch label, now dubbed "World Music."

The works.

William Bolcom's *Black Host* was a fave scary organ record on that label. Dad had a lot of music around on 78s, LPs, and box sets of 45s on colored vinyl. None were rock 'n' roll.

Dad would tell me, now this is jazz, now this is classical, and this is avant-garde...and so on. To me it was all just music. I either thought it was bitchin', or it wasn't. To me, classical is a period encompassing approximately the years 1730 to 1820, not a type of music. Igor Stravinsky and Bela Bartok are certainly not classical.

To this day I am loathe to use the rock muso colloquial terms such as "prog." Makes my ears hurt.

What the fuck is "World Music" anyway? I hate labels, especially the ones attached to rock by geeky prog rock sorts starting in the 1990s, for example, "Symph Prog," "Prog Metal," "Neo Prog," "Avant Prog" and so on. Groan.

Come on. None of that nonsense existed when I was a kid.

I surmise these people need a comfort zone of some kind. It's either GOOD MUSIC, or the other kind.

Your choice.

More on that later on.

People sometimes ask me what is my favorite style of music, and all I can come up with is, *organic*. People ask me "oh, what type of music do you play?" Again, the answer is *organic*. As long as PEOPLE are playing ACTUAL musical instruments, I'll give anything a shot. My compass runs all over the map, and if you look at my catalogue, it is also rather varied. My music collection is alphabetical which is the only thing that works for me. We have SO MUCH in the house now.

My dad's best friend for years from the late 1950s to the 1980s was Sophocles Papas. His *Method for the Classic Guitar* is famous—Charlie 'Bird' Parker studied with him. Sophocles was instrumental in documenting Andre' Segovia's music and making it known in the USA. He and my dad became good friends when I was a tot. Many times, dad took me with him to visit Sophocles. His house was literally a music museum. He gave me a letter written to him from Segovia, but stupidly, I lost track of it. DC folks will remember his place, The Guitar Shop in downtown DC. Sophocles has been called the Johnny Appleseed of the guitar. The shop opened in 1922, and had a rich history. It operated for more than 90 years.

Mr. Papas lived near Wolf Trap in Virginia and had the only full-size vertical grand piano I have ever seen that was not in a museum. He told me he traded a guitar for it. He passed away in 1986.

My dad's other very close friend was a retired Hungarian doctor named Claudius Mayer. He was on 39th Street, just blocks from where we lived at the intersection of 39th Street and Military Road. In his house, he had a mondo three-manual electric organ with bass pedals. It had six speaker cabinets, stacked high behind two posh couches.

Dr. Mayer wrote medical textbooks that I think are still

used in Hungary. This guy hated prerecorded music and would sometimes hire small ensembles or an organist to play whatever he wanted to hear, LIVE, maybe once a month, JUST FOR HIM and a few friends, and sometimes at Blessed Sacrament Church. Apparently, he had money to burn, as his house was exotically *wallpapered with red sculpted silk damask fabric.*

He would sit with his chin resting on his cane and love the live music.

Lovely guy.

What a character.

1960's—Rock Bands, DC

THERE WAS ANOTHER (of course) large family three-four blocks down from us on Military Road, the Welch family, and they seemed to always have all the stuff that attracted neighborhood kids, including a pool, trampoline and this cool little blue motorized electric tractor with a trailer. We would take turns putting up and down the block on the sidewalk with a couple of kids riding in the trailer.

Around 1965, they acquired, of all things, an *electric guitar, and an amp—the FIRST I was able to actually touch. It* may have been one of those Sears Silvertone combo setups that had an amp and speaker built right in to the guitar case. I forget.

I have many fond memories revolving around the Welch family. They were two doors down from other family friends, the Hackett family. The Hackett parents were close friends with mine. All three of their sons, Mike, Pete, and John were very good singers and were in my dad's choir. Later on, one of the Welch daughters went on to play guitar in local DC area rock groups.

Starting in 1967 and 1968, it seemed that there were two or three bands on every block forming in the upper NW Washington, DC neighborhood my parents chose to settle in. In those days, kids in my neighborhood were outside running around, riding bicycles, at home, or at friend's houses learning to operate musical instruments in order to impress the gals.

The hippie scene was going full swing in the Georgetown area of Washington, DC. Just blocks from my house, Fort Reno Park started having all sorts of concerts during 1968 and 1969.

I had tried the trumpet, autoharp, bass and guitar before finding out the drums came much more naturally than anything else.

I can remember being in my garage with a neighbor, Jimmy Thackery, (a great guitarist, now quite well known) teaching me how to play *Kicks* by Paul Revere and the Raiders on my Japanese Kapa Continental guitar.

My first experience on drums was around 1966 at the local 41st Street playground office where some kids had set up and were playing stuff like Batman.

A cowbell was involved.

I think the drums belonged to a fellow named Joe Bernot. The problem with this new fascination with the drums was that neither of my parents were really thrilled by the new development of this sudden interest in hitting stuff that was loud.

They were fine with just about any other instrument.

I had to beg and borrow drums to get going. Fortunately, I knew several local drummers that were a huge help, and lent me stuff back then, including Doug Mendelson, Bruce Oliver, Geoff Wright, Mark Klieger and a guy that taught me quite a lot of the basics, Kirk Degler.

I think the first time I ever played with a whole band was in his front yard in 1967. He was an amazing player, and loud—the first guy I ever saw who played real serious flams. He played with some of the first people in our area that had full Monty, i.e. Marshall amplifier stacks. His ears did not last long and he had to quit playing before he was twenty.

I noticed his hearing loss and since then have been very careful to never have a high-output speaker aimed at me. At one festival, a tech rolled a monitor speaker next to me that looked like a refrigerator.

No.

Behind me, and aim at my back, please. There was another fantastic drummer that is a few years older than I around the hood in those days named Louis Rozier. He went pro very early. I went to see him whenever he was gigging to try to learn something and cop some of his licks.

Back in ye olden days he was in a cool power trio called SRT with Chris Sonnenberg on guitar and Tom Transtrum on bass. Louis and I have both played in recent years with Philadelphia's staple woodwind/saxman Elliott Levin.

Small world.

I found out later that Louis is the guy that Elvin Jones replaces on drums in the wacky, but truly great movie *Zachariah*.

Crazy.

Musical Neighborhoods and my First Actual Band

In these ancient 1960s times, there were a lot of kids forming bands right around the corner. My friend Carl Peachey was on his way to becoming one of the best guitarists in the neighborhood, and we would often jam wherever I could set up the drums I borrowed from a friend—in a living room, basement or upstairs bedroom—anywhere the stuff would fit.

Carl wrote a tune for my 18th birthday called *Lost in The Sauce*. Sadly, we never recorded this gem—it was a fine instrumental. Later, in 1973, we would be in a band, Tinsel'd Sin (yes, lifted from a King Crimson Lyric). Today, Carl is an author, boat captain and blues guitar god in Florida.

In my neighborhood, two or three other teenage bands were within an easy walking distance.

More on this coming.

Sometime around 1968 I had become enamored of a certain local gal named Peggy who lived quite near Washington National Cathedral. Her brother Bobby had some Latino pals that lived in the Mount Pleasant area of Washington, DC, and suggested I connect up with them.

They had a band that practiced on 18th Street in NW Washington, DC called Sour Cream. Great sense of humor, these guys, I thought. The band was Ernie Herrera on guitar and vocals, Pepe Gonalez on bass and Rudy Morales on drumkit. We hit it off jamming, and later we decided to be a band; I ended up on drums, with Rudy moving to congas and other percussion. Ernie's brother Mike aka Miguel—who later on called himself Mick—joined on lead guitar and vocals.

The guys called this band Zapata, after Emiliano Zapata, a leader of the movement called Zapatismo, related to the agrarian movement that was part of the Mexican revolution in the early 20th century. When my drums arrived late in 1968, practice was moved to my house. This band played a lot of covers with a cool mixture of Santana, Crosby Stills and Nash, Savoy Brown, and later even Black Sabbath.

They had a pal named George who had a full-blown, large orange diesel trash truck, and he would drive us around to gigs at schools, churches, and parks for most of time I was in this band. Fort Reno Park stands out in my memory as we could just back this big ass truck up to the side of the stage, and thus setup and tear down took mere minutes.

The odor in the back of that rig was somewhat less than flowery, but it sure as fuck was convenient.

We would also play at the park in the middle of the Mount Pleasant neighborhood.

These guys had great humor.

One day they showed up for practice and had a present for me. Inside the box or bag was a pair of pointy toed shoes they called Puerto Rican fence climbers, a real switchblade and a certificate proclaiming me an honorary SPIC.

My parents laughed so hard I thought they would pee their pants. My mom got ten years of stories out of that. Mick & Ernie have since passed away. Pepe and Rudy are still around, and are lifelong friends. During 1967, because I ran around with some older kids, I was lucky enough to see both Jimi Hendrix and The Doors.

My first real concerts.

Hendrix played at The Ambassador Theatre, and I recall my friend Chip Stanard, who was a couple of years older than me and working at the show heading backstage for some reason, and on his way through a curtain, stepped on Jimi's feet.

My old pal Ernie Herrera from my first band made an 8mm video of this concert, but, *horrors,* no audio. Hendrix also played at a Hilton Hotel Ballroom nearby, as did The Doors. These were not big places, holding only a few hundred at most.

We had no clue at the time, of course, that we were witnessing rock 'n' roll history. Jimi also played Baltimore Civics center with a great DC band, Crank, as an opener. As I recall the tix for these shows added up to about 15 bucks total. All this (except Baltimore) was not far from where I grew up—we walked to these DC gigs. I may have been with pals Casey Garza, and/or Bruce Oliver and/or a dude called Marcus Aurelius.

Never did know his real name. He was older than all of us, maybe 18. 1967-8 was the start of hippie heaven in DC, when the Georgetown area of DC had head shops/paraphernalia shops like The Dungeon, and Yonders Wall. So-called underground comix like Zap with R. Crumb, S. Clay Wilson, Spain, and Gilbert Shelton's Fabulous Furry Freak Bothers books helped to fuel these rebellious times.

I still enjoy these comix and buy them when I run across them today. Fringe jackets, Beatle Boots, leather, and Nehru shirts were all the rage. One store in DC, FLAGG Bros on F Street NW, sold a shit-ton of Beatle Boots. They seemed to have the local monopoly on those.

A shop called The Sunflower Seed sold the usual incense, sandals, clothes and underground (and under the counter, some of them) comix, but also sold the material with which to manufacture one's own hip outfits was right in our upper NW neighborhood on Wisconsin Avenue. There was a guy called

Wonder Wart Hog who would actually sell the free LA Free Press to unsuspecting freak teens in Georgetown at the corner of Wisconsin Ave and M Street NW for a quarter. Wonder Wart Hog was quite the dancing fool, and we would see him whirling around at shows everywhere. He had wild frizzy red hair. When he would show up at Fort Reno Park or P Street Beach for a concert, he sometimes would practice dancing for an hour before the music even started. He also had orange-framed Coke bottle glasses that were held together with paper clips.

What a character.

Also saw The Lovin' Spoonful with neighbors who took me to, I think, Constitution Hall where The Who had just played, (missed that one) and the Spoonful's opener was a great psych band called Green Glass World.

I can't find any information on them. Great show. All in 1967 and 8.

There was a head shop on Connecticut Avenue three blocks from Chevy Chase Circle called Before and After that was run by cool guy, a biker and former math teacher named Moe. One could go there at midnight to buy clothes. The place was a magnet for local hippie teens. These guys kept their Harleys IN the store, and would just ride up over the curb and putt right in.

They had those giant drip candles that you see in hipster boutique shops now, but some of these bad boys were gigantic; five-foot tall, and 14-16 inches in circumference. Houses around there where I grew up are now $1M+, and I don't think that behavior would fly in that Chevy Chase, DC neighborhood today.

Around then, and right up the street from me, a very talented piano/organ player named Wayne Brown founded a long-lived and almost all cover band called The Louie Alphontz Conspiracy. (I recorded Wayne on a reel to reel machine playing pipe organ too at National City Christian Church in DC long ago) He was the leader, ran a tight ship, always had great players in this band and gigged around the area for ages and ages. One of their early guitarists was a guy named Tom McGrath, and I fondly recall his green jacket with THINK SNOW written in white paint on it. He is an entertainment bigwig in CA nowadays. Local producer Caltrick Simone also played with them off and on. I sat in with them more than a few times, and did at least one show with them at the Circus Maximus club in Tenleytown, DC.

The place was nuts.

Picture this: live bands on a stage next to a disco, and booths with telephones for calling other booths. Analog Hootie Call Internet.

All red decor as I recall.

The place was just five or ten minutes into DC, and some folks that were scared of really going downtown would go there so they could say they "partied in DC." With an abundance of morons, (most from the suburbs) machismo, and testosterone at this venue, there were many fights. Saw an ambulance there after midnight while driving by on more than one occasion.

Once I was there at Circus in 1973 or thereabouts with pal Greg Yaskovich, (later in the space band Mars Everywhere) and a guy was tossed off an indoor balcony and landed on and smashed the table next to us…FUGROON. Just like in a wild west movie.

I did not hang out there often. Wayne knows cars, and for moving the band around, he had modified what I think was an old school bus into a transport for the band. Half the body was gone; at least the roof. It was huge, eerie, and flat black. Would have fit nicely in a ROAD WARRIOR movie.

Wayne later renamed this band 2nd Conspiracy, with some different players and gigged right up into the 21st century. Wayne is capable of playing just about any music he wants, (he was also competent on electric bass) and, last I heard, is still active in a local area DC oldies cover band doing keys and vocals.

There was yet another band, on my own 3900 block of Military Road block no less, run by a guy named Gus. I forget the band name. I remember they had a good bassist named

Henry Arrington. I also remember they had the first plush blue sparkle tuck and roll PA system made by Kustom that I ever saw. Cheezy sounding, barely adequate even for vocals, but it sure looked cool.

Back in 1970 or so, a local church hosted a battle of the bands with Gus's group and Louie Alphontz, and the latter won hands down.

One fond memory of Louie Alphontz was their unique take on the Iron Butterfly tune In a Gadda Da Vida. You know, the long LP side tune with organ intro, then a long groove and long drum solo. Louie Alphontz did not bother with the groove, or the drum solo. They would just play the organ intro and then jump right to the da daa dada da dat ending.

Hilarious.

Applause every time.

Even looking like you played music was a fashionable thing to do in those days. There was a sort of goofy hippie looking dude (forget his name) that trolled around our hood, and hung out at Fort Reno Park. He always carried around a guitar case. One day, he ended up at my house in the basement with a few others, and so I, of course, asked him to whip out the guitar. He sheepishly told me there was NO guitar in the case.

He used the case to con chicks into thinking he was a muso.

Brilliant.

When I was a teenager, before I got my drums, and was still learning how to drive, I would spend time with my neighbor Alvin Liu, whose dad owned the Peking Restaurant near Connecticut Ave and Morrison Street NW.

It was at the end of the indoor Arcade (where the barber shop with the tube tester was) at Connecticut Avenue and Morrison Street. Not only did Alvin let me drive his cars, but also play his Telecaster and amp. Alvin was Chinese American, and two or three years older than I. We also rode bicycles all over downtown DC at night with two or three other guys, back when that was a safe thing to do.

I would not do that now.

He lived nearby on Livingston Street, and his next door neighbor was John Martin, then a well known cellist in Washington's National Symphony. Alvin also had a gorgeous older sister named Juanita who dated a popular Maryland rockabilly guy back in the 1960s.

She used to answer the door in a diaphanous nightgown.

That, I certainly didn't mind.

Her boyfriend may have been where Alvin got the guitar and amp. I forget the name of the guy his sister dated. Alvin also had this nice Fender Twin Reverb or Vox amp, I think.

For whatever reason, Alvin's family did not get along well with the Martin household.

Every now and then he would say, let's go "Martin Crashing", which was his terminology for putting the amp out on the front porch and blasting loud guitar towards the Martin house.

By the time I got to my second band, Sane Day, we upped our game and were similarly annoying to J. Edgar Hoover.

True.

More on that later.

One more funny thing: Alvin's mom had this vile tempered chihuahua named Yoyo, who would dart out from under the couch as soon as you came through the door screaming the battle cry YYIYIPYAPYIYI, nip both your ankles and be back under the couch before you knew what hit you.

Alvin's mom would come to the rescue, and pick up this pup—who would sit on her bosom, just SHAKIN' atcha and growling.

I could imagine the pup thinking, "If I ever get down off this here boobie, imma eat yo ass."

1968 First Drum Set

DURING THE SUMMER of 1968, my mom's mom sold her property in Coatesville, PA, and came to live with us in DC. She paid for an addition to our house, in which she lived. Right around my 15th birthday in October, she agreed to write the check for whatever drums I wanted.

She also bought my mom a 1969 Impala, which I quickly appropriated at age 16. (My pal Bobby Siegel called this car the Palimpa. Sometimes I would. Folks would ask what I was driving these days, and I would say oh, a 69 Palimpa.)

At the time, Rogers drums were very highly thought of, and so that's what I got. I had been to drum clinics at Drums Unlimited in nearby Bethesda; one with Buddy Rich, and one with The Tonight Show's Ed Shaughnessy as I recall, and Rogers drums are what we played. I of course went for the gold while I had grandma's support, and got double bass drums, with 4 tom toms, and double floor toms. Effectively 2 drum sets, or one large.

I still have this kit, although *some asshole* (named John M. I was told) stole the spare Dynasonic snare from the coffeehouse at Washington National Cathedral in 1975, and a couple of toms were stolen from a storage space in the mid 1990s.

I promised grandma in 1968 that I would never part with

them.

These drums stay in my studio now, and are on almost every record I have played on since 1972. These are all maple wood, got beat up from decades of gigs, and have been beautifully refinished (for the 2nd time) a dark purple with blue/red hues some years ago by Tom Scott, with whom I was in The Muffins.

Now they are mic'd up permanently for recording and don't move out of my studio.

As I mentioned, both of my parents were from Coatesville, PA. Some early memories include listening to the racket emanating from the huge and now mostly deserted Lukens Steel Mill, which was visible from where they lived. My mom's pop Oscar Jackson worked there for thirty-some years.

They lived on Oak Street in Coatesville, and one could see

sparks and hear loud booms all night long during the early 1960s. Freight trains were also nonstop. Now, it's ghostly since the U.S. steel biz went in the toilet. My dad's parents were nearby, however, they were never as close to the family as my mom's were. I never got to meet my real grandpa on that side.

My mom's mom—grandma Iva—who bought me those drums also happened be a racist, and had a plethora of prejudices. She was 70 when she moved in with us in 1968. She was born in 1898, grew up through the Great Depression in and around Coatesville, which was then a productive steel town in eastern PA.

She used expressions such as, "sit on the davenport and have a highball," "consarned whippersnapper," and my favorite, if one fell down, she would say "fell ass over tincups." She hated just about everyone; Jews, blacks, Latinos, wops, krauts, etc. In those heady 1960s days and living in the big city, Washington DC, I had a lot of friends who happened to be of these various persuasions disapproved of by grandma.

One day, during the 1968 Martin Luther King riots in DC, she looked up and out the window from watching the TV news and saw me walking towards the house down 39th Street in the middle of the street, with not one, but two actual black guys.

My mom told me grandma nearly had a heart attack, and that I should keep these guys out of the house, or at least just in the basement. I adamantly refused, and insisted that she meet them. These were great pals Richard Taliaferro, nicknamed Kuzz, and Chuck Simmons, who also played drums, was a fantastic cartoonist and was one of the funniest people I have ever known. Grandma was hesitant, but ended up loving these guys, and I am eternally grateful both to both those two, and the guys in my first band, Zapata, who were all Latinos, for helping to cure grandma Iva of her horrible racism.

It was hard to break the ice at first, but she finally accepted and eventually liked all of both mine, and my sister's friends. She even got to asking for them if she had not seen any of them for a few days.

It warmed my heart.

SUCCESS.

A Chapter for—and an Appreciation of— my Parents

I was very fortunate to have the support of my family during the early years between 1968 and 1975. All the time, really. Most of the time in those days, bands were playing in the basement. Friend's bands were playing in the basement.

We started out with Fender, Ampeg and Vox amplifiers when I was in Zapata back in 1968-1970. That was loud, but not too. One or two Ampeg SVTs passed through, and a Marshall Major. By the time Tinsel'd Sin, my third band happened, we had an assortment of Marshalls and Hiwatt stacks, a thirty-inch bass speaker and a PA.

Between 1968-1973 there must have been 30 different loud amps there during those years, including at least one cool Vox Super Beatle. When I had the Magick Theatre band there in 1975-1976, we had an Acoustic 360 for bass, which was serious amp then. Band practice occurred often and we were seldom asked to turn stuff down.

It got pretty damned loud.

My poor grandma was confined to the first floor, and so watching TV in the living room over us while we were playing was impossible. Sadly, she passed away in 1973. My mom would always say that she at least knew where I was and what I was doing.

My dad, Larry, had more than a passing resemblance to Joe Flynn who played Captain Binghamton on the TV show *McHale's Navy*, and many of my friends called my dad Leadbottom behind his back, which was the Captain's nickname on that show.

It was pretty funny. Once in awhile my dad would stick his head down the stairs and yell "can you please keep it to a low roar?" My dad also worked part time for Jordan Kitt's Music in

DC, helping them with organ projects. He also worked part time for Campbell's Music in DC selling Bosendorfer grand pianos to folks with very deep pockets.

Our basement was underground with a private entrance, had a cement floor, and was brick-walled on all four sides. I lived down there from time to time starting in 1967 at age fourteen. I had my own key and could come and go as I pleased. The caveat was that IF I got into ANY trouble whatsoever, that privilege would disappear and I would go to military school.

So I kept my ass out of trouble through my teen years. To this day I have never been arrested. Amazing, but true. There were certainly times I should have been.

When I moved and cleared out a lot of stuff in the mid 1970s, there were piles and piles of brick dust about 3" high behind speakers lining the wall. The sound over the years had begun to disintegrate the front wall where most of the amps were lined up for years and years. This I did not show my parents.

By the time I was in The Muffins, both of my parents would actually come to shows. They came to see The Muffins at Fort Reno Park. They hosted a soiree' for us the night of my 23rd birthday, on which was my first gig with The Muffins. They were excited and supportive when our first LP, Manna/Mirage came out in 1978.

My dad subscribed to Fanfare, which was, and is, a very nice, but hoighty-toighty glossy periodical print mag that covered "serious" music, and my dad freaked out when he saw a favorable review of The Muffins in the M section just after Mozart.

He was amazed.

He also had a great sense of humor, and when he was asked about updating his listing in the Washington Blue Book social register, he made sure to include me and The Muffins to see if they would print it. They did. So, The Muffins were officially boojy. Sadly, I no longer have a copy of the book.

My mom, Doris, in particular got along with pretty much everyone, and if my friends or my sister's friends would come by and we weren't there, they would hang with Doris. She was people savvy, and could spot a bad egg a mile away.

Once, when the hood was in mini-bike and Go-kart mode in 1967-8, I, and two or three other kids on Rupp mini-bikes (illegal then) were being chased by the cops. We flew into the garage, shut the door and ran into the house. Cops pulled up and asked my mom who was on the back porch if she had seen these hooligans.

No, she said.

Bless 'er.

My dad also had great humor, which would surface when least expected. Once, when I was around thirteen, he took me to watch the National Symphony rehearse. He was showing me how to follow a score up in a balcony at, I think, the then new Kennedy Center. At about ten pages into this thing, he slyly said to just watch the face of so and so onstage when we get to, say page twelve, bar so and so.

He had put porn photos from skin mags in someone's music. Hilarious. They knew full well who the jokester was.

A Chapter for My Sons

In January of 1986, my first son, Adrian was born. He was a big baby. Grew real fast. When he was little, and when he was with me, I kept him away from normal TV. We would sometimes watch Pee Wee's Playhouse, which my mom loved as well. We watched tons of my vintage cartoons.

I did, and still do, collect them. I had acres of old toons and old shows on video in those days. I think one of the first films he saw, if not the first, was Tod Browning's *Freaks*, from 1932. A friend had taped early Mr. Bean and crazy Bollywood music videos from Channel 4 in England and copied these for me. We also romped around the 41st Street Playground near my house many times. He would play the drums once in awhile, and came to recording sessions during the Chainsaw Jazz period in the early 1990s.

A little later, he and his mom moved to Baltimore and he went to school there. One of his art teachers happened to be an actress, Susan Lowe, and she was in the great John Waters movie Desperate Living. She played Mole McHenry, a gal wrestler who had a sex change. Great movie. Still later, his mom and he moved to England, and there, Adrian attended Dartington College of Arts in Totnes, Devon. Igor Stravinsky taught a little bit there in the 1950s, and pianist Keith Tippett, with Julie Tippett and Saxophonist Paul Dunmall were involved at some point with Dartington.

Adrian had by then learned a lot about music theory, and had taken up cello after a very brief stint with guitar. He also met his wife to be, Vicki, there. During the mid 2000s, he ended up at clinics with Karlheinz Stockhausen in Germany. Once visiting us in Baltimore in 2006, we were on our way home from picking him up at BWI airport, (he also got busted in customs trying to sneak me some real Absinthe) he hands me a videocassette, and says "open it up, dad."

A video of Momente by Stockhausen from the 1960s.

I said, "Wow, THANKS."

Then he says "take OUT the cassette, dad". In the box with the cassette was a handwritten note to me from Stockhausen.

Talk about making daddy proud.

I sincerely wished my parents had lived to see all the great stuff he and his brother had accomplished. My dad did not live to meet my sons. Adrian and Vicki got married, and ended up living on a narrowboat in and around the area of Bath, Somerset mostly in the Kennett/Avon Canal. Not too long after, he and Vicki had a son, my grandson Rowan. They then decided they needed a bigger boat, so they got what is called a Dutch Barge that had a bit more elbow room, and was wider than a narrowboat.

I spent a few weeks on these watercraft, and let me tell you, canal living ain't for sissies. I was continually amazed at the amount of work he and Vicki had to do to maintain the barge, AND look after a toddler. Winter there is not easy. Lots of good people live on the canal, and they are a unique, and tight community. It was quite something to experience.

Most of the boat dwellers know each other and look out for one another. Maritime law applies there. It's inexpensive. One pays the National Trust (I think) a modest monthly fee, and this buys you the use of hundreds & hundreds of miles of canals, the use of marinas and use of the fresh water stops. One can moor up for a week or two.

We saw one boat over there that was launched in 1899. Ade, Vicki, and Roro returned to being landlubbers in nearby Frome a couple of years ago, and are doing well.

My younger son, Niall, was born in 1989. He developed quickly and was even speaking rhetorically by age three. Amazing. Very clever kid. He also developed a quite early and intense interest in piano. We still had an upright in the house, and he played it a lot.

An interesting event occurred when he was very young. I believe children can see things we do not. Not very long after my mom passed in 1991, we were lying on the big bed I had, and out of the blue he starts talking about nana. His mom and I were startled by this, and asked him where he thought nana was. Immediately he points to the window and says "right there."

Wow, we thought.

He got quite good at piano and was very active in sports. Soccer, ice hockey, frisbee; whatever he wanted, he could do. As time went on his interest in music grew serious, and he entered music school, and later went to England to join his brother at Dartington College of Arts, in Totnes, Devon. He had also grown sort of cocky and rebellious and sometimes his rambunctious personality did not help him at Dartington.

I was hoping he would love it, do well, and end up staying in England with his brother. This did not work out, so he returned, resumed music study and playing here in the U.S., and worked at a few odd jobs.

It was he that hipped me to The Tick, Opeth, and South Park. A great story from our Baltimore neighborhood involved kind of a redneck sports bar called The Sharks Tooth. We had a few friends there. They also had an Internet juke. It accessed, among other things, music by Sun Ra. My dear son Niall, inherited some of my sense of humor did the following while we were there playing pool. Just as the bar filled up anticipating a football game on the TVs, Niall would play SPACE IS THE PLACE by Sun Ra to entertain a bar full of sports fans before game time. That is also a treasured memory from 2007 or so.

He got quite good on guitar, both electric and acoustic.

His grandpa was a Marine. For a long time. He retired as Colonel. A great guy with a zillion stories. By the time Niall was 18, he was still working odd jobs, even as a waiter at a DuPont Circle DC hipster joint. I believe that his mom's family played the major part in talking him into becoming a Marine. When I learned of this development, given the world situation, I was unhappy, but accepted this, if that's what he really wanted. Given the world today, and his personality, I pleaded with him to do anything as a Marine, except infantry. I wanted him to be a POG, which means Person Other Than Grunt.

There were so many options.

He ignored me, and went on to become an excellent shot, in the top few of the 400+ guys that graduated boot camp with him at Parris Island. In his words, he liked to get paid to "blow shit up" which apparently they did bunches of.

When he learned I was moving to Arizona, he requested to be stationed at 29 Palms in California so that we could visit, and when he rotated back and got out, he would live with me. He went to Japan for awhile and was also stationed in Virginia.

A little over three years into his 5 year contract, it looked like he would be deployed to a war zone. He was in USMC 1/7, Dog Company.

It happened.

I was a wreck about this deployment news, but did not mention that to him. He ended up in Afghanistan, and stepped on what is called a pressure plate IED on June 23, 2012, two days after his 23rd birthday. When I saw two uniformed Sergeants walk up my driveway my heart and soul hit bottom before they even got to the door. I knew what they were going to tell me. I spoke with him, for the last time, a little over a week before his birthday.

I must take a moment and thank the USMC for all the support they provided, to his squad mates and commander who phoned me from Afghanistan, and to his squad leader, who has actually visited me here in Arizona. The USMC is very well prepared to provide assistance in these situations—they have folks dedicated to these functions. It took a long time to settle everything. I am still in touch with some of the guys he knew, and some of their family members. Not long after he died, we received a gorgeous and unexpected musical tribute from the great Patrick Moraz, who, among a ton of other things, has played keyboards with Mainhorse, Refugee, Yes, and The Moody Blues.

Patrick reworked, and sent to us a version of a tune called *Flags* from a record he did with drummer Bill Bruford many years ago. I often think to myself…

Why the fuck could my son not have had Elvis's luck, being in the Army with no conflicts happening, and rotating home as a Sergeant?

June 2018 Facebook Thread by Bruce Hellington

Paul. Your sons are awesome. I will never forget what Niall did for 9353. There we were in 2007 at your house, plugging in for the first time in years. Looking at each other with a serious, comical uncertainty. Are we really doing this? Can we really do this? Knowing of course yes we can physically do it but can we actually physically still be it? I was, to say the least, a little uncomfortable having no insight one way or another as to what was about to happen. I will never forget how the rumble from the very first song hadn't even cleared yet when Niall came running downstairs to tell us how cool and great he thought this was. 66% of my fear was instantly gone. Niall gave us something in that moment that we couldn't get ourselves and he tipped the scale in our favor that very first hour. I never thought getting the thumbs up from a seventeen-year-old could mean so much. We knew he would've just stayed upstairs and said nothing if he really thought it sucked.

He certainly would have waited till we were done and not have appeared after one song only if he was only giving us some kind of encouraging elderly charity pity praise. Niall seriously validated 9353 that day. I will always love him dearly. The wonderful guy he is. This entire thread is one of many proving how thoroughly he touched so many people during his time on Earth.

—Bruce Hellington

I must also thank the great bassist in Belgium, Guy Segers, who sent me music via email almost every day for months and months starting not long after Niall was killed. Over 250 tunes. An amazing gesture from this great composer/bassist.

My son, Adrian aka Kozzie, Remembers

My father gave me a miniature drum set when I was four years old, maybe even three. He set it up in the living room (1989-90) with a forty-inch Paiste gong behind it. I spent a lot of time playing gongs and cymbals in his house and would let rip on his drums whenever I got the chance.

For some reason, when I played myself into a sweaty frenzy with my eyes closed, I would sometimes see the Magma 'griffe' pulsating in my mind's eye; one of the things seared into my consciousness from those developmental years.

Paul Sears

It would be heedless not to mention the ubiquity of Magma music at the Military Road house. Of all the records which were played at 'live gig' volume through the living room 'PA' (Prince *Controversy*, Parliament *Uncle Jam*, Stravinsky *Symphony of Wind Instruments*, Tony Williams *Emergency*, and the organ music of Olivier Messiaen), *Udu Wudu* stands out as being particularly evocative and *De Futura* grabbed me more than any other tune (for there was nowhere to run), and remains redolent of my early experience of life.

During this same period, Chainsaw Jazz were rehearsing regularly in the basement, the "Obsidian Cavern" as it was dubbed on account of the black glossy paint which seemed to cover every visible square inch of this dark space of possibility. "Once they start playing, nobody can hear you scream", is the ponderous advice I remember receiving.

Ed Maguire ('Big Ed' to me), probably the tallest person I had met at that time, played electric violin and mandolin slightly hunched over and had a thing about jumping around while he played. Music was a natural thing that happened, part of life; something people do. By the time I started going to school, I could whistle the opening saxophone motif of *Neon Baby*.

Another educational factor was the truly vast archive of VHS tapes of obscure cartoons from the 1920's-1940's, the animations of Wladyslaw Starewicz, underground 'music videos', and Tod Browning's *Freaks* (1932) which, along with the newly available *Santa Sangre* of Joderowsky had to be one of the first feature-length films I ever sat through. Normal television was strongly discouraged. Instead, I was privy to 'alternative programming' in the form of 'Ralph Records Shorts'.

Ten Years Later...

I was thirteen years old, and by that time living in England, when I started to spin my mother's cat-shredded record collection. Among these were Nina Hagen, Robert Wyatt, Mahavishnu Orchestra and...The Muffins; a band I could not

32

remember having heard before at all despite growing up with Lynn Pruitt's 'Manna/Mirage' sculpture hanging on the wall in 'the Purple Room' of the Sears house.

It didn't take long before I had every ripple of sound from 'Manna/Mirage', '185' and 'Open City' fully uploaded in my mind, ready to play from memory at my leisure; my punk records got less and less spin as The Muffins became 'my favorite pop combo'.

Simultaneously, The Muffins were actually meeting regularly at Carl Merson's house to record tracks for what would become *Bandwidth*, and I started receiving cassette tapes of this raw material in the post. After what must have been several weeks of listening to these tapes (in full darkness), I detuned my guitar and started to record improvisations by plugging in directly to the tape deck.

Before I realized it, the Muffin's assumed a semi-mythical status for me as I began to reorientate and explore other music orthogonal to their 'world map.' Henry Cow, Sun Ra, Stravinsky, Zappa, Faust, Fela Kuti...semi-mythical because none of this matched the reality I found myself in, living in London in 1999, yet corresponded to a sort of pre-history that seemed consistent in itself; a sort of alternate universe.

This is where my head was at when I arrived in the U.S. for the summer, in July of 2000. My plan was to meet The Muffins and spend as much time with them as possible. It was beyond surreal for me to have my father arrive to pick me up with Billy Swann waiting in the car. It was all I could do to keep from gushing and I kept my ears open for any clues about musical subculture, with my pre-internet mentality.

It was at Tom Scott's Hobart Headquarters—somewhere in the Blue Ridge Mountains—that I believe my musical education began. For several days I was able to hear material from '185', 'Manna Mirage,' and a host of newer compositions, played endlessly throughout the day; knowing it all by heart, I could get lost in the never-ending minutia.

At Carl Merson's house, the journey up to Tribeca began. The Muffins were to play their first gig in New York since the 1978 Zu Fest at The Knitting Factory and to squeeze in a radio session at WFMU in New Jersey beforehand. My designation as 'roadie' began with piling gear into Tom Scott's van, 'the Big Brown Turd.' This vehicle proved something of a war-horse, the long drive made more accommodating by the fact that most fellow travelers were afraid to get anywhere near us, a fact which proved a charm for a squeezing into the Holland Tunnel en route to Lower Manhattan. I remember a snare drum being stuck in the back as the last thing before we left, and it sat there against the door, rattling softly like an incredibly long drum roll.

Arriving at 'The Knit' and stretching my legs during the unloading, I observed a man standing by the entrance to the club watching the four Muffins and looking oddly enraptured. Dressed head to foot in garish nylon, and his legs aglint with silver spider-webs, he earnestly introduced himself to me as 'Big Toe,' and said he was looking for Paul Sears.

This was Joe Paoli. Upstairs in the club was a small room with a window looking out at the stage; it was here that the distinguished company gathered. Joe says breathlessly "I can't believe I'm in the same room with you guys." to which Billy replies "I like your pants." Nick Didkovsky brought some cymbals in from the van. Beers are opened. Bill Milkowski pops in for a chat. Later on, I catch wind that there are people gathering downstairs who were at Zu Fest, twenty-two years prior. I also learned my second music lesson at the Knitting Factory; setting up quickly.

—August 2018, by Adrian Bronson aka Cosmos Organon

About Adrian Bronson

Composer and cellist Adrian Bronson lives in Somerset, UK and studied at Dartington College of Arts, Devon, UK. He also studied with the composer Karlheinz Stockhausen in Germany.

Tommy Linthicum, Old Friend and Audio Genius

In 1970, I met a guy named Ken Smithson (we used to go roller skating, of all things, with pals Nick Brown and guitarist Carl Peachey) who knew a lot about audio and worked part time for TAL Sound, which was run by an electronics and audio genius named Tommy Linthicum and a blind fellow named Greg Lukens who was and is also an audio genius.

At that time, these guys had the only PA system in town capable of doing large rock shows.

This was in the days of green panel Altec amps, and enormous speaker cabinets. I met these guys through Ken, and wound up as a cable guy and cabinet schlepper, and sometimes provided eyes for Greg. Greg had unbelievable hearing. He could stand a hundred-feet back from Black Sabbath at sound check and point at exactly the speaker cabinet that was not working at optimum. No one else could do that. Tommy also kept a trashcan full of cold Budweiser sometimes for the crew. I did not drink then.

We did so many shows, I can't recall them all.

Oldmanititus has set in.

Here's a few I worked from about age 16-19, running cables, schlepping large speaker cabs, amps, being eyes for Greg, and whatever else was needed:

Mountain	Black Sabbath
Alice Cooper	Humble Pie
Poco	Edgar Winter
Jethro Tull	James Gang
Deep Purple	Yes
Mark Stein's Boomerang	Renaissance (original)
Procol Harum (with Robin Trower)	Rory Gallagher
Atomic Rooster	Grin
Crank	Joy

Claude Jones	Rosslyn Mountain Boys
T. Rex	Bloodstone
Modern Jazz Quartet	Wayne Feeds

We worked with some bands more than once. The Atomic Rooster drummer on that 1971 tour, their only U.S. tour, Ric Parnell of Spinal Tap fame, was their drummer. They played at The Emergency in Washington, DC, and another show somewhere in Virginia, I think. We also did tons of local gigs in DC at Fort Reno Park, P Street Beach and Sylvan Theatre at the Washington Monument.

The most bizarre lineup award goes to a gig at the American University Amphitheatre in 1971, I think, that had three bands. Mountain as headliner, Bloodstone (Natural High.) and the opener was the Modern Jazz Quartet. As I recall, Tommy also did work with Shrader Sound, one of the early high end stereo stores in DC.

At one gig we did at the Alexandria Roller Rink (many shows there) in Virginia, Alice Cooper, I think it was, the MC was a local DJ and radio personality named Barry Richards. He decided to clown around after announcements by hanging monkey bar style from a lighting truss on stage right and it collapsed. Damn good thing no one was under this thing, or they could have been maimed or killed.

I can't thank Tommy Linthicum enough for all the stuff I learned from him about live sound, how to coil cables, what different types of microphones were, etc. He also lent me from time to time a small Hi-Z PA with a Shure Vocal Master amp/mixer and a pair of Altec 1205 speakers for my first band, Zapata in 1969-70. He would drive this stuff over from a warehouse in Virginia in a step van and personally help load it into my basement. In the rain at least once. This guy had a big heart.

Years later after I started playing more and more and long after I stopped working with him, he worked for the Canadian band Rush for many years. His name is on their albums. After Rush, he returned to the DC area and with a larger company, I think named National Sound, he provided PA for presidential inaugurations, other large events and believe, even did sound for the Dalai Lama on the Washington Mall back in 2000. When I was a kid I razzed him about doing sound for me sometime. He laughed. It happened in 1989 when Chainsaw Jazz played DC's huge Riverfest. We had a nice chat and a good laugh. He passed away in 2007, and as of this writing there is a memorial website for him under his name. A really great guy who is missed by many folks.

Another thing that I want to mention is that back in these heady early 1970s days was that with a mere $50 cash deposit and only a driver license, one could walk into a U-Haul rental place and drive away with a nice new twenty-four-foot box truck. Today this is a $50,000 truck. Back then, no credit card was required—we would do this to move gear to shows, for taking a bunch of kids to the beach, or whatever. Not the safest practice in the world, shoving a bunch of kids in the back of one of these things, but we did it more than once without incident. Unbelievable, but true. $50. We must have done this nearly a dozen times from 1971-1973. I got to be pretty good at driving those things.

Funny story:

What viola? While still in high school, I became enamored of a gal named Anne, aka Goldie, that I met in my 10th grade driver education class, and she also later became one of my younger sister's best friends, and nearly part of our family.

I was at her house off of 16th Street NW in DC one night in 1971 or so, and she showed me a viola and mentioned that no one played it, and would I like to have it? Sure, but she said we had to sneak it out of the house somehow. It had a hard case, so one of us dropped it out the window two floors down into the soft bushes in a side yard. Not too much later that evening, her mom's little dog found it, and mom came upstairs with it and asked us how could this viola possibly be in the bushes? Anne and I looked at each and said "What viola?" It took awhile, but I finally got it. Over forty years later—after I moved to Arizona—she up and sent me this viola; it hangs on a wall next to the Dali print she gave me in 1991. It is a beautiful signed large print of Dali's *Atavistic Vestiges after the Rain.*

Anne was one of very few people that helped me go through my mom's house when she passed. Her mom was an art collector, and out of the blue one day she asked if I would like this framed print. A lovely gal and family friend that I am still in touch with and dearly miss.

Audio VooDoo

All of my adult life I have been listening to music in stereo. Kind of like live.

I will stay this way.

I do not buy into the optimized 5.1. surround craze. There is no way any music sounds like that in real life. I consider this just a ploy to sell people more stuff, and repurchase old music you may already have, to take advantage of this 5.1 craze. I see a parallel here with Blu-Ray. Take a fifty-year-old movie that already looks great on DVD, but because of the Blu-Ray format, you must go BUY new hardware. Bollocks. Who remembers the quad fad? Most people can't tell the difference as it is between an MP3, a high resolution digital wav file (CD format), or even an analog recording anymore for that matter.

Here's a case: I have a friend in Maryland that has no problem spending $750 for a cable to go from his preamp to his high end and pricy mono-bloc amplifiers. One for each channel. I have even seen exotic speaker cables that sell for $5K.

I think I might have splurged once and spent $40 on a preamp cable with gold plated connectors. Anyway, we were sitting there in his spacious living room listening to a Bartok string quartet record on his system that cost as much as a car. It was an excellent analog recording, done direct to vinyl disc. He was waxing in poetic rapture at the stereo image coming out of his expensive electrostatic speakers that he assured me were positioned just so, for the resulting immaculate stereo image.

So, after a few minutes we need to play side 2. Side 2 starts. He is again enraptured. Five minutes go by. Then I popped his bubble by saying it did not sound "right." He's going whaddya mean doesn't sound right?? It's GORGEOUS. While he was occupied with turning the record over, I covertly set the stereo preamp to mono, and he did not even notice. POOF.

I like good sound as much as anyone, but I am not going to spend twelve grand on two speakers. I do have mid-fi JBL towers and double 18" Cerwin Vega subwoofers, and they sound just peachy to me, and plenty big. I have a lot of old U.S. made Crown equipment that I love. My amps and preamps are already 30-40+ years old and will likely outlive me.

For recording, I use small, inexpensive what are called near-field monitor speakers. These provide at close range an average reproduction of whatever I have recorded across the frequency range. I then listen to mixes on my bigger system, boomboxes, and in car CD players. I also make MP3s, (usually for compact transport via computer, never for production) even though I rarely listen to any MP3, the exception being our radio show.

I usually start a mix using a five-position stereo live (to my ear) audio image, and then fine tune.

Far left side—any instrument
Mid left side—any instrument
Center—bass always, other low frequencies
Mid right side—any instrument
Far right side—any instrument

Live: For strung musical instruments, I prefer an actual tube amp. Tubes distort harmonically, similar to the way strings vibrate harmonically. Most guitar amp purists and some bassists prefer tubes. In this guitar amp application tube distortion is infinitely variable, and can be used creatively with respect to volumes and frequencies, (Jimi Hendrix provides damn good examples of the creative control of high gain tube amp distortion) whereas a transistor circuit tends to distort everything in the signal all at once when overloaded. This can be an unpleasant sound. With tubes, clipping is usually smooth, which is widely considered to be more musical than transistors.

However, on the negative side, tube amps are heavy as hell, and folks don't want to schlep them around anymore.

For power, I believe in headroom. I use older Crown DC300 laboratory class high current amplifiers in my sound system. They are sort of bulletproof in the sense that they can provide extremely high output wattage at a variety of impedances without working too hard, and thus seldom get warm.

They are also pretty flat, which means they amplify all frequencies at the same rate without having their own frequency preferences, or adding their own "color" as that characteristic is often called. They sport very low distortion of around 0.05% when used correctly. They have in the past been called the closest thing one can get to a piece of wire with gain. They provide a fairly honest representation of the signal they receive without adding "color" to it.

I use the Crown IC 150 preamp with unique features I have not seen on other preamps. It has two sets of stereo outputs, so I am able drive two separate stereo power amps with it. One amp has high pass filters on the inputs at 200 Hz for subwoofers. This preamp also has an infinite stereo panorama control, a FLAT setting, and when desired, excellent EQ. I usually listen FLAT, with no added bass or other frequency coloration.

My Major Musical Influences

Having a somewhat different childhood than many, by the time more adventurous rock music appeared, I was already familiar with where some were getting influences from, Stravinsky, Messiaen, Holst, Prokofiev, Mussorgsky, Varese, Poulenc, Alain, etc. My compass was fairly wide compared to most other teenagers around me at that time.

I was ready when actual ROCK bands started nodding to, and quoting a lot of this music. After The Yardbirds, Jimi Hendrix, The Doors, Beach Boys, West Coast Pop Art Experimental Band, and so on, I was wrapped, rapt, ready for delivery when King Crimson, early Genesis, Renaissance, etc. records hit the market. I liked ELP too, early on. Chicago's first LP. The Flock. IF. Savoy Brown's first few LPs are great records.

Not long after, I discovered Magma, Sun Ra, Zappa/Beefheart, Henry Cow, Van der Graaf Generator, Art Zoyd, Faust, Canterbury school stuff and so my interest in new and different music just snowballed, and still does just that.

I am always eager to hear something I haven't. I also loved heavy stuff like Blue Cheer, Led Zeppelin and Black Sabbath. I was always amused that Black Sabbath's first release was a cover; a 45 of *Evil Woman*, which is actually a song by a Minnesota band I liked back then too, called Crow. Crow were a great band and were tremendous live. I am amazed that Frank Zappa got the commentary on his first several albums out on a major label. Much of what he sang about back in the 1960s is still very relevant today.

Here's a short list of people and bands, on the rock/jazz side that I truly love and that have had some influence on me—in no particular order.

More fun this way.

Think of the fun you will have looking some of them up.

King Crimson	Art Zoyd
Original Mahavishnu Orchestra	Original Genesis
Magma	Henry Cow
Art Bears	Mike Oldfield
Frank Zappa	Jimi Hendrix

The Yardbirds	Pre-Parsons Pink Floyd
Fred Frith	Tim Hodgkinson
John Greaves	Peter Blegvad
Balletto Di Bronzo	Banco
Premiata Forneria Marconi	Present
Univers Zero	Henry Kaiser
Area	Moody Blues
Sun Records era Elvis Presley	Danny Gatton
Billy Hancock	Robert Fripp
Faun Fables	John McLaughlin
Psychic TV	Throbbing Gristle
Suicide	Public Image Limited
Joe Zawinul	Miles Davis
Link Wray	The Insect Surfers
Ilhan Mimaroglu	Dick Dale
Larry Coryell—all but *11th House*	9353
Jethro Tull	Atomic Rooster
ELP	Yes—*Relayer*
Peter Gabriel	David Bowie
Brian Eno	Johnny Cash
Guru Guru	Kraan
Focus	Can
Tom Cora	Chris Cutler
Buddy Rich	Christian Vander
Kraldjursanstalten	Beach Boys
Tony Williams	Thinking Plague
Van Morrison—*Astral Weeks*	The Doors
Free Salamander Exhibit	Albert Marcoeur
Esperanto	Cream
Copernicus	Jack Bruce
John Mayall	The Residents
The Bluesbreakers	Tuxedo Moon
The Flock	TS Henry Webb
Jack Dupon	Nick Prol
Daevid Allen	Gong

Steve Hillage
Motorhead
Alan Davey
Iggy Pop
Michael Manring
Lazuli
Copernicus
Jannick Top
Faust
Moondog
Clearlight
Black Sabbath
Cecil Taylor
Cloud Over Jupiter
Manna / Mirage
James Brown
George Clinton
Jon Sindelman
5UUs
Crazy Backwars Alphabet
Don Preston
The Work
Grits
Bob Drake
Savoy Brown
Barkays
Spirits Burning
See You On Tuesday
Jonas Hellborg
Guapo
The Cardiacs
Zao
Neffesh Music
Punishment of Luxury
Buckethead

Hawkwind
Lemmy Kilminster
Captain Beefheart
Herbie Hancock
Patrick Moraz
Morglbl
Cheer Accident
Alamaailman Vasarat
Prince
Cyrille Verdeaux
Lobotomatic
Alice Cooper
Doctor Nerve
Moon Men
4S'd
The Funkadelics
Skeleton Crew
Penguin Cafe
Karda Estra
Syd Barrett
Bunk Gardner
Crank (DC Area band)
Dzyan
Sun Ra
Muddy Waters
Al Kooper
Harlingtox A.D.
Behold The Arctopus
Eberhard Weber
Knifeworld
Yochk'o Seffer
Joni Mitchell
Manster
Bill Laswell
Crispin Hellion Glover

Charles Mingus	Eric Dolphy
Art Ensemble of Chicago	Nona Hendryx
Nico	John Cale
Chicago	The Tubes
8 Eyed Spy	Public Image Limited
Lydia Lunch	The Contortions
One Shot	Bloodrock
Brian Jones era Rolling Stones	The Troggs
Brian Wilson/Beach Boys	Peter Hammill
Van Der Graaf Generator	

And, I can't forget The West Coast Pop Art Experimental Band.

Scratching the surface, here.

Here's a funny Mahavishnu Orchestra story…while my dad was a music critic for The Evening Star newspaper in DC in the early 1970s, he got me tickets to see something I had never heard of…The Mahavishnu Orchestra at Lisner Auditorium in Washington, DC. The press blurb said ex-Miles Davis players, John McLaughlin on guitar and Billy Cobham on drums. My gal Lesley and I were expecting an evening of jazz. With press passes, we got in early. We saw tons and tons of amps and drums set up and wondered if this was the right concert. It was the first time I saw a transparent plastic FIBES drumset. Just before show time, John McLaughlin walked on stage amongst the sticks of incense that were burning, stuck on mic stands and all over the stage. He had a Gibson ES-1275 double neck guitar and was in front of several Marshall amps. He then spoke very quietly while the band silently took their places and John asked for a minute of silence. Then…the earth shifted beneath my very feet. To this day, I have never been hit that hard by a live band I have never heard of. Holy crap. The first King Crimson record made a similar impression on me.

One more thing about this show—right in the middle of *A*

Lotus On Irish Streams, an acoustic piece, the cops came on stage and stopped the show because of a bomb scare. They cleared out the theatre for about thirty minutes while they checked it out, then finding nothing, let all back in and the show resumed. I saw and chatted with their drummer Billy Cobham here in Mesa, AZ in July of 2018, and he remembered this event quite well. "Glad we're still alive," he said.

I have a large collection of music, and enjoy playing music on the Victrola for people that don't possess wide musical compasses. Lots of the stuff on my shelf most people have certainly never heard of. I have fun with it. I ask someone what artist or music they love, and in almost every case I can pull something off the shelf that they don't know, and in most cases they end up really liking it.

I always had difficulty finding other folks that gave a rat's ass about new and different music up until I met The Muffins and the Random Radar collective in 1976. I find it somewhat amazing that I have actually gotten to play or record with many of my tender years heroes, such as Fred Frith, Jerry Goodman, Cyrille Verdeaux, Tom Webb, John Greaves, Peter Blegvad, Marshall Allen, Don Preston and Bunk Gardner from Zappa/Mothers, Yochk'o Seffer from Magma/Zao and so on. (Now, if can I somehow cause ways to work with Robert Fripp, Pat Moraz, and John McGlaughlin...) Speaking of Robert Fripp, later on, I was to meet him socially in NYC in 1978. There was no King Crimson at that time, and he was checking things out in NYC. We had a nice chin wag at Giorgio Gomelsky's place in Chelsea, and then he came, with Debbie Harry aka Blondie, to the Zu Festival. Walking into Gomelsky's place in 1978 and running into those two was a real surprise. More on that later. We have been in touch for many years. A few years back, he invited me for a visit while I was in England visiting family, and he picked me up at the Worcester train station and took me out for tea and a snack at Worcester Cathedral. He also gave me a short tour of that beautiful cathedral.

Improvisation

Going back to 1972, I don't remember how, but I met a piano teacher named Steve Freeman. He also had a buddy that played rock guitar named Ed Marshall. Fast Eddie. Maybe I met Eddie first; I don't recall. We would jam at my place sometimes, with Steve playing a Fender Rhodes, and a bassist who was great, but I can't recall his name. Steve also had a Steinway baby grand in his apartment in a development called Pepper Tree something or other out by the intersection of Connecticut and Georgia Avenues in Maryland.

Steve suggested bringing a small drum kit to his place to do some piano/drum improvisations. So I did, and it was one of the most fun days I had back then. He was one hell of a player. Improvising was totally new to me. He set up a Sony reel to reel and we recorded two or three pieces of just piano and drums that I thought were great. Sadly, I no longer have these recordings. Years later, I would have Dave Newhouse add woodwinds to these, and Steve Feigenbaum added some guitar, back in 1976. Don't know if they even have copies. During 1975 and early 76 lots of improvising occurred with the band Magick theatre, which prepared me for my encounter with The Muffins that summer and fall of 1976.

Steve Freeman also asked me to do the qualified absurd a year or two later—1973, I think. He had a recital at Catholic University in a small hall where there were two married grand pianos on stage. This is where the pianos are set up opposite each other and joined where the sides curve into each other with the pianists facing each other. I am sure you have seen this common two-piano setup. He asked me to play the piano. I don't play the piano. I did this day. The idea was, I would just play a few random clusters of pseudo chords and so on, and he would *immediately* react and play around whatever I played making whatever I did seem sort of legit. His cue was to look across at me—that was my cue to immediately become Cecil Taylor for ten seconds or so. I may have thrown in a Keith Jarrett moan or two for effect.

Ha-ha.

He had me come out in the middle of his recital, and we did this trade off thing for about five minutes. I was trying hard not to laugh. Applause. He was unbelievable. To this day I don't know if we fooled 'em. At the time, my dad was teaching choral music at this University part time, and nearly fell out of his chair when I told him about this.

"You did WHAT, now???"

Ensemble Playing

I have always been of the opinion that if one is going to have a band, whatever the instrumentation is intended to be, IF there is a bass player and drummer involved, the bass and drums must work, or anything additional won't. I have a bass ear, and that is my first priority when listening to anything, actually. When starting from scratch, which I have no problem with, the first thing I do is find a bassist that I am compatible with.

An example is the band Chainsaw Jazz I started with Mark Smoot in 1988. Mark is a tremendous player, listens, can improvise and write and arrange music. The desire to do so along with simpatico vis-a-vis musical tastes are also damned good things. These things we have. So, we spent many days getting used to each other by just improvising and playing some cool systems that Mark conjured up. When we were comfortable playing with each other, and had some idea of what we wanted in a band, THEN we brought in other players. We ended up with whole band, called Next at first, and then became Chainsaw Jazz.

We could both improvise, and play tightly arranged music. Our Chainsaw Jazz recording Disconcerto on Cuneiform Records provides a good whiff of that band. There are also videos online.

Much of The Muffins material was tightly arranged, and we would rehearse different systems for weeks on end and then learn how to play whatever it was pasted together as a whole piece. Some of these were real buggers to learn. In those days, Dave Newhouse was writing the bulk of the tunes. We appreciated how difficult some of these 1970s arrangements are when we decided to perform some of them in the 21st century. Train wrecks, and clam bakes. For the non-muso types, clams are bad notes. In The Muffins lexicon a large clam is a quahog, and a small one is a cherrystone. Heh.

Another example is a loose consortium of improvisers called Thee Maximalists that was founded by NYC bassist Keith Macksoud and me. I had heard Keith on the Present CD *High Infidelity*, and he just knocked me out. Keith and I became pals, and he would come down from NYC to Baltimore and we would spend days just improvising. Bass and drums only. He can also read, and played some amazing, very tightly arranged music with Present. Look them up. After some time with just the two of us knocking about, we concluded that we were hip enough at improvising to actually do shows with no rehearsal whatsoever.

So, we started a list of people that we liked to invite along for this ride. Not everyone can, or is comfortable with the prospect of playing entirely improvisations for an audience with absolutely no rehearsal. Happily, between the two us, we know a whole passel of musical bungee jumpers. Our first victim was Yanni Papadopoulos, the great Philadelphia guitarist with the gothy death-jazz band Stinking Lizaveta, who are a fave band of mine. (9353 also did shows with them) Sort of a Black Sabbath plays jazz kind of vibe. Then Dave Newhouse from The Muffins came aboard with woodwinds and keyboards. We have at various times had different configurations since 2003 that have included these great players:

Cyndee Lee Rule—violin
Werbinox—vocals
Louisa Morgan—vocals, harmonica
Mark Stanley—guitar

Marshall Allen—saxophone, EVI
Elliott Levin—saxes, flutes, poetry
Charles Cohen—electronics
Jim Rezek—Mellotron, Mini-moog
Chester Hawkins—electronics, graphics
Rick Iannacone—guitar
Adrian Bronson—cello
Dave Newhouse—keys, woodwinds
Vonorn—Theremin

Drum Solos

I don't really like to play them. A short section, maybe. Over my entire recording career, I think have recorded maybe a whopping four minutes of drum solos. I prefer solos, including mine, to occur while the whole ensemble is playing, and for a solo, mine or others, to compliment whatever else is happening.

I have never pushed myself as some kind of superman type drum solo guy, thus saving me from upholding some imagined exalted reputation. I can do some flashy stuff, but I am there to support and hopefully contribute to the quality of the music, not to showboat my "amazing" technique.

Some drummers like to have a gazillion drums, and all kinds of percussion instruments and some electronic gadgetry integrated into their kits. I even saw a guy with double bass drum pedal driven cowbells a few years ago. Not my style. I am not doing performance art, here.

Electronic drum pads? No.

Roto-toms? No.

I play a fairly basic setup, but do often indulge myself with very large cymbals. I went through a phase of having a ton of tom toms and other stuff back in the early 1970s, but not for long. Fashionable nowadays is to have an extra smaller snare drum next to the high hat.

Why?

Technique is nothing more than failed style.
—Cecil B. Demented

*I believe the quality of expression to be of more value than
form itself.*
—Paul Sears

Teaching

Once in awhile I get the question, "do you teach?" I have, long ago, and consider this from time to time on a strictly case by case basis. I am flattered that anyone thinks I can teach them anything. I see myself as more of a drum kit coach and adviser on music to avoid.

Long ago, I coached a quite young fellow named John Hage (I was seeing his older sister) who lived just a few blocks away. As a youngster, under ten-years-old, he would come over all the time wanting me to show him stuff, and wanting to play my drums. Totally infatuated with drums. If his parents could not find him, they knew where he likely was. I helped him learn rudiments, some basic beats, counting measures and encouraged him to take every chance available to play with other folks in the neighborhood. I also provided recommendations for music to listen to that I thought he might like and that has some emphasis on the drums. As a teen, he roadied for The Muffins for awhile. As soon as he was able to, he acquired a nice set of Gretsch drums, and in short order became a great player and gigged around with DC area bands. Today, he runs a music program in a high school near Frederick, Maryland.

Later in the 1970s, I coached another local DC fellow named Eric Smith aka E. Doctor Smith. He was not a youngster, but a friend, and a guy I had known for some time. He could already play, and just wanted coaching, some pointers, tips and tricks. He would watch me practice, intensely, for hours at a time and we played opposing drum kits for awhile. He went off to NYC, and on to work with Madonna, Brian Eno, Warren

Zevon, and many others. He also became an inventor along the way, coming up with a hand held electronic drum/percussion device called the Drummstick. He is in California now and easy to find on the Internet. He still calls me "Sensei."

E. Doctor Smith Remembers

Paul "Sensei" Sears...back in 1971, I was a wide-eyed kid, absorbing many of the musical influences of my youth back in the day. At my High School orientation at Woodrow Wilson in Washington, D.C., we were treated to a power rock band from the senior class, something none of us expected to see. The seniors were our musical mentors; guys like guitarist Carl Peachey, bassist Pepe Gonzales and drummer Paul Sears; Paul was an ambidextrous, whirling dervish on a his monster Rogers kit, a kit that almost seemed to swallow him, yet Paul flew around those toms like nothing we had ever seen. As the weeks and months went by, I began regularly going to concerts, and delving into more and more progressive music and jazz; groups like King Crimson, Weather Report, Return to Forever, Larry Coryell's Eleventh House and the Mahavishnu Orchestra featuring the one and only Billy Cobham. Their legendary free concert at American University blew my mind. Paul Sears could play just like Cobham.

I, like so many others were mesmerized by Cobham's prodigious talent, and his open-handed, ambidextrous playing. I desperately wanted to play like Cobham; I convinced my Mom to help me buy a new, six-piece, clear Ludwig Vistalite kit (Nick Mason model), from Veneman's in Silver Spring, Maryland; next I got my Dad to help me buy three more Ludwig Vistalite toms from Chuck Levin's Bennett Goldstein in Wheaton, Maryland to complete my nine- piece "Cobham kit", then set about taking lessons with the D.C. Youth Orchestra for basic rudiments, and soon after with the Alan Massey Studios in Northwest D.C. When I told the teachers at Alan Massey I wanted to learn how to play ambidextrously like Cobham, they told me they were only comfortable teaching right handed, traditional and match grip. I continued for a bit longer, but I knew that it wasn't going to last.

That was a bit deflating, but undaunted, I pressed on; going to concerts and jamming with friends. After attending one of the fabled Fort Reno concerts, and the Emergency, and Coffee House shows at the National Cathedral; I saw Paul and asked him if he could teach me how to play like him and Cobham. Paul asked me how much Alan Massey charged me; I told him $40 and he said, "Deal. Bring your entire kit over to my house and we'll take it from there." Paul lived in Chevy Chase, right on Military Road. His Mom would greet me and say, "Paul's downstairs," and nod to the basement door. Paul had me set up my Ludwig kit facing his Rogers kit, and we began months of "call and response" drumming after school, weeknights and weekends.

Paul was absolutely amazing, and I don't think I could ever sufficiently duplicate most of what he did. Nevertheless, he taught me about independence; paradiddles, flams, ratamacues and more. Paul then took me on a prog-rock musical journey that would shape my musical path to this day. We listened to King Crimson, (and we even attended their '74 Kennedy Center show with another idol: Bill Bruford); We listened to groups like Magma, Gong, Tony Williams Lifetime, Miles Davis, Herbie Hancock, National Health, Fred Frith, Henry Cow, Gentle Giant, Genesis, Yes, and Frank Zappa, to name just a few. Paul once prank called me at Midnight on New Year's Eve by playing the obscure "Wild Man Fisher" album by Zappa.

I also followed Paul to many of his own gigs; with The Muffins, with Fred Frith at the Entermedia Theatre (ZU festival 1978) in NYC, and many, many other shows. His sessions at Track Recording Studios, his recordings on the Cuneiform label, and his later work with the group 9353 were part of my regular diet. Paul also taught me about acoustic drums and how they are made. To pay for more lessons, Paul asked me to help him strip his entire nine-piece, vintage Rogers kit to be refinished. We bagged and tagged every lug, bolt, vent, tension rods, and screws; and when the drums came back, we put them all back together, tom-by-tom, lug-by-lug. I can't count how many custom-made drums I've built since then, but suffice it to say it was Paul who taught me how to do it.

As time went by, I left D.C. and ultimately moved to NYC in 1980. Before I knew it, I found myself in the company of folks like drummer/composer Stephen Bray, his girlfriend Madonna, and the Breakfast Club with the Gilroy Brothers; Playing percussion with Bray and bassist Stanley Adler (Lydia Lunch, Crazy World of Arthur Brown), and the group "The Same", led by keyboardist Carter Burwell, (Raising Arizona, Barton Fink, Fargo), guitarist Chip Johanssen, singer Clodagh Simmons, (Mike Oldfield), and often performing with and featuring the legendary Brian Eno. Those were heady days indeed, and the rest is history. My love of "open-handed" drummers in particular, continues to this day; Billy Cobham, Lenny White, Simon Phillips, Rayford Griffin, and of course, Paul. I owe much of my drumming expertise and musical formation to the man I affectionately call *Sensei*, the inimitable Paul Sears.

About E. Doctor Smith

E. Doctor Smith is a drummer, producer, electronic percussionist and recording artist with Edgetone Records, who has worked with the likes of Brian Eno, Madonna, Warren Zevon, Mickey Hart, Howard Levy and many, many others. He is also the Arts & Entertainment editor for Beyond Chron and the inventor of the musical instrument, the Drummstick.

My Mentor, Paul Sears, by John Hage

Paul Sears is my Mentor. My big brother. My friend. He is the reason I started playing drums and why I'll always keep playing drums. He's the reason I pursued music and discovered all types of music and musicians. He was hugely influential to my life in music when he showed me the basics of playing drums.

He was so much more than a teacher, however, and taught me about things that can't be put into words. He told me music was 50% talent and 50% attitude and those words have always stayed with me.

I first met Paul when I was eight-years-old. I was trying to learn guitar which was difficult and I wanted to do something different and for whatever reason, my older sister introduced me to Paul to try drums. He had this big drum set in the basement (and coke cans everywhere). I couldn't reach the pedals at first but he showed me some basics. They were never formal lessons and I realized later he never charged me a cent. I would just sit and play and he would say "try this" or "use the left hand and foot as much as the right" etc.

These were not half hour lessons. I would play and play and he would come down periodically and suggest some things. It was heaven. His best advice over the years was often "just play". Later, when I was reluctant to join a more formal concert band in school he suggested I do so. He told me it may not be the music I was interested in but I'm still playing and I could still learn something. That has always proved to be valuable advice.

It was more than the lessons, though. I remember calling my mother on several occasions asking if I could go to lunch, a pool party or some other excursion with Paul that was more fascinating than the last. I think what attracted me the most was the way he treated me as an equal. I never felt like just a kid tagging along but a part of whatever was going on. He's a somewhat eccentric character and I was amused by his unique observations of the world around him. I remember going to McDonald's once and he drove in through the exit. I pointed this out to him and he promptly responded that he was going to leave through the entrance. He was always deliberately doing the opposite of what was expected. He had a fresh and unusual and very positive way of looking at things that I found refreshing.

Paul also introduced me to all types of music. Bebop,

Stravinsky, Henry Cow, Faust, Captain Beefheart, John Cage, and so much more. He introduced me to drummers like Elvin Jones, Tony Williams and Billy Cobham and literally introduced me to Chris Cutler. I was especially taken with the Magma Live recording he gave me and the power of Christian Vander's drumming and music. (I know my wife really loves me because I introduced her to Paul Sears and we saw Magma on the same night-and she's still around.)

We stayed in touch and eventually I started to be a roadie for his band The Muffins. We're talking a full-size, double-bass drum kit with tons of cymbals, not to mention the gong, xylophone and many more percussive instruments that the band would all play. I loved it though, and I loved hanging out at the "Muffin House." I would just soak in all this music they were into. They would let me sit in on the rehearsals and their recording sessions with Fred Frith. They would even let me play drums with them for little jam sessions. It wasn't just music but literature, art, film and all kinds of unique artists they were into.

The Muffins were one of the best bands in DC. They were all incredibly talented and able to play complex rhythms and time signatures with cohesion and ease. Despite the sophisticated nature of the band, they also had a sense of humor and lightness to their music. It certainly showcased Paul's unique style of playing. Paul always plays with such ferocity and intensity. He's also very dynamic and plays soft patterns and then really lays down some thunderous beats. He is a very unique drummer and there's no one who can play like Paul plays.

Above all, Paul is fun to be around. Every time I see him or talk to him I learn something new and exciting. He has been through a lot, I know, but he's always full of life and new experiences. It's incredible really, and inspiring. We're family. We always have been.

—John Hage, September 2018

About John Hage

Drummer, Composer, Producer, Performing Arts Director,
Music Educator from Frederick, MD

He is a drummer and multi-instrumentalist who has performed and recorded extensively. He has been in numerous bands including Beaver (with Tom Lyle of Government Issue) New Potato Caboose, Party Akimbo, Glassoline and Bittersweet Manics. He has a degree in percussion and has performed at CBGB's, 9:30 Club, Carnegie Hall and The Kennedy Center. He has played in rock, punk and jazz bands, symphony orchestras and numerous musicals. He has released numerous recordings in all styles of music.

Recently he produced an album with brother Joe Hage (*Still Hungry*) and a solo record (*Still Waiting*). He just completed a stint with the Market Street Big Band that he played in for several years. He is the Performing Arts Director at a private school in Frederick, directing bands, chorus, musicals and providing instruction on percussion, guitar, piano and brass and woodwind instruments. He is currently working on a new solo project of energetic, driving rock songs, half in Spanish, and half in English.

Drummers

There are so many good ones, I cannot pick one favorite. Here are some I like:

Tony Williams	Christian Vander
Morgan Agren	Chris Cutler
Weasel Walter	David Kerman
Phil Collins	Bill Ward
Paul Whaley	John Bonham
Buddy Rich	Louie Bellson
Viola Smith	Daniel Denis
Ginger Baker	Billy Cobham

Angels and Demons that Play

Bill Bruford
Alan White
Pete Ragusa
Denny Craswell
Robert Wyatt
Brain
Charles Hayward
Thymme Jones
John Guerin
John Weathers
Ken Pustelnik
Mike Shrieve
Clyde Stubblefield
Louis Rozier

Jamie Muir
Charlie Zeleny
Dave Ellliott
Nick Mason
John Marshall
Dave Clark
Ric Parnell
Aynsley Dunbar
Malcolm Mortimer
Joey Baron
Marco Minneman
Tatsuya Yoshida
Giulio Capiozzo
Jimmy Carl Black

While I am on the subject, and I hope not to be TOO vilified by Beatles fans for this, but I really don't think Ringo played on all the Beatles records. For example, if you listen to the songs *Ticket to Ride*, and *Tell Me Why*, the drums on those tracks, to my ears, have glaringly different feels and drum sound than most other Beatles tunes. It would be interesting to know how much help the Beatles got from other musicians someday. I will duck now.

NEW(er) Music and Bare, Ruined Stages

THERE IS SO much good music being made today that it is impossible to keep up with it. All of it from disparate locations around the world, and self released or released via small record labels. You really gotta search it out. You won't hear any of it via the painfully whitebread mass media. What I have zero tolerance for is what I call non-musical instrument generated digital entertainment, or, so-called "music" with no actual musicians or musical instruments involved. Lots of RAP & Hip Hop are rife with these "features." You know, the sound when a car goes by rattling, and going BOOM BOOM Ssss, BOOM BOOM Ssss, really loud, (sometimes horrible sounding too) and often with someone talking birdbrain over this ridonkulous noise, or rather, yelling hateful rhymes over it.

Simply put, I hate this shit.

My parents generation thought what we listened was racket, but at least actual, tangible musical talent was present. PARENTS. HEAR-HEAR. If there was ever a time to lobby for bringing back actual music classes, and band, in schools , HERE IT IS. Actually, many years ago was the time. Or how about those DJs folks? No doubt some are talented, but call yourself a musician?

Wait a minute.

No pal, you are not.

Tired of your teen thinking this is somehow music, and not knowing to pull pants up like a grownup? Turn that hat around. You are lame. Ask grandma. She'll not put up with this shit. Hated disco didja? Little did you or I know what evil was lurking in the shadows of a steadily growing, opportunistic, dumbed down, and narrow "entertainment" business model that has hijacked and decimated what USED to be the music business.

Just like TV and movies, folks.

Personally, I will give ANY music a shot, as long as it involves folks operating actual musical instruments and singing. Check out The Last Poets, or Gil Scott Heron's classic The Revolution Will Not Be Televised, for some of the meaningful and musical foundations of what later became the Rap/Hip Hop horror we know now.

For all that hated disco, punk, and new wave, little did we know what crap was waiting in the wings. Remember, this is just my opinion. How many people REALLY want to pay to go see some poseur on a stage with a laptop?

Right.

Fuck that.

Musical entertainment in general now is almost purely a nostalgia trip. Music and entertainment necrophilia. Much easier and cheaper to just keep selling the same—as generic as possible—formula over and over.

Just like TV and movies. If a unique, or original act like, for instance, say a Jimi Hendrix, James Brown, Elvis Presley, The Doors, Janis Joplin, or a Miles Davis came along today, they would not have a prayer with the way the biz works now. As Frank Zappa so aptly put it in his book, nobody knew what the fuck was going on back in the 1960s. A happy consequence of this fact was that lots of good stuff slipped through.

Take jazz. I seriously doubt there are very many folks making serious money with jazz the way Miles Davis was back in 1970, which according to his book was around $400K per year. This would be over $2.5M in today's dollars.

The "music biz" today wants to, and does stomp any hint of originality, or god forbid, new ideas, into the ground. To hell in a handbasket with these "talent" TV shows. Laughable to many in my generation that grew up with TV that occasionally showcased real rock bands. The stuff on TV now is so whitebread it causes me physical pain. I blame Star Search and Ed McMahon for that vile practice that got its' start in the 1980s.

The only hope today seems to be doing stuff yourself, or working with one of the dwindling independent record labels that makes and pays actual money. There are not many of those. Almost all of them are hurting, especially ones trying to sell physical products. Hell, I buy vinyls and CDs. Never owned an MP3 player. Who needs to carry 22,000 songs around? I carry a few CDs in the car, and that's plenty. Digital sharing and streaming have not helped the biz either. I read a book some years ago about the music biz. I wish I still had the book. Can't recall the title or author. Maybe some of you will recall these instances...

Many artists were screwed hugely over the years, and some of them sued record labels for unpaid royalties on sales, publishing, songwriting, etc. Some of the artists won, with the excuse being "accounting mistakes." One lawyer was famous for advocating the artists in court cases and became an expensive pain in the ass to some major record labels. One of the record labels asked "When will you STOP harassing us with these goddamn lawsuits?" Response: "When I hear of ONE "accounting mistake" that's in favor of the artist, I'll stop."

Wish I could recall the name of this book.

Karaoke, whoo hoo, I used to find mildly amusing—back when I did not encounter it too often, that is. I avoid it like I do TV, hip hop, rap, and DJs now.

Here's a funny.

Once, The Muffins bassist Billy Swann and I were somewhere in Bethesda, MD in the late 1970s and stopped somewhere on Old Georgetown Road for a bite. Karaoke broke out. We had no fucking clue what was going on and thought it was a comedy performance. We busted up laughing and clapping. Nobody else there thought it was funny and they all gave us the evil eye. So, we split quick. Years later, Deb and I went to The Castle, a then popular restaurant and bar on Route 2 in The Brooklyn area of Baltimore where we lived, for Saint Patrick's day dinner in 2002 right after we moved there.

Well, it happened to be senior citizen heavy metal kilt wearing karaoke night. Had we known, we would have brought a video camera. THAT was entertainment. A treasured memory from that evening is some 75-year-old guy prancing around in a kilt getting down to business, gesticulating wildy, and singing Black Sabbath's IRON MAN. I think a couple of zaftig gals also belted out some Heart that evening.

A friend told me years ago he thought the only real progress in rock was being made by metal bands, and suggested a few of the extreme ones. I tend to agree with him. Cookie monster vocals, though, I can only take so much of, but a lot of the music is great. There is a lot of excellent music being made today, but one must really make an effort to look for it. My hat is off to folks that get STUFF DONE like Michel Besset in France that has put on hundreds of concerts, and music festivals.

He also does the RIO Festival near Carmaux, France, taking chances on newer bands that write all their own stuff, or improvise. Hats off to George Roldan, who took a chance starting RosFest, which caters mostly to the so-called neo-prog rock audience. Hats off to Chad Hutchinson and Rob Laduca who ran NEARfest successfully for many years. There is also Mike Bennett and his team at Progday in NC that still goes on as the longest running, but smaller, fest in the USA. There are a few more in Germany, Portugal, England, & France, and elsewhere in Europe. There is a wealth of great music being made, but, sadly will never get any support from evil mass media.

Forget FM radio airplay, until your stuff is old enough to have no influence and get on the classic stations. The Internet has helped to make music nearly valueless, and also compromised the quality of the actual products they DO sell by compressing stuff to MP3 files. Some do sell lossless formats, like FLAC, but this is not nearly as popular as the evil old MP3, of which many are small enough to actually attach to an email, and helped make bootlegging rampant.

The Internet has helped me personally, though. By using FTP and various sharing technologies, I have been able to exchange music files with people all over the world. The Internet also allows some broadcasters to play whatever music they damned well want to play. Sometimes I get paid up front for playing on other peoples records, and lo and behold, some of these products even appear in…vinyl format.

It is now possible again to go to a show, and buy a vinyl, direct from the band, just like in the previous century, folks. Vinyls are a helluva lot harder to bootleg than a CD file. DIY merchandising is the thing of the present and future. Services like gofundme can also be a big help.

A scene that originated in Washington DC, called Go-Go appeared during the 1960s. Sort of quiet then, and into the

1970s, but gradually took hold and became very popular by the 1980s and 1990s. Great alternative to the mostly samey punk scene, rap and hip-hop. Bands like Rare Essence, Chuck Brown and the Soul Searchers, The Junkyard Band, Eminence, Experience Unlimited, Young Senators, and many others were just packing them in at outdoor shows and in clubs.

Go-Go sports an infectious syncopated signature almost non-stop beat, and lo and behold, there are actual musicians involved. Most of them have a bassist, drums and additional percussion such as timbales, roto-toms, congas, & keyboards, guitars, and some even sport brass and saxes etc. For awhile a DC cable channel had a show called Metroworld that was dedicated to this scene. The host was great, and reminded me a little bit of Mr. T.

I have hours of this show on videotape, thanks to my buddy Jamil Guellal. There is even some footage of the late DC Mayor Marion Barry groovin' with the Junkyard Band. I got to play with Eminence back in 2002 at a DC party, and it was a blast, and those guys can play. The reach of this scene went far and wide. Miles Davis heard Chuck Brown, loved the rhythm, and done stole Chucks drummer Ricky "Sugarfoot" Wellman. Local legend has it that Ricky had to call Miles' office back because Ricky's mom did not know who Miles Davis was when they called and so she took a message. Ricky can be seen on many YouTube vids of later Miles appearances.

Another coincidence was that after The Muffins split in 1981, Tom Scott and his Black Pond studio was popular with the DC punk scene, even recording some of the band Government Issue's tracks. Later, when Chris Biondo took over that studio, he became very tight with Chuck Brown.

Small world.

Stuff about Playing Drums

When I was a kid of 14, and did not know much about drum kits, I watched people play standard right handed drums with the ride cymbal on the right betwixt tom toms, with the hi-hat over on the left, which required one to cross arms to play the hi-hat. I was comfy with the drums going to around the right, but not comfy riding with my right arm. I was much better at it with my left. I also play matched grip. So, I moved the ride cymbal over on the left hand side where the hi-hat lives and play both with my left arm. Having the ride cymbal inches away from the hi-hat just made more sense to me, and I can use both easily without contorting. Been that way ever since 1967.

Other drummers thought this weird. Some years passed, and I saw Billy Cobham play with the Mahavishnu Orchestra, and noticed he sets up and plays this way as well. I thought that if this drum god also does it, it must be acceptable.

I am exonerated.

I now see that this sort of style has a name now. Open Handed Lead. Just heard the term recently. Nowadays I have a ride cymbal on both sides and this provides more options, and I will sometimes play the right hand side ride cymbal with my right arm.

I have always preferred drums to have both top and bottom heads installed. The kits I borrowed as a kid from friends before I got drums were nice early 1960s Rogers and Ludwig drums with all heads present. So I became used to the feel of high quality drums with all drum heads installed.

Later, I had the opportunity play drums with the bottom heads on the tom toms removed and I hated the lack of tone, & non-responsiveness because there was no air to compress in the drum, and the stick just dies there instead of bouncing back. I like a little ring tone in all the drums, and bounce from a double headed drum.

If you listen to 1970s rock drums you will notice most sound totally dead with no tone, because conventional wisdom du jour was to pull off the bottom head, muffle the drum and even pull off the front bass drum head, and put a pillow with a brick on it in there, thus killing tone, along with any shot at acoustic dynamics from the player. Tons of rock records from the 1970s exhibit this dull tone drum aura.

My own preference is an all wood drum, with the tom heads a little tighter on the bottom than the top, and on larger floor toms, the opposite. I go back and forth between using two real bass drums, and one. Don't care much for the double beater pedals used with one bass drum that are popular with metal bands. I can play them, but it's a whole different bag than two real bass drums. For one thing, you can play a serious forte' with two real drums, BOOM, and not at all with the double beater pedal, which just sort of lamely goes thwop if you try it. Rolls and syncopated beats sound way better to me with two real bass drums.

If you play fast rolls on the double beater pedal, one stroke can interfere with the other as the drum head does not snap back fast enough to hear, or feel them separately. Roto-toms are not even drums to me. You've probably seen them; a metal ring with a drum head on it that one spins to change the pitch. Usually in sets of multiples of two or three. I guess they are okay for melodic percussion, which I tried, and now don't play. The thinnest sound imaginable with no tone. I have inherited them on occasion from other drummers, and I just give them away.

I have never liked electronic drums, and only play those for fun or amusement. For sticks, I use a 5B hickory wood tip most of the time. When I was a kid, I tried every option there was, including plastic ones, and wood sticks with plastic tips which would always fly off. I tried oak sticks, but they are quite stiff & brittle and break easily. I like the hickory because they flex a little bit, which means they can take a battering. I often play on the louder side, but always try to play appropriately to the music and environment.

My original Rogers Swivomatic bass drum pedals from 1968 came with leather straps attaching the actual pedal to the beater mechanism. I kept stretching and breaking these damn things. I decided to replace the straps with bicycle chain. Much sturdier and efficient because they did not stretch. I should have patented this idea. Nobody else had a chain driven pedal. Chain driven bass drum pedals are now everywhere. One of my original 1968 pedals with the bike chain is at Tom Scott's Mountain Studio with my spare Sonor drum kit.

For drum heads, the standard Remo Ambassador or Emperor style batter heads are fine for every day, but I record with Remo Fibreskins, as they are reverberant and can make the smallest drum sound like a cannon.

My first experience with these heads was during the year 2000 when The Muffins played The Knitting Factory in Tribeca, NYC for the first time. They asked me about drums and said they had what I needed. When we got there, the stage manager went to get the drums out, and it was a small kit with an 18" bass, 12" tom and 14" floor tom. When I grumbled about the small sizes, he said "wait till you play and hear them."

He was right. The kit sounded great onstage and through their sound system and can be heard on The Muffins Loveletter # 1 CD. I always have front heads on bass drums, usually with a hole for exhaust and a microphone. I do have nice painted front heads with no hole and that's okay, too.

For cymbals, my taste is all over the map, using Paiste Sound Edge hi-hats, after twenty years with Zildjian hats which are a tad brittle. The Sound Edge are also very present, needing only a tickle to get to a microphone. I use a fifty-year-old 22" Zildjian A ride, and an assortment of other cymbals of varying vintages, by Wuhan, Ufips, Stagg, Zildjian and Paiste going from 18" to 30".

Never went in for small crashes or so-called splash cymbals. Nope.

No cowbell. I do have a set of Crotales, and a percussion tree made of various circular saw blades, farm equipment, and antique gongs that I use during overdubs. My old original mid-1960s Rogers kit for recording is set up, ready to go, and mic'd as of this writing.

Stuff about Playing other Instruments—Guitar

I have always loved to play guitar, but never learned proper. Drums took precedence. (I didn't learn drums proper either, but that did not stop me.) I can, however, get the point across in certain instances. When The Muffins were doing the Bandwidth CD back in 2000, I suggested a known entity to play guitar. When that did not pan out, I asked the guys if I could try. If it did not work, no big whoop and we would take another path.

Amazingly they said okay.

So, the first guitar track I ever did on a record was a solo on Essay R on the Bandwidth CD. For some reason, I had my pal John Logan's Telecaster at my house, so that's what I used. I had a Tube Overdrive pedal and some big amp and it was real loud. The Muffin boys insisted on actually being in the room for this, and I think to this day they regret THAT ear toasting decision. I had headphones; they didn't. So, the boys approved, and I ended up playing on several tunes on that record, as well as on the next 2 CDs, Double Negative, and Loveletter #2.

A long time ago, I heard the great Bob Quine play fucking crazy stuff that sounds beautifully out of place (not all the time) on Lydia Lunch's wonderful *Queen of Siam* record. That's kind of my approach to guitar. I sure ain't no shredder, nor do I aspire to be one.

I have since accumulated several guitars, and big tube amps by Marshall, Hiwatt, and Soldano (Soldano courtesy Rich Mueller). Other folks use this stuff in my studio.

Stuff about Playing other Instruments—Bass

Bass I can play if I have practice time. Only played live a few times, and do keep a nice old Fender P-bass around to prevent rust. For a solo record…someday. Wish the collector that has my early 1970s Rickenbacker 4001 would sell it back to me. I tried many times to buy it back, but he just won't budge. So, I finally gave up on that.

Stuff about Playing other Instruments—
Saxophone

Back when I joined The Muffins, Dave Newhouse offered me his Borgani soprano sax to honk/squeak on from time to time. I actually got tone out of this, and my embouchre would sometimes last a whole ten minutes. I had to use a light reed.

I don't own one, but would love to learn a low sax, like Baritone.

Not long after the Washington, DC metro opened in late 70s or 1980, The Muffins decided to do a walk around DC Sax quartet. Dave on bari, Tom on alto, Billy on tenor and myself on soprano. We went inside the Metro Center metro station stop to try this out. It is like a huge church...you can easily hear a whisper fifty feet away. It was so fucking loud I think you could hear us in the next two stations in both directions. Needless to say, the metro officials kicked our mugs out of there but fast. Too bad we did not record that cathedral-like natural reverb.

Stuff about Playing other Instruments—
Trombone

I have always loved the bone.

The well-known player, and purveyor of Doug Elliott brass mouthpieces, Doug Elliott, has played bone on several records by The Muffins. He's an old friend. For years, he was the guy you auditioned for to get in the excellent U.S. Air Force brass band, The Airmen of Note. He is currently lead trombone for the Artie Shaw Orchestra, and with the Smithsonian Jazz Masterworks Orchestra.

Fantastic player.

Back in the early 2000s when I lived in Baltimore, we went to Dewey Beach Delaware many times, as it is dog friendly. In Georgetown, DE, I scored an antique playable Pan American tenor trombone in a pawn shop for $75.

When The Muffins were doing the Loveletter # 2 CD,

Doug Elliott was not available, so Dave Newhouse had me learn an actual small sectional part, and I played it passably on this old instrument.

Since then, I also scored a nice copy of a Bach Bass trombone bone with a low F trigger. Much easier to play. I lent it to Doug Robinson, a pro player here in AZ, and he approved of it, and gave me a nicer proper bass bone mouthpiece than the one I had. I practice when no one is around.

Big sound.

I like the low end CHAWWW tone you can get from one of these.

During the late 1960s and early 1970s, the live music scene in Washington, DC was starting to get interesting, with seemingly a ton of bands playing original music. Shows were going on all the time at Fort Reno Park, P Street Beach, local schools, churches, and the Washington Monument grounds at Sylvan Theatre, which was outdoors.

The top-two bands in the area doing their own stuff included Grin, which was fronted by Nils Lofgren, who also dated my little sister for years, up until he hooked up with Bruce Springsteen, and the hard hitting Crank, who remain my fave local rock band from back then. I am still friends with Crank's Johnny Castle, who has been playing with The Nighthawks, and Geoff Richardson the Crank guitarist. Johnny also has or had another band in the DC area, The Thrillbillys.

Geoff lives in SoCal & visited me in AZ a few years back. I have a hazy memory of jamming with Crank at some farm type place in the days of yore, but wine, (I did not drink hardly at all in those days...) was involved.

Other great bands included Sageworth And Drums, Snake, Still Roven, Itchy Brother, Claude Jones, Wayne Feeds, Babe (Babe guitarist Steuart Smith plays with The Eagles now) and the first all synth band I ever saw in 1970 or 71, called Joy.

A band called Grits came on the scene in 1970, and were a bit Zappa-ish, and at times very Canterbury sounding, but, they had never even heard of any of the British Canterbury scene bands (Hatfield and The North, Caravan, National Health, etc.) Their leader and main composer Rick Barse loved Wagner, and one tune they did reminded me very much of Wagner's Siegfried Idyll. They were a big influence on The Muffins, and my first show with The Muffins was opening for them at American University in DC in October of 1976—on October 2nd, my 23rd birthday.

I used to see Grits regularly at Mr. Henry's bar at Tenley Circle, and I think once at The Emergency club in Georgetown, DC. I have some great recordings of Nils Lofgren with Grin from there. Crank played there. The Emergency also had some shows that have entered the realm of legend. The original Renaissance with Keith and Jane Relf played there. Atomic

Rooster during their only U.S. tour in 1971 with Ric Parnell of Spinal Tap fame on drums. I was on crew for the Rooster show, and the Renaissance gig.

After Vanilla Fudge melted, organist Mark Stein had a great band called Boomerang that played there. They had a teenage guitarist, Ricky Ramirez who was only 17 or 18, and great. Boomerang did one great LP on RCA. Many of these groups also played a cool venue called My Mother's Place near Connecticut Avenue in DC. I was on sound crew for Boomerang, and Rory Gallagher there.

There was a band called Watch that was comprised mostly of well heeled kids from out in the MD suburbs. They had the lot; red, white, blue, and even purple full Marshall stacks, Hammond organ and nice guitars. A shit-ton of expensive gear. Clean rock star clothes, too. They had a cool shtick where at the end of their set, the guitarist would throw his cherry wood Les Paul way up in the air while the band was doing the Quaalude thunder ending and stop on a dime when he caught the guitar.

What a crowd pleaser.

Once at the Sylvan Theatre near the Washington Monument, when he did the guitar toss, the guitar's headstock got caught in lighting wires, dangling there for a few seconds, and then it came down on the cement in front of the stage. Plugged into a Marshall stack. What a noise THAT was.

By 1971, I only knew two guys that had any experience at all with professional audio recording. These guys were Tom Robinson aka Tom True, (he helped record my band Tinsel'd Sin in 1973) and a guy named Chip Stanard who lived nearby in Chevy Chase, MD. Both of them are great at audio. Chip was a couple of years older than I, and had a whole audio lab in his house with Revox tape decks, signal generators, audio oscillators, microphones, oscilloscopes, the works. He was also a whiz at editing and splicing 1/4" audio tape. He would play tones on a sine wave generator, record them, then splice the tape together to obtain renditions of popular tunes. Chip obtained a contract with the Smithsonian to record various sound stages at the annual Smithsonian Folklife festival in 1971, held on the Washington, DC mall. This was then and still is a large event.

Chip took me under his wing, and trained me on the use of a Nagra-Kudelski IVs portable stereo reel-to-reel tape deck, and hired me to record the African stage. I think the microphones were Electrovoice RE11s, which are nice dynamic supercardioid mics. Nagra audio tape decks are the highest quality portable analog reel to reel tape decks ever manufactured. Expensive then, and now. The one I used even had extensions on the transport to accommodate 10" NAB tape reels if desired. When you used to see news reporters running around in the 1960s and 70s, they usually had someone right behind them carrying a Nagra in a briefcase. That is what the reporter's microphone was attached to in order to record stuff for later broadcast.

Coolest gig ever, to get paid while recording African music and drinking beer. The music was mostly great, and consisted of small acoustic acts to entire bands with horns.

Second Band Sane Day and Third Band Tinsel'd Sin

Sometime in 1971, guitarist and singer Bobby Siegel asked me if I wanted to play with his power trio, SANE DAY. He was about to, or was already dating my younger sister. I forget. Peter Olson was on bass. This was a fun band, and the first I played in that that did only original tunes.

We rehearsed at Bobby's house in the so-called "Hannukah Heights", which was and likely still is a large wealthy Jewish neighborhood in DC. His family acquired the house from Lyndon Johnson. Johnson's huge multiline telephone switch was still in a back room in the basement.

Another feature was that it was situated almost directly across the street from J. Edgar Hoover's house. Hoover would sometimes arrive at home while we were in front of the house hanging out and would NOT get out of his police escorted car while we were there. So, we would of course dilly dally on purpose for awhile and make him wait.

Fuck him, we thought.

I remember once we put a big PA speaker out in the driveway and pointed at his house. We certainly could be obnoxious little shits. There were always two cop cars in front of that house. They never bugged us. It was lit up at night with floodlights, too. Sane Day played at least a dozen or more shows during 1971 and two at Fort Reno Park in NW Washington, DC, several coffeehouses, and small clubs.

Our first gig was in a church set up by a super cute gal named Patty Palm. I was infatuated with Patty, this gal with long curly hair who hung out at the National Cathedral Coffeehouse. The place was then called the Green Door, and the same place I managed later as Pipeline Coffeehouse.

Patty's dad was Mike Palm, who was a well known restaurateur in DC and had Mike Palm's, a popular place for ages among the countless hootersuckers from central casting on and around Capitol Hill. Sane Day even had a Spinal Tap experience, when, I forget exactly how this happened, we ended up with a gig at the Fort Belvoir Army Officers club in Northern VA.

The military base scene in the movie Spinal Tap provides a pretty good whiff of how that went down. Sometime in 1972 we tried another singer, (forgot his name) who financed a 45 RPM single recording session in DC with the great engineer Ted Bodnar, who was about to expand to Merrifield, VA, where he later built and ran American Star studios.

This day we recorded live to 1/4" stereo tape. Ted also happened to have a cutting lathe, and so we got a few 45 RPM acetates cut that same day, and then, not knowing a damn thing about the business, never released the single. I don't even have one now. Be nice to have. We cut a song called "Susie" and our theme toon *Sane Day*.

Sane Day and Tinsel'd Sin's Bob Siegel Remembers

If I am remembering correctly—I met Peter Olson, the bass player of Sane Day and Tinsel'd Sin around the end of my tenth grade year—around May or June of 1970.

I believe he knew my "junior high school drummer" and neighbor, Wayne Price. Wayne, Peter and I jammed several times, and we got along well. Peter, then, dropped out of high school and hitchhiked out to Colorado, where he lived the western hippy life for several months. I remember he left his equipment here and a friend was borrowing his Fender bass. When he returned from Colorado, expanded mind and all—we re-connected and Sane Day was formed around the summer of 1971 with me on guitar, Matt McBride on vocals, and Jim Durham on the drums.

After some pretty wild times, and at least one show at Bethesda Chevy Chase High School—Matt and Jim went their separate ways—and "I think" maybe, we got our "over the top.." drummer, Paul Sears. Peter might have met Paul thru his Chevy Chase friend, Cary Secrest—and the "real Sane Day" was formed. I was drafted to be lead singer, and we started writing songs and doing our best to be rock stars.

At that point we mainly rehearsed in my parent's basement on 30th Place, NW DC—So, Paul and I were DC boys, living in Chevy Chase, DC, and Peter lived in Chevy Chase, Maryland.

We had to do some hitchhiking from house to house in those days, but that was pretty easy to do. If you were a "long hair" chances are it did not take very long, to get a lift from some other "long hair" who was driving. Paul seemed to be the best connected to find us gigs—we played at Coffee Houses (particularly the St Albans Coffee House, also known as The Pipeline, various Church teen affairs, private parties, a Frat Party or two in College Park, Maryland, and our "home away from home, Fort Reno, the big park in between Woodrow Wilson

High School, and Alice Deal Junior High School in upper NW Washington, DC.

George T. Dennis the Priest (a real Jesuit priest) was very involved with the "hippie youth" in the neighborhood, and I seem to remember since Paul was a very colorful teenager in the neighborhood (at age twelve or thirteen, Paul was famous for riding his stingray bicycle wheelie style for blocks and blocks all over the place—and was certainly the best drummer for miles and miles) He was also a champion on the trampoline—I basically think Paul was just not afraid of anything. I think he was drinking twenty Cokes a day by the time he was fourteen or fifteen, so that probably gave him lots of energy.

Fort Reno is where Nils Lofgren and his awesome band Grin played several times in the summer of 1970. By 1971, when Sane Day started playing Fort Reno, Grin had a record deal, and Nils had recorded with Neil Young and was on his way, to his well deserved fame and success.

In 1971, with George the Priest in our corner, we were being booked at Fort Reno a few times every month over the summer. We often were called in when somebody else canceled, and I believe George arranged paying us with a case of Budweiser Beer. Paul was the only one who could legally drink, being 18, but he didn't drink (I don't think beer mixed well with Coca Cola) George didn't care at the time that he was providing beer for underage kids—Sane Day had a pretty good fan base at Fort Reno.

And we sort of became young budding rock stars in the neighborhood. We did shows at Fort Reno in summer 1971, and tons of shows in summer 1972) I remember Crank, Itchy Brother, a band called Snake (I think), Sageworth and Drums (with Walter Eagen later of Magnet and Steel fame) and other very popular, talented young bands were also playing at Fort Reno.

Before Sane Day broke up, Paul and Peter got a little sick of my vocal abilities (Peter did sing some songs too)—so we enlisted a sort of "night club style singer" who could carry a tune a bit better, but did not seem quite as gritty as us. He financed our first recording—a song he wrote called Susie (a love song to some girl who I don't think he ever got to first base with)—backed with one of my personal favorite Sane Day songs, called, appropriately *Sane Day*.

Then, after all of our hard work, doing many gigs, even going as far south as Richmond, for some club gig—we broke up. Peter and Paul, then formed Tinsel'd Sin, replacing me with Carl Peachey on guitar and Lenny Puglisi on vocals—Lenny and Carl wrote some pretty controversial songs, but they were having fun.

Before long, I believe Peter campaigned for me to rejoin the boys as a second lead guitarist. I think they knew I liked to play long solos, with my wah-wah pedal, etc, so we could play longer shows. Then we also got Jim Panek on keyboards.

We sort of became the "house band" at Fort Reno in 1973. Lenny in his inimitable style, could work the crowd in a rather antisocial fashion—and we had lots of fans that enjoyed our hard rock "Alice Cooper" style show. Lenny used my motorcycle on stage as a prop for one of our most popular "cover songs" Ace Supreme" (was the prince of his team)—a song by a British band called Silverhead—who's singer became an actor of sorts and married the world's most famous groupie. (Pamela *I'm with the Band* Des Barres).

Then, I think Carl and Peter wanted a singer who could carry a tune better (sounds familiar) and we recruited Bill Thomas who could sing—as our new lead singer. He was not that keen on singing the lyrics that Lenny and Carl had written, but he took one for the team, and we carried on.

One other really fun story, about the Sane Day era—when we were rehearsing at my parents house, at 4921 30th Place, NW, DC (purchased from Lyndon Baines Johnson, when he became Vice President, and he moved to a much larger house in the Spring Valley neighborhood of DC)—my across the street neighbor was J. Edgar Hoover, director (and founder) of the FBI. When Hoover would return from work in his limousine—often, the band, plus maybe another rough looking teenager or two or three, would be hanging out in my front yard. Hoover was not too excited about being greeted on his street by a bunch of hippies—and he would not get out of the car, until we went inside. Needless to say, we thought this was hilarious, so we would regularly torment him by just hanging out for an additional twenty to forty minutes or so, and laugh about him hiding in his car.

On the day that Hoover died in 1972, TV news people were on my street, and they asked me (as a hippy looking kid) what was it like to have Hoover as a neighbor—and I told the "keep Hoover in his car story" and it was on the national news. It became a part of the documentation of Hoover being a bit paranoid. A few years later, investigative journalist Jack Anderson actually referred to my interview in describing some of Hoover's social awkwardness.

—Bob Siegel

Fort Reno Park, near my house, became a hub for hanging out as there were shows there every week. I played so many shows there, (Most were with Sane Day) and rented my Altec Lansing A7 Voice of the Theatre speakers to so many bands, that the Park office there gave me a parking pass so I could always drive right up on the grass to the stage whenever I wanted.

My days of scoping for street parking were over. This park also had a full on soccer field, a gazebo with enough room for a band and picnic tables, and is situated right next to Deal Hill, the highest elevation in the DC area. There were two TV stations nearby, and back in the days of Hi-Z PA systems a TV station audio signal would sometimes leak into the band PA during a show.

Kind of inconvenient.

Instrument amps sometimes had this same problem. If one had cheap unshielded cables...look out. Some crowds there got up to many hundreds of people and once in awhile there would be live classical/orchestral music back in the 1970s.

I played there with Zapata, the first band I was in during 1970, Then several shows with Sane Day in 1971-1972, and then with Tinsel'd Sin in 1973 which was the Sane Day trio with added Fender Rhodes played by Jim Panek, my dear teenage pal Carl Peachey on guitar, and first Lenny Puglisi, and then Bill Thomas on vocals. By then I had also acquired a 30" Electro-Voice bass speaker, which we had to build a very large and heavy cabinet for. (The band I was in during 1975-1976, Magick Theatre, played there, as did The Muffins later on after they moved the stage away from the woods to the other side of Fort Reno over near Wilson High School—where it still is. The old location I thought was much nicer, closer to the pavilion, had some tree shade, and had a basketball court.)

George Dennis, the local long haired Jesuit priest, who was involved with Fort Reno Park and area youth groups had a full wood shop in his garage nearby and helped me build it. We did not have enough screws holding the back on, and first time this was used, I was behind it, and after about 2 seconds it blew the heavy 3/4" plywood back cover off nearly taking my nuts with it.

This speaker came with a ten-pound toroidal crossover that sent everything over 200Hz to another speaker cabinet. Oddly, there was another band in DC, Sageworth and Drums, and their bassist had this same setup. My friend the bassist Jerry Moore actually had two of these things, and I ended up with one. I still don't know why 30" bass speakers were around in DC at that time in that scene. I have not seen one since those days.

They were also used in large stereo speaker cabinets that Electrovoice built and sold called Patricians. They sometimes pop up for sale on the Internet. I also had acquired from Tom Linthicum, a pair of Altec Lansing 210 exponential bass horns for the PA, (look them up) which were so large they could not be brought into the house, nor would they fit in a cargo van. They lived in my garage. When we used these bad boys at Fort Reno Park, we would put one on top of pal Nick Brown's station wagon, and the other on the roof of a van and just park the vehicles on either side of the stage.

Sometime in the very early 1970s, I ended up doing sound, for the first time all by myself, (Ken Smithson may have been guiding me) for a local singer named Liz Meyer. Her backup band was called The Fat Boys. The bassist I already knew, Billy Hancock, as I had met he and brother Dale some years before. I had not met drummer Dave Elliott, and had never seen or heard of their guitarist, Danny Gatton before. He looked like a guy from an auto parts counter. I had to rub my eyes repeatedly. While this style of rock and roll was not exactly my style of rock music, I *just had never seen anyone play the guitar like that before*, nor had anyone else who witnessed early Gatton appearances.

What an eye opener.

Astounding.

It wasn't too long before every guitarist in the DC area was checking him out. The Fat Boys eventually became their own entity sans Liz.

Gatton's influence on guitar players everywhere is nearly inestimable, and also amazing, considering how long it took for him to really get noticed. He appeared to be bored to death much of the time, or wishing he was someplace else while playing this just...incredible....guitar.

Being a whiz at electronics, Gatton developed this doo-dad he called the Magic Dingus Box which was attached near or over the tailpiece of his black Les Paul. It controlled a variety of effects including an Echoplex and a Leslie rotating horn. The rest of the time, as far as I know, he played ancient Telecasters. Years later, he was rehearsing with a guy named Johnny Seaton directly across the street from my house in Bruce Cornwell's basement, and so I saw these guys all the time. They needed a drum kit, so I lent them my spare 1980s Rogers drumkit, and they ended up liking it a lot and the drummer bought it. (Later on the kit was owned by Pete Ragusa from the Nighthawks—dunno where it is now) I had several opportunities to jam with Danny Gatton, but my dumb ass did not jump on any of them.

When the great guitarist Henry Kaiser was visiting from California and playing with The Muffins in 1980, almost the first thing he said after unpacking was "Is there a way we can go see Danny Gatton?" He happened to be playing regularly at a place called Beneath It All, which was located under the Crazy Horse club in Georgetown, Washington, DC.

So, Steve Feigenbaum and I took Henry to see him. There are a lot of Gatton vids on the web, but I don't think any are from this place. A great show, and Henry loved it. An old friend and roommate of mine, Jimmy Cavanaugh, played bass with Gatton often and had funny stories about leaving smelly cheese in the back of each others' amps.

Nice.

Both Danny and Billy Hancock have since passed away. Sometime in 1995, James Burton (Elvis, Ricky Nelson) and even Les Paul himself played at a Gatton memorial. Fender made a Danny Gatton model Telecaster for awhile.

Music Machine or Drum Machine

Sometime in 1972 or 3, I was approached by the manager of a club called The Rabbit's Foot in Washington, DC on Wisconsin Avenue, not far from where I lived, who threw me a curve ball over beers with this idea: play LIVE drums to canned music blasting through their large disco sound system. Sometimes they actually had live acts on Friday and Saturdays, but this was a four-nights-a-week Mondays to Thursdays gig.

However, I declined this paying gig because I would not be able to choose ANY of the music. Playing 1972/3 vanilla top-40 hits such as *Free Bird*, *The Joker*, and *Ramblin' Man* was not really my thing. I made mention of this event on social media some years ago, and heard from the guy that actually took the gig.

Small world.

New Jersey Adventures

During 1972 or 1973, my friend, guitarist/trumpet player Greg Yaskovich (we played a gig together once as Fast Food) introduced me to a guy he met at Maryland University named Stu Paskow, who lived in New Jersey. One weekend, Greg was going up to visit Stu in NJ, and invited me to tag along.

Stu was leaving college and starting a band playing bass with two guitarists, then called Whisssk. One was Bruce Pucciarello, now a quite successful jewelry designer and Kenny Segall, since of the popular Snarling Dog effects pedals fame. He designed those things. Kenny still plays in area bands in NJ.

We played for a bit, and they invited to move up there, Scotch Plains/Fanwood area off on NJ 22 and play in this band. I said okay, sort of pissed off my girlfriend Lesley and did it. This group played kind of an odd mixture of originals and a few covers. We played some King Crimson, Zappa, and tunes from Stanley Clarke's first great solo LP. It was getting to be a tight band.

For most of its existence during my time the band

rehearsed in a large ex chicken coop with a big roll-up loading door behind an enormous mid 18th century home with 75 acres of land, known as the Van Der Veer Harris house in Hillsborough, NJ on RT 206 South.

At that time, across from the coop was a garage that would easily hold ten cars. It was all thick forested land, except for a small lawn around the house, and very private. As of this writing it has a website. The Van Der Veer Harris House website does not show that all the surrounding land has since been carved into strip malls, condos, and gas stations.

Pretty depressing.

A few miles down the same road is Drumthwacket, the NJ governor mansion (I want that job.) and the other way towards Somerville is the estate of Doris Duke, where I later read someplace that Imelda Marcos had been hiding from the authorities. It is now a tourist attraction with gorgeous gardens.

That part of NJ was gorgeous at the time. Sparsely populated. Not anymore.

Anyway, this Harris house was huge, and had two kitchens and front and back staircases. It was not hard to go a day without seeing anyone else. Also on the property was a little servant's house out near the road. It was a wreck and uninhabitable.

One day when I was either visiting, or in the process of moving to NJ my mom who was working part time at Georgetown University informed me they were casting extras for The Exorcist and I could not get down there then. Darn.

One fine day, I was there with Stu Paskow our bassist, and Jean or Tuffy (I forget the last names) who lived there (We also used Tuffy's big step van sometimes) and the sheriff of either Hillsborough or Somerset County came by with NO HUNTING signs that he wanted to post on the property.

Okay, fine.

Here's a funny: he lingered a bit, and said that property owned by the Kennedy family wrapped around about 15 acres of the property. No one knew that. He said the Kennedys had a horse path cut through the property, and could he open the gates? Let them come ask was the response. The gates were never unlocked for the couple of years I was with the band.

Sometimes, besides having the band in that huge chicken coop, we rehearsed in the actual house, or at our bassist's home in Scotch Plains, NJ. The coop was large enough to have a small audience in it, which we often did. There were some great parties at the big house, and local NJ proggers Fireballet, who were popular at the time would sometimes come hang out.

There was giant old Sylvan pool there with about two feet of mud and debris in it, and we spent ages cleaning that out, and actually used it one summer. These guys all had Joisy accents as in.."ay, Pully, are youse goin' to the batroom?" Another expression I heard there and love, akin to "catch ya later" was, "later, baluba". I still use that one.

Gigs, however, were in the not-too-many category, and after some months I found out my girlfriend had spent a night or two with a member of Larry Coryell's fusion band, 11th House. This fact pissed me off enough to return to the DC area and find out if Lesley and I would last.

Meanwhile, a great drummer, and pal, Neil Collier, replaced me in the band. So, knocking around DC and not getting much done, the gal and I separated. For awhile. The NJ guys invited me back with a possibility of more potential gigs, and "by the way, we are joining the union; you in?" So we all joined the American Federation of Musicians and got a booking agent.

Stu was also related to a powerful ABKCO attorney named Alan Kahn, who was general counsel at the time for ABKCO (Beatles, Stones, etc., etc.) and Apple Records. He drew up a band contract too. He was a nice guy. The booking agents, whose names I forget, (somebody and Boyd) got us quite a few more gigs. They did try as I recall to get us a tour with a major, (I never found out who it was) but The Pousette Dart Band, who were a bit softer than us I heard later, landed whatever that was;

may have even been Yes. After some months of okay local NJ shows and sheckels, I went back to visit my folks via metroliner for Christmas.

On that trip in late 1974 or early 1975, I think it was, two things happened.

My gal Lesley wanted us to try the relationship again. She was my first real love. She was also close friends with my sister and my parents.

So, she had some pull.

Pepe Gonzalez, the bassist from my first band Zapata, who had by then gotten heavy into Miles Davis suggested I come back and why don't we do a Weather Report/electric Miles Davis type project? This music was more my style, so I said okay. This would be with he and Ernie Hererra who also played guitar in the first band I was ever in, Zapata.

So, I said goodbye to Whisssk, all of whom I am still friends with, and came back to DC with the help of old friend, Nick Brown, who very graciously drove up from DC to NJ with a U-haul and back I went. I had to sign a release from the band contract with Alan Kahn, too. He wrote me a very nice letter wishing me luck, that I wish I still had.

At that time, this move back to DC was a good idea I thought, so I returned, staying with Lesley, and back and forth to my parents' house nearby where my drums ended up. We ended calling this pop combo Magick Theatre. The three of us original Zapata guys managed to convince a great woodwind player, Moshesh Akhbab, the now Texas based percussionist Rudy Morales, also from Zapata, and Greg Hutchinson on Fender Rhodes to join us.

Last to join was Don Lax on violin. Don built his own instruments and is one hell of a player. Today, he is very well known performer on the Island of Maui, HI. We rehearsed in my basement during the day.

Sometimes I would sleep in, and if I did not answer the door, Don would stand in the back yard and practice his primal screaming to wake me up. That worked, and occasionally freaked out some of the neighbors. He sounded like he was being chased by Leatherface from the Texas Chainsaw Massacre. One day while rehearsing, Don was doing a solo and playing some really great and frantic violin, and suddenly, he stopped, looked puzzled, and started looking around. The violin had vanished. It was a tad creepy. The whole band stopped and were looking around, mystified.

What the fuck happened?

We thought maybe we pissed off the spirit world or something. It took us a good five minutes to realize that the violin had sailed past all of us, over the seated pianist, and wedged itself, undamaged, in the frame of my mom's unused exercycle on the other side of the room. A good twenty-five feet or more. That room was as big as the entire house footprint. Bizarre occurrence. We must have all really been into the tune, as no one noticed a flying violin go by. This group only had two or three tunes, but they were long. We had an acoustic, almost jazz set, and a long electric Miles style piece maybe twenty-five minutes long called *No Words Need to Be Spoken*.

Music and Les Femmes

FOR MOST OF my life, the music I listened to and played seemed to quite the turn off for the mums. I mostly grew up with classical and twentieth century music thanks to my parents, who always had Gershwin, Bernstein, Delius, Moussorgsky, Borodin, Wagner, (my mom always accused my dad of having a crush on Birgit Nilsson, a very famous Wagnerian singer) and sometimes Gregorian chant playing on the family Magnavox.

This was a problem even when I was a sometimes sullen "outsider teen" early on, listening mostly to a mixture of King Crimson, Wagner, Bartok, Stockhausen, Varese, Zappa, West Coast Pop Art Experimental Band, and Carl Orff; you get the gist.

Most of the west coast hippie vibe stuff like Grateful Dead/Jefferson Airplane, etc. just did not speak to me. I tried to like the Dead, as folks I knew loved them, but the dope-laden sissy-assed jams (my opinion) just never roped me in. The audience at the two shows I saw back in the early 1970s made me want to put lots of geography between us. Airplane's bassist Jack Casady is actually from my neighborhood, and I had several of the same teachers he did at Alice Deal Jr. High in DC back in the 1960s.

Back in the 1970s, there were not terribly many females

that enjoyed Henry Cow, Faust, Pere Ubu, Tin Huey, Frank Zappa, The Residents, Art Zoyd, Magma, or Bartok, Stravinsky, Stockhausen, King Crimson, and so on. Progressive rock fests and concerts throughout time have often been called sausage fests (with no line at ladies room) for this reason.

I see now that this has changed in recent years.

So...

The gals thought I was on the peculiar side. Go figure. I felt like I was becoming quite a Steppenwolf in this respect before I was even 30. Back then I attempted to keep these two relationships, music and gals, completely separate, and did so for many years up through my first marriage. Wife #1 kind of tolerated my stuff, but was certainly not what one could call a fan.

We had been through a lot of stuff, and I thought we were committed to each other, and would tough it out. No. She left, and that was that.

Depressing.

Up until my second marriage, I could count the gals that actually liked the music stuff I did on the fingers of one hand.

What the hell was I thinking?

Get with a gal that gets it.

My Second Wife

Late into 2001, I met and eventually married, Deb, my second wife, who IS into the music, is very supportive and has had, and still does, her own progressive rock radio show on cable and Internet since 1991. (Internet came later)

Late in 2001, I was hunting for radio stations that played new music, and WEBR, now Radio Fairfax, came up in a search. I sent an email into the general mailbox, and not too long after wards heard back from Deb, who had the Prog Rock Diner show. She was on the band committee at the Progday festival in Chapel Hill, NC that we had just played that past Labor Day.

I did not know they even had a committee.

I did not even know who she was, nor did I meet her at

Progday. A few weeks later, we did an interview, and the rest is history.

She was single, and came to me like a life preserver after the very depressing failure of my first marriage. I have been her co-host on the radio show since January 2014, presenting the Paul Sears Radio Hour as the second half of her Prog Rock Diner show on Radio Fairfax. It's a blast, and I can play whatever I want. Like for instance Stockhausen's entire Kontakte, or if I feel like it, Jimi Hendrix. Once in awhile I even play prog rock.

She is also one of the most reasonable, even-tempered person I have ever met. Type A as am I, I can always use grounding.

We lived for awhile in DC, and late in 2002, bought a house in Baltimore. We got involved with Orion Sound Studios and helped out with shows there for about seven years.

The ongoing decline of our Baltimore neighborhood (I was ambushed and mugged while on a bicycle) was getting unbearable, so we decided that we had enough of the east coast.

We were going to bail from the U.S. completely, and go live in France, but that proved to be expensive, (moving our stuff) traumatic (quarantining dogs) and involved impressive amounts of paperwork. One can buy a house there, no problem. Vacating the U.S. to actually live there is not a walk in the park.

Deb had lived in Arizona and I have friends here; one that had been razzing me for years to come live out here, so we moved in 2010.

She, of course, ended up finding a place we could afford.

As far as music goes, we do not have identical taste. I learn from her, and she learns from me, and between the two of us, it's a huge music collection. Our CD collection alone takes up most of a wall twenty-three feet long and shelves five or so feet high. We still have vinyls as well, but not nearly as many. For instance, she hipped me to Karda Estra with Richard Wileman, which was new music to me.

I love his work.

I have since done several CDs with Karda Estra.

For awhile, Thee Maximalists, which started life as a loud all improvising power trio, and resembled a sorta "Blue Cheer plays Coltrane" kinda vibe played at our home in Baltimore. The joke then amongst Thee Maxis was, if she likes this racket, I'm home free.

We have been to festivals in the U.S. and other countries. It was she that got involved with the folks here in Superior a year before I did, and we are here as a direct result.

We have a small extra house here that she used as an art getaway for a couple of years. I had the bigger building next to our house in Apache Junction all to myself as my Garage Mahal studio. She wanted for us to move here to Superior. It took ages to find a suitable house with room for our stuff and my studio, but, she did it.

To boot, her family and I get along great, thankfully. Refreshing, when contrasted against some past relationships I have had.

If your partner's family does not care for you, you are very likely doomed.

The Muffins

WHILE I WAS in the band Pepe Gonzalez and I founded in 1975, Magick Theatre, I had gotten more into improvising with an ensemble. Besides Pepe on bass, we had Moshesh Akhbab on sax and flute, myself on drums, Rudy Morales on congas and percussion, Ernie Herrera on guitar, and a Fender Rhodes player named Greg Hutchinson. Don Lax on violin.

Magick Theatre was influenced in part by electric Miles Davis, mid-1970s Weather Report, Mahavishnu Orchestra and other like minded "fusion" music, with some acoustic jazz influence thrown in the mix.

By then I had also spent a lot of time absorbing British and European groups such as Magma, Henry Cow, Soft Machine, Faust, PFM, older Genesis, King Crimson, Van der Graaf Generator, and many other "similarly different" obscure-at-the-time European groups.

I had a friend named Tom Fenwick who told me about a group of people he knew that were also into the *VERY SAME*.

Tom never had a phone number for these folks. Tom often came to my house in Washington, DC, or we would meet at Fort Reno Park nearby for shows. These people he was on about I found out later turned out to be The Muffins and the Random Radar Records folks that were getting going out in the Maryland suburbs.

So, then, this happened: Michael Zentner, (guitar, violin) who had left The Muffins (along with Stu Abramowitz, their drummer) contacted Pepe Gonzalez about playing, and Pepe was not really interested in the progressive rock scene, i.e. Henry Cow, etc. but told Michael... hey...that *his drummer was*, and gave Michael my number. Michael called me up and suggested getting together. (Michael and I still have never have played together)

He brought over lots of live boot tapes of Henry Cow (he had visited them), Robert Wyatt, and other great stuff. He then filled me in about The Muffins, Random Radar, and that scene going on out in Gaithersburg and other nearby MD suburbs.

Pepe Gonzalez was getting more and more involved with straight jazz, which was not a direction I wanted to go. (Today, Pepe and I are still pals, and he is now a very influential force in the jazz community in Washington, DC, and teaches music there).

Shortly after our meeting, Michael told me that The Muffins were doing shows as a trio, with Dave Newhouse, (keys, woodwinds) Billy Swann, (bass) and Tom Scott, (woodwinds) improvising, and...that they were even playing a Henry Cow tune, *Solemn Music*.

During the summer of 1976, Michael took me from DC to see The Muffins, who had built a stage in their backyard in Gaithersburg, MD. They did a trio show. I could not believe this. Gaithersburg? This town was generally regarded as being on the podunk side of the tracks back then by us Washington, DC city sophistos.

I was flabbergasted that out in the Maryland 'burbs was a whole passel of people into music like this. Very few in DC where I lived were at the time. The camaraderie was instant, and they invited me to play with them sometime and see if it could work. On that fateful life-changing first day, Dave Newhouse came to pick me up in DC.

His car sounded like a babbling brook. About halfway to

The Muffin house, I asked what was up with the weird noise the car was making? Well. He had an eight-track tape player with Edgar Froese's Aqua tape stuck in there, and could not turn it off. Right when the car started it was blub-gurgle-blub.

Hilarious.

After two or three sessions, they asked me to join the band, and said "by the way, Stu, their ex-drummer, was about move out and would I like to move in?"

So, throughout late summer into September of 1976, as a quartet, we worked incessantly, both improvising, and got started writing *Amelia Earhart*, which appears on our first record Manna/Mirage.

I also learned a long tune, *Not Alone*, that they kept from the five-piece version of the band. That kept me busy for ages. There's more.

The Muffins, along with pals Steve Feigenbaum, John Paige, Ernie Falcone, and a few others had already formed a record company, Random Radar, and had been in touch both Fred Frith, and Lol Coxhill. I could not believe that here was a readymade music collective up and running that I had lots of stuff in common with.

Consanguinity.

To boot, I previously knew none of these Random Radar/The Muffins people. I was still a kid, only 22. Prior to my arrival, they had already recorded an unreleased, at that time, sampler LP that included The Muffins, Fred Frith, Lol Coxhill, Mars Everywhere (then a duo—Tom Fenwick & Ernie Falcone) and some offshoots such as Illegal Aliens. This was the Random Radar Sampler. Vinyl only, never re-released.

We played our first gig together with a great DC band called Grits on my 23rd birthday October 2nd, 1976 at American University.

An early as yet unreleased version of the tune Amelia Earhart on our first record, Manna/Mirage was recorded there in Gaithersburg on Dave's four-track TEAC 2340.

Paul Sears

The Muffins Relocate to Rockville, Maryland, 1977-1978

Sometime in late 1977 or early 1978 we decided to move closer to DC. We needed more room, as Tom Scott and wife Colleen were going to move in so The Muffins would all be together.

We ended up settling on a brick house with an underground basement on Portree Drive near downtown Rockville, MD. I actually went and met the neighbors first to let them know what we were up to beforehand before we signed a lease, and they were fine with it. A couple of the neighborhood kids are now grown, and friends of ours today. One, Matt Romasco (whose dad occasionally let us hop the fence and use their pool back then) is now a tube guitar amp whiz.

Not long after the move, our friend Denise K, by now Billy's girlfriend, was also living with us. She owned a woodworking company with her brother, and did most of the work building a wall in the basement towards the end of soundproofing. We had a twelve-channel Peavey mixer, several average dynamic microphones, and Tom bought a TASCAM 80-8 half inch eight-track tape machine.

CATCH -A-BUZZ STUDIO Rockville location was shortly up and running. The control room was in Tom and Colleen's bedroom in the basement. Tom and Dave were now also working together at Washington Music Center running the horn and woodwind repair shop there. So these two lads had to look at each other morning, noon, and night.

I was working at a record store in Gaithersburg and running the Pipeline Coffeehouse at the Washington Cathedral in Washington, DC. An easy gig to get. I had been a patron for many years, played there a few times, and knew the Cathedral admin staff, as my dad also worked at Washington Cathedral. He consulted on their three pipe organs and worked in their gorgeous libraries.

They probably still have the enormous Skinner pipe organ.

They also had a smaller one in a chapel, and one that rolled around, called a Portativ. It was the size of a small house. Both Helen Keller and President Woodrow Wilson are buried at the National Cathedral. While I was working there, there was a full pottery shop/classroom and offices in the basement of the building the coffeehouse was located in.

There were kilns and all the other supplies needed to do this stuff. The pottery teacher, whose name I forget and I were clearing out a basement room, ripped down some big shelves that had been attached to the wall long ago, and found a huge hidden metal door on rollers. Lo and behold, this is an entrance to the catacombs that run under the National Cathedral and Saint Albans grounds.

We had been hearing rumors about these so called secret underground passages for ages, but here was an actual entrance. I remember exactly where it is. A friend and I went in, and bingo. The light switch worked. We explored, but only a little. Being employees, we did not want to get busted in there.

Billy was a manager at a pre-Starbucks-era coffee shop at the now defunct White Flint Mall. We rehearsed four nights a week and did shows throughout the Washington, DC area at clubs such as the Childe Harolde, the Psychedelly, coffee shops, Fort Reno Park and even in churches. We, of course, did many shows at the Pipeline Coffeehouse.

We would haul our stuff in Tom's old brown Ford Econoline van, affectionately called "The Brown Turd." Sometimes Lynn Pruitt, the Manna/Mirage cover artist, would help us out with her slightly larger van.

Carlos Garza, later keys player in Mars Everywhere also provided transport services with his big van. An awful lot of music occurred in that Rockville house. Guests of The Muffins included Fred Frith, John Greaves, Peter Blegvad, Chris Cutler, Yochk'o Seffer, Francious Lazeau, Hector Zazou, along with Giorgio Gomelsky and Jean Luc Karakos.

Chris Cutler came to visit alone sometime in the late

1970s, and was curious to know if we could give him a lift to California to visit The Residents. We had to tell him that it was 3,000 miles away.

Kinda funny.

He wanted to go see Pere Ubu, and fortunately they were playing a scant distance away at the Psychedelly in Bethesda, Maryland, so I drove him to meet them for the first time. A great gig, too. Chris also recorded a solo percussion piece at Tom Scott's new Black Pond studio. It's pretty cool, but I don't think he ever released it.

Late into the 1970s, I became reacquainted with old friend Richard Womeldorf, whom I knew fairly well back the 1960s. He came into an inheritance and spent about $400 in one fell swoop at the record store I worked at.

An average new LP was only $5 including tax in those days; A LARGE pile of LPs. He also decided to help out The Muffins and just gave us about three grand, which we promptly spent a chunk of on PA amps and speakers. He also tried valiantly, as did many, to help my younger sister, and took her on a vacation to Colorado to help her clean up her act. That ultimately didn't work. Bless 'm.

Our friend George Daoust had a large white van and transported us to shows many times. George also drove me to NYC to deliver the stereo master tape for our <185> LP to Fred Frith. He was a quiet, sweet guy, and absolutely the most unpunctual cat I have ever known; I soon learned that if we needed him at 3:00 PM, to tell him noon, and MAYBE he would arrive by maybe 3:00 PM.

Up into the 2000s, he would come to a show I was doing and walk in on the downbeat of the last bar of the last tune and say "did I miss it?"

Back in the early 2000s when we were in Baltimore, George brought me a box of seven-inch tape reels and sez, howza bout digitizing these? I said waaaait a minute. Most of them had MY handwriting on them.

I said dude, you are not getting these back. He did help me move once back in 1981…hmmm.

RIP, George.

Miss the guy.

Brian Rapp and Grits, a Great Washington, DC Band

When I was around 17, I was dating a gal named Meg in Garrett Park, Maryland. There was a guy that lived down the street from her named Brian, who had a sarcastic sense of humor and a gruff vibe that appealed to me.

He was also a very sharp guy, and was well spoken. The gal and I broke up, and I did not see Brian again until I was 18 and old enough to go in a bar, Mister Henry's at Tenley Circle, to see live bands. This was the bar closest to my house that had live music. 1971 or so. One of the bands that played there was a great group that played all originals, called Grits.

Rick Barse seemed to be the leader, and played keys and also sang. I remember he was the first guy in a DC rock band to acquire a Yamaha CP70 electric baby grand piano. I also remember an RMI Rocksichord. His wife Amy played bass, violin and sang. Tom Wright was on guitar and viola with Bob Sims on drums. Great group. Sound at times was not unlike a mixture of Frank Zappa and Richard Wagner.

They had a tune that reminded me very much of Wagner's *Siegfried Idyll*. Very unique style and they were all serious players. They had great humor sprinkled within their lyrics. I developed a crush on Amy, who had long wild hair and played excellent bass and violin—unique for a woman in the area back then. Plus, it was amazing to see a band like this one in a bar.

Anyway, I walk in the live-performance room at Mister Henry's one night while Grits were playing, and there's the gruff Garrett Park kid Brian Rapp, now decked out with long hair and a full beard. He was working with Grits as their road manager and sound man, and did this for many, many years. This was a few years before I joined The Muffins, and I later found out The Muffins posse and their friends were also big Grits fans.

Grits music also had a bit of a Canterbury scene vibe to it, (Hatfield and The North particularly) and I was surprised when I learned they had never even heard any of that British progressive rock music.

When The Muffins got going, there was tight camaraderie with Grits. As I mentioned, my first show with The Muffins actually was opening for Grits at American University on my 23rd birthday, Oct 2, 1976. When Grits started to wind down close to or during 1979-80, Brian Rapp came and worked with us part time.

Brian moved in to our Portree Drive house in Rockville. When Grits called it quits, he worked with The Muffins full time for the last year and a half of the first go round of The Muffins quartet life cycle—which ended in 1981. Brian was an absolute whiz at electronics.

Billy Swann has an old no name (he calls it Voice of God) fuzz box pedal for what we called Zoom Bass. (on most of our records—the really hairy bass sound).

When that pedal started to deteriorate, Brian disassembled and re-soldered it. More than once I think. Billy had that pedal when I joined The Muffins in 1976, so it is old! Someone spilled a drink on one of our Crown amps at a Psychedelly Club show in Bethesda, and Brian repaired it while we were playing.

When we split in 1981, Brian ended up teaching electronics at a trade school. He passed away some years back. Billy still has that amazing sounding fuzz box pedal and I think of Brian whenever I see it. Tom Wright the Grits guitarist/viola player eventually scored a gig in the Chicago Symphony Orchestra where he still is, I think. Rick Barse passed away some years ago. Amy Taylor (Barse) has played violin on two later CDs by The Muffins, Bandwidth and Double Negative. Drummer Bob Sims is still around, but I don't know if he is playing these days.

Sometime in the Mid-1970s Pipeline Coffeehouse

When I was running the Pipeline Coffeehouse at the National Cathedral, I was visited there late one afternoon before a show by two teenaged kids. One was Dave Byers, a guitarist, and the other, Jonathan Gibson, a bass player. (I later found out they had actually met through The Muffins) They gave me a little blue cassette that I wish I still had. This was of their band The Dancing Flower Pots and a song on the tape was *Mr. America and the Swastika Girls*.

They wanted a gig at the coffeehouse.

This was too cool to pass up, so I gave them a show. May have been Dave and Jon's first ever gig. Later on, when the hardcore punk scene was starting, Dave worked all over the DC area, and got involved with bigger things; folks like Henry Rollins, Chucky Sluggo, The Enzymes, Static Disruptors, and others. Same with Jon. I also remember a band called Tony Perkins and The Psychotics, and later Human Rights, and one of their songs (Dave's I think) was covered later by the group 311.

Dave, Jon, and I remained friends over the years. Late in the 1990s, Dave Byers took a 90 degree turn and got into playing jazz guitar. He asked me to record with him at Norman Van Der Sluys's studio which was very close to where I was living in the Mount Pleasant area of Washington, DC. We recorded some tunes, but they never came out.

Later, Jon Gibson had a studio and helped The Muffins with some ADAT transfers for our Loveletter # 1 CD. Dave sadly passed away in the early 2000s. Jonathan Gibson is today a muso and software developer, and I think, designs virtual instruments.

Jonathan Gibson, Bassist and DC Scenester Remembers

Like most teens, when I discovered music, I was both moved and motivated. I had to hear every note of every song by every band I discovered. I got my first bass in the fall of 1974 and never looked back. I was a passionate collector of sounds and utterly fascinated by the diversity of musical idioms. And all these sounds, beats and melodies, got mixed up in my mind, as what would later be called mash-ups.

During this passionate consumption of music, I discovered WGTB Georgetown University radio. WGTB was my home for all the diverse music I could consume. One day, I heard a local band called The Muffins play on the air. At the end of their segment, they gave out their phone number.

Naturally, I had to call. I don't remember who I talked to, but toward the end of the conversation he told me about this guy in NE DC who had some brilliantly weird guitar sounds and performances, and gave me his number. And that is how I met David Byers.

After our first jam, we decided to form a band to further expand and express our love of experimental, abstract timbres and free improvisation. This gave birth to The Dancing Flowerpots.

The Flowerpots found a venue at the Pipeline Coffeehouse on the grounds of Saint Albans near the National Cathedral. The Pipeline was home to a variety of underground and experimental bands. There, The Flowerpots played our first show—in 1976. Once again, the common denominator was The Muffins: not only did they play there often, but the curator of the Pipeline's Friday night shows was none other than Paul Sears, drummer from The Muffins.

Time passed as did many musical adventures, and The Flowerpots evolved into The Enzymes, a punk band with a streak of Flowerpot experimentalism. David was lead guitarist, and sang lead on most of our songs, and in addition to bass, I played prepared guitar, inspired by Fred Frith of British band Henry Cow. Other original Enzymes included Chris Haskett on guitar, later of Rollins Band and now pursuing his own music in Europe, and Craig Rosen of Static Disruptors, now a writer in LA. An interesting bit of trivia: Craig and I were fifth-grade classmates of Henry Rollins.

And David Byers was, and always would be, no one but himself, a true genius. The history of his career is very much the story of DC music from Jazz to Funk to Punk in the 70's, 80's and 90's. A DC and indeed an American original, there will only be just the one. Of all my experiences and accomplishments in music, I consider my work with him to have been the greatest honor I will ever have.

After the Enzymes, I played in Tony Perkins and the Psychotics, a diversely influenced funk-punk band 1980-87, that also featured David Byers, Mission for Christ 1983-86 (punk), Cocktail Music 1984-85 (Jazz) and Penguin's Exploding Octopus 1986-87 (improv). In 1993 I started my studio, Electric Naschyland, where I worked with such artists as Englishman and Shango Band (Reggae), The Skinnys (Punk) and MK Ultra (Post-Punk) among many others. I was recently working on a project with Phil Duarte, who was the original guitarist in the Psychotics, and played in several other bands. My new limited-space studio will be home to my personal music, and small-scale collaborations. The story goes on from there, but I write these memories to give a shout-out to my friends the Muffins. For introducing David and me, I owe my career and meeting my greatest musical collaborator to the Muffins.

—Jon Gibson

In hindsight, I regret not thinking at the time to find more symbiosis with some of the DC punk scene. The Muffins had a similar attitude; we were a bit older and played different music. Some of the bands I liked, especially the ones Dave Byers/Jon Gibson were involved with and Government Issue. 9353, was, of course, loosely connected to that scene when they appeared in the early 1980s, jarring quite a few, and they were WAY different. (I was a fan and played with them, but not until much later.) The Muffins, I think now, had in some ways a similar

"Punk Jazz" approach, if you will.

We were older and did not have the passion for fashion that some of these people seemed to be possessed by. Sort of a "White Dopes on Punk" syndrome. I liked the hardcore rock punks a little better then the much prettier middle-of-the-road "new wave" thing that was happening contemporaneously.

Around that same time, 1976 I think, I was visited at the coffeehouse by a huge guy wanting a gig. This monster sort of resembled Hagrid from the Harry Potter films, resplendent in his everyday chain mail. I first thought he was running recon as part of a Viking horde coming to storm the cathedral.

Ha-ha.

Just kidding.

This was way before Harry Potter, but he should have had that part. His name was Rupert Chappelle; he had a cool schtick and ended up a friend. He mostly played solo synthesizer and sang, often with an array of TVs showing early computer graphics and other arty stuff. Of course, I gave him his own show. He later did shows with The Muffins.

One day, he gave me a ride to Montgomery college for some reason—might have been an interview on their radio station. When we were leaving the campus, he made an illegal turn and a cop blipped him to pull over. He was dressed Hagrid style. He got out of the car to see what the cop wanted and the cop saw him, turned around and hauled ass out of there. Guess it looked like a lot of paperwork. Later on, Rupert teamed up with Theremin player and guru Arthur Harrison, and they did duo gigs around the area for years.

You know those Tiny Desk concerts on NPR? That originates with a band called Tiny Desk Unit that was around the DC area back in the 1970s. They played at Pipeline Coffeehouse during my reign.

Saint Albans School on the Cathedral grounds also put on plays at the Pipeline Coffeehouse from time to time. One was to be on a Saturday afternoon where I would be for a meeting before setting up for a show.

This was Woody Allen's *God*.

This is a short play, and they were short some people and I was asked if I wanted to read a part, and ended up playing Hepatitis. It was pretty funny.

One More Ungood Pipeline Coffeehouse Story

I forget how, but I ended up booking Timmy Meadows' (little brother of Punky Meadows, then in the Casablanca Records band Angel) rock band in the coffeehouse.

What a fucking, shambolic nightmare.

They were way too loud for the room. The band, whose name I forget, were nice enough guys, but their whitebread suburban Maryland redneck fans absolutely trashed the place. This is not some fucking Prince Georges county warehouse you schmucks, this is a very nice facility at the Washington National Cathedral and I am responsible for it.

Some cocksucker even stole the vintage fur coat my grandma gave me. This was a cold winter night, too. No polite way to put it. Assholes. Not cool. I had to physically run them out of the building after the show.

The fans somehow thought it would be okay to just hang out after their set—drinking all night. I advised them to never show up there again. The only get-the-fuck-out-of-here-now type problem night I ever had there. Took me ages to pick up all the trash and debris they left in the place and I had to hide all the evidence of booze from Sara, my boss.

I only saw her about twice a month. She managed the building and all the events that went on there, including the chapel, pottery and art classes and the Pipeline. I would pick up the keys from the office on show days, and put them back in a mail slot after I cleaned and locked up. She was actually very cool, and never bugged me once during the thirty or forty shows I did during Pipeline's last year. The Cathedral also paid for press releases that I wrote for the shows to be sent out.

A fun gig.

The Muffins must have played there ten times. This building was Guild Hall, and it was re-purposed sometime during 1980 by Saint Albans and Washington National Cathedral.

A Hilarious Rock 'n' Roll Coincidence

There was a very popular band called (the) Razz in the area back then, the late 1970s in the DC area. We were friends, and Billy Swann in The Muffins did projects with one of their guitarists, Bill Craig. Bill Craig also did a show with The Muffins when we did *Dancing in the Street* with my sister Marianne on vocals.

Prior to that, my sister had appeared in Playboy—*The Girls of Washington* issue with Liz Ray in 1976. I think also later collections. Somebody in Razz saw her in Playboy and they wrote and recorded a tune for her called *Marianne* that appears on their 1979 Air Time vinyl EP.

Though, against all advice, she used her real name, the Razz folks did not realize she was my sister. I think Billy Swann said to Bill Craig "You do know that's Paul's sister, right?" They didn't and they went…uh-oh, omigod, or similar. I met Bill Craig for coffee and he explained that they did not know, etc. and were concerned she might be upset.

She LOVED it when she found out, and all was good. It's a great song. At a Razz reunion at the 9:30 club during the 1990s, I was backstage trolling for free food and a beer. Heading towards me was Doug Tull, the great Razz drummer (they even rehearsed at my DC house for a bit) with two hot teenaged girls headed for a dressing room. I rubbed my eyes, and thought NOOoo, I'm not seeing this. Then he stopped me with, "Paul, I'd like you to meet my daughters…"

A good laugh.

Their singer, Mike Reidy, is a very fine artist and did many great posters for their shows. Razz bassist Jim Crenca recently wrote to me wanting to jam. He thought I still lived in DC. Ha.

A Funny Story involving Greg Yaskovich—Late 1970s

Sometime in the late 1970s, while I was in The Muffins, my friend Greg Yaskovich introduced me to the John Waters (Pink Flamingos, Polyester, Hairspray, etc.) film-making crowd, called Dreamlanders. This was before, I think, Greg joined Mars Everywhere, a Random Radar band.

He took me to a gig where Edith Massey of John Waters movie fame (Edie the Egg Lady) was playing with her punk band L'enfant Terribles at the old Psychedelly in Bethesda, MD.

What a trip.

The ever so zaftig Divine was there, along with Waters and a whole cast of odd characters. Edie's band started up in loud, bouncing-cut time, and then Edie came out in a leather corset, black fishnet stockings, plastic spiders on her boobs, a black veil, crazy makeup and started screaming "I wanna see somebody die." over and over.

Add to that she was less than 5' tall and on the heavy side, so this was quite a sight to behold. The audience adored her. The punk scene in DC was getting started then. That was quite an evening. Greg introduced me to those folks and Edie, who seemed kind of sweet.

All show biz, folks.

Some months later, this band came and did another show at DC Arts Center on 18th Street in DC, and again Greg took me. Edie was like "how have ya been sweetie?", and gave me a hug. Another crazy show. She later changed the band name to Edie & The Eggs.

First Album, The Muffins MANNA/MIRAGE— 1978

By 1978, we felt ready to record our first album. Tom was itching to test his engineering chops on the new gear. By then we had been playing live the tunes *Expected Freedom*, *Not Alone*, *Solemn*

Music, and a song Dave and I whipped up in Gaithersburg, called *Amelia Earhart*, (I recall helping with ideas for the end. Dave did the bulk of the writing) improvising a bit, & a long tune that we sadly never properly recorded, *Lady In a Brown Paper Bag*, and our rocker finale *Hobart Got Burned*.

Up through this time, Dave Newhouse was doing the bulk of the writing with input from us guys in terms of practical arrangement. Often we would rehearse tunes in sections, then glue them together as we learned the systems. By this time, we were rehearsing three-four nights per week and doing occasional local gigs. Dave would write stuff we could not play, and then we would spend ages working on the systems....i. e. "Start again at letter C" and so on. For weeks. The cover art was by Lynn Pruitt. (RIP) We picked out some stuff from the very interesting Dada-esque house in Rockville, MD that she and her daughter Shawn lived in.

The first tune we recorded on the eight-track was *Expected Freedom*, which did not make it to MANNA/MIRAGE, but was tarted up and included later on both the vinyl/CD release called OPEN CITY. One of my fave tunes. We recorded lots of improvisation, *Amelia Earhart*, *Hobart Got Burned*, (which we knew how to play) and then *The Adventures of Captain Boomerang*, which as I recall was still sort of in the arrangement stage and thus took donkeys ages to record. All of side two. Despite being an average mid-fi multitrack recording, it remains our most constant seller. We did not have one condenser mic.

This record, like the Random Random Radar sampler, was mastered in Allentown, PA, by a fellow named Peter Hellfrich. He had his studio situated in a nice old church. He also cut over two-hundred sides for Nonesuch Records. He usually signed these up near the end spiral on the vinyls, where you can see mastering, and other information. I have several of these Nonesuch vinyls with his signature up in the end spiral.

During the tune Amelia Earhart, at 7:19 for about twenty seconds if you listen carefully, you can hear kids laughing and screaming. I forget whose idea this was, but our good friend Pat Fahey aka Gunther the Clown, got he and I into a day care center in Kensington, MD to record the kids for a few minutes. 1978 sometime. I think he had done clown gigs there and knew the folks that ran the place. I don't think this is documented anywhere else.

Steven Feigenbaum Remembers

By the time of fall, 1976, I had been hanging out with the Muffins for about three years. I was younger and they were the older, cooler guys—in a band. In a GREAT band. They were always very nice to me. Nicer than I probably deserved, but that's for them to say. We and a few like-minded other folks had even started a collective to release music by them and others; Random Radar. But nothing concrete had come of it yet. But, The Muffins had fallen on tough times by then. Always a quintet, they had gone through a number of drummers, finally arriving at Stu Abramowitz by summer 1975 and seemingly finding the right guy.

Seemingly not.

On July 9, 1976, Stu played his last show with the band (he had given his notice a month earlier) and sold his drums right off of the stage. And guitarist Michael Zentner decided it was time to throw in the towel as well. This left a core trio of Dave Newhouse (keyboards/reeds), Billy Swann (bass, etc), and Tom Scott (reeds, etc). They actually played shows in this unlikely configuration a few times, improvising and taking their inspiration from the drumless Art Ensemble of Chicago. But honestly, I think they were as confused by this turn of events as could be and were just treading water.

Somewhere along the way, Paul appeared. I can't remember if I saw him play or rehearse with them before their first show together on October 2, 1976, but I did meet him before the gig. I remember he was a hyper-animated guy, he had a beautiful girlfriend, he ran a weekly coffeehouse (The Pipeline

Coffeehouse that only served tea) that hosted bands at Saint Albans Church on the grounds of the Washington Cathedral on Wisconsin Ave, NW and that he actually lived in Washington, DC.

I was a suburban kid through and through and I had never met a peer (read 'a white musician, middle-class kid') who lived in DC before. It was a small revelation and so sophisticated. I mean, where did you park? Paul joined The Muffins and started rehearsing with them and the band, now happily settled into being a quartet of keyboards/reeds, bass and drums, threw out all the old material and started fresh. That meant a couple of tunes and a lot of improvising. Listening back now, the biggest, most obvious influence that I hear on his early days with the band is Tony Williams circa "Believe It". The Muffins' music became looser and a bit more jazz rock.

Paul moved into the band house in Gaithersburg then Rockville, and somewhere along the way he got a job in a record store a good twelve miles down the road; did he really hitchhike to work everyday?[1] The band kept rehearsing seriously, as they always had, Sunday-Thursday nights in the basement. New material starting cropping up, but they kept improvising as well and improvisations become a bigger part of their live sets than previously.

Random Radar had been working towards getting our first release out, which was a sampler album featuring all of the participants in the collective and a few famous friends, done very consciously to draw attention to the effort. I'm not really quite certain why The Muffin's track featured on the sampler was by the old five piece lineup, but by time "A Random Sampler" appeared in fall 1977, give or take, the Muffins were a very different band than what someone buying that sampler would know.

---

[1] Yes. Used to be a fifteen minute walk from the Gaitherburg house
—PS

Another important thing that happened in late 1976/early 1977 is that Tom bought a semi-pro eight-track tape recorder and some microphones and voila, The Muffins had a decent studio to use. They wrote material, they gigged a bit, they rehearsed and by 1977, they were recording material with an eye towards it being the band's debut.

They spent a lot of time recording and mixing what would become Manna/Mirage; something like four months recording and four months mixing. No computerized mixing decks in those days. Eight-channels, each recorded very fully and very, very sectionally (a track might have an oboe, then a baritone sax, then a guitar, then a tambourine), four band members = eight hands to move the sliders up and down and tweak the EQ, as the tape ran by.

Phew.

But it was done and came out really nicely and it became the third release on Random Radar and helped gain the band the notice and respect that they would enjoy, in a small way, for the rest of their career and resurrection later.

While racking my brain about all of this, I have also just remembered that not too long after Manna/Mirage came out, Tom was involved in an accident playing softball during summer 1978 and had his jaw wired shut for some months and couldn't play.

The band continued and the material got edgier and edgier and less 'jazz/rock', culminating in the material that was found on their second Random Radar album, <185>, which was recorded in September 1980 and released in early 1981. By June 1981 or so, Tom, who was expecting his first child, had left and the band dissolved.

There was a short lived follow-up bands called Weekend and Blowout with Paul, Dave, Billy and a guitarist friend named Peter Hoepfner. I saw a show by them, which I remember as being really good, but they didn't last long.

The band's break up really depressed me, although I had

seen it coming; they'd been working very hard for a very long time with very little notice and success and the musical fashions were changing in a way that were very much against the basic building blocks of the music that they did.

I was less involved with the band for the last 18 months of their existence because in the fall of 1979 I had an idea. I was tired of going to college and working in record stores part time and was trying to figure out a way to do something that really interested me.

I was really interested in this obscure, unpopular conglomeration of jazz, rock, 20th century classical etc, music that I found myself involved with The Muffins and Random Radar and I (kind of) knew a little bit about having a store from my work at record stores. Luckily, even at 21, I had enough sense to know that opening a store specializing in this unpopular stuff was a terrible idea. But still…but still….

So, the idea hit me of instead of having a store and needing to attract locals, which there wouldn't be enough of, I would have a mail order store; less overhead to start up with and I had the advantage of reaching worldwide.

So, I bought inventory and built shelves and got shipping supplies. With the help of Random Radar/The Muffins' mailing list, which they had built up over the years (ooops. sorry guys. I guess I should have asked first, right?), in very, very early January, 1980, I mailed out paper copies of a catalog filled with bargain priced releases in rather small print and Wayside Music was on its way.

I saw Paul and the ex-Muffies less and less. Time passed. I got married. I did what I thought was the next step in making the world a better place for edgy music and started Cuneiform Records.

Then in the late, late 1980s, Paul got in touch again. He had a new band. He wanted me to hear them. I wanted to hear them. I did. They were totally different than The Muffins, but they were totally great too.

Chainsaw Jazz was a five piece of guitar, bass, drums, saxes and electric violin/mandolin. The music was aggressive hard jazz/rock with a healthy touch of the 'downtown jazz/punk' scene from NYC.

I really liked them and I was happy to see Paul playing again in a great band. Eventually they recorded an album and I released it on Cuneiform. They were never that stable or played that many gigs, but they lasted a few years and played a few great shows that I saw—and the record came out great. So, once again our paths were crossing.

—Steven Feigenbaum

During the late 1970s, John Paige, a DJ at WGTB FM in DC and big muso fan was president of our record label, Random Radar. He arranged a few live broadcasts for The Muffins, and one really cool one with Mike Bass and His Moderately Sized Orchestra aka P.D. Pop Studio Orchestra, which also included The Muffins and several other players.

Mike is a former drummer in The Muffins, and a fine composer and percussionist. He had two LPs on Random Radar, Parcheesi Pi and Painting By Numbers that The Muffins guest on.

Racing on, WGTB-FM at Georgetown University was linked to a recording studio called Sounds Reasonable that was located near DuPont Circle. The radio show John did these shows on was called Take One, and were, of course, all live. Three tracks from one of The Muffins Take One show are included on our Open City LP and CD. This one was done on 3/3/1977. The Mike Bass one was done 5/18/1978, and is great, but, was never released.

John Paige of WGTB/Random Radar Remembers

I was an 'underground' DJ at Washington, DC's WGTB-FM when I first heard about The Muffins. My program had a focus on the Soft Machine and the other bands in their axis (this was before the term 'Canterbury' was used to describe this genre).

I was taken aback to travel to a performance at a sort of Maryland roadhouse to find this talented (at the time) five-piece ensemble clearly influenced by the music I loved. This was prior to the time of Paul's joining the band when they had Michael Zentner as the fifth member on guitar and violin. In no time, the Muffins became my favorite local band and I featured them on my radio program, promoted some performances with them— including a 1978 Trinity Theatre concert which included Fred Frith, John Greaves and Peter Blegvad amongst others and went on to establish a record label with them and the liked-minded groups working with them. Thus Random Radar Records was born.

When Paul Sears joined the group in 1976, he replaced the previous drummer, who happened to be my best friend from High School, Gary Mayne, who had left the band. So, initially, I might have been a bit predisposed against this self-possessed new drummer, (who was nicknamed 'Clubfoot' for his strong bass drum beat) but he quickly proved his worth and became in integral member of this adventurous ensemble and provided an insistent and undeniable energy to this challenging music.[2]

In amongst the myriad of memories I have of amazing Muffins gigs throughout the years that I was privileged to attend was one we decided to do live from the WGTB-FM Studios on New Year's Eve, 1976. I had always remembered the New Years programs of my youth, with some vaguely Guy Lombardo-esque lounge band playing live from a hotel ballroom, so we decided to do our version of the same (which also doubled as an in-studio New Year's Party with plenty of friends, guests, refreshments, etc.).

But not content to let things totally devolve into the after

---

[2] I replaced Stu Abramowitz, not Gary. Stu must have been clubfoot. I had some colorful nicknames for sure, but not clubfoot. Ha!
—PS

midnight anarchy that these events can be, The Muffins had provided the guests with all manner of musical (and other) instruments (such as, if I remember correctly, penny whistles, egg beaters, washboards etc.) that could be used as instruments during the piece the Muffins had prepared.

So, after I did the NYE countdown from the control room, we brought up the microphones in the studio for a musical performance of The Muffins playing a new composition with the help the musical and percussive additions from the party-goers (who were being loosely conducted by Dave), which wove into a wonderful blend of composed and improvised music to welcome in the New Year. You can hear a snippet of the New Year's Countdown and revelry at the beginning of the Muffin's song *Countdown* on their 'Secret Signals 1' album.

I often marvel about the level of interest and attention audiences were willing to pay to new music in those days, and it was into this musical world of Canterbury, Improvisation, Jazz and Progressive music that Paul Sears was about to make his appearance.

—John Paige

Giorgio Gomelsky—Zu Festival, 1978

I have known this name Giorgio Gomelsky for most of my life, as he was mixed up in the British rock music scene back in the early 1960s, and was involved with The Rolling Stones. During the mid 1960s, I discovered The Yardbirds, and their better-known records were produced by...again, that familiar name.

The Yardbirds remain one of my favorite groups. A little later during the 1970s, I discovered the groups Gong, Magma, Vangelis and John McLaughlin's great Extrapolation record. There again on these LPs was his name as producer. I got to wondering over the years who the hell this guy with the Russki sounding name was, and how he came to be involved with all this music I loved. We seemed to have similar tastes.

During early spring/summer of 1978 the phone rang at The Muffins house in Rockville MD. I answered. I heard an indiscernible gruff euro accent: "This is Giorgio Gomelsky and I am trying to reach The Muffins."

GAAAH.

I nearly fell over. I nearly said that I was Tyrone Power and that he had the wrong number. He was *following me* all this time…ha. Turned out he was living in Chelsea, NYC on West 24th Street and was putting together what was to be the first-ever progressive rock fest in the U.S., and wanted our participation. He needed a lot of help. Never did find out how he got our phone number.

I jumped on the train that next week and went up to meet him. He had a fair sized three-story loft on West 24th, which was a quick ten-block New York walk from Penn Station. He made me dinner—Rosti potatoes and red wine. I recall a couple of dogs living there as well. We talked almost all night.

What crazy stories. Stuff like how the Yardbirds insisted on touring with their own drinking water, and Magma touring youth hostel churches in France. I could not get enough of this shit. I was a goggle eyed twenty-five-year-old at the time, and in absolute awe of this dude. This would change to becoming absolutely frustrated with him later. He reminded me on first encounter to be a mix of Castro and Stalin.

Todd Rundgren's Secret Sound studio was literally right across the street from his place on West 24th Street in NYC. Out for a stroll the next day, we could actually hear the Mahavishnu Orchestra rehearsing in the neighborhood. The great percussionist Dom Um Romao's Black Beans studio was two or three doors down from Gomelsky's place.

What a scene.

So, Giorgio was looking to get Daevid Allen, Gilli Smyth, Fred Frith, Chis Cutler, Peter Blegvad, Yochk'o Seffer, and a bunch of new, no-wave NYC bands involved in this here Zu Festival. At the time, Bill Laswell seemed to me to be sort of

Giorgio's adjutant. I liked Bill a lot, and he took me for my one and only trip on the NYC metro train to show me around and go record shopping.

He showed me a place that had an incredible selection of live bootlegs. Tom Verlaine was in there browsing that day as well. Bill also had a pocket trumpet in his coat pocket this day, and when the train station got crowded and we needed a hole to cut through, he pulled out the trumpet real fast, went THWADEEP which startled people and we then had a hole to cut through.

One morning, this short little guy comes over in a gray felt jogging suit to meet with Giorgio. He introduced me to another guy, Ron Delsener—I had no clue who he was. Turns out he was a major concert promoter that has done many shows at Madison Square Garden and other large venues. They talked about the Rolling Stones. All I could overhear…this was nuts.

Arrangements were made for us to appear at this Zu Festival thingie, which was at the Entermedia Theatre at 2nd Ave and East 12th St, NYC on October 8th, 1978. Yochk'o Seffer (Magma-Zao-Neffesh Music) needed a bassist to present his Neffesh Music set at Zu, so he came over and stayed with The Muffins and we lined up Dave Kasler, a bassist for he and his drummer Francois Lazeau. Georges Leton, then manager of Magma, was along with them and helped translate as Yochk'o and Francois understood and spoke little English. Seffer also wrote a tune, "Inkosz" to play with The Muffins at the fest.

So, I went up there two or three days early, as the sound man that was lined up canceled, and Giorgio drafted me—over the phone—as FOH[3] sound guy. It was around then I met and played a bit in Gomelsky's basement with the Zu Band; a basically unknown Bill Laswell, Mike Beinhorn, Cliff Cultreri, and also met drummer Fred Maher who were then known briefly as the Zu Band, and would end up backing Daevid Allen,

---

[3] Front of House

becoming NY Gong, and then of course, becoming the excellent band/collective Material.

Laswell and Beinhorn later went on to much bigger things. Between the two of them, they worked with Herbie Hancock, Mick Jagger, Iggy Pop, Public Image Limited, the Red Hot Chili Peppers, and many others. When I arrived at Gomelsky's place a few days early I met Fred Frith for the first time, and quite unexpectedly, Robert Fripp and Debbie Harry, who were at Gomelsky's the day I got there.

Fripp was hanging out in NYC back in those days.

We had a nice chat over wine that evening. A night or two before the fest, I received a (very) little training on the sound system, as Art Ensemble of Chicago were doing a show then at the Entermedia Theatre. This was one of Pink Floyd's rental PA systems.

The Pink Floyd guy was leaving the morning of the fest, and so I was on my own after cursory training, (with Art Ensemble as the guinea pig) and zero documentation as to routing, block diagrams, subs or anything else useful.

He showed up the morning of the fest to make sure everything at least worked, then hauled ass out of there. Sort of, here ya go man. See ya...good luck. Don't blow it up. I remember a 36 or 48 channel Midas mixer just behind center right of house, and up under the stage a dozen or so amps in racks that appeared to be Phase Linear 700s with "PINK FLOYD 700" silk screened on the front panels.

Pretty cool.

I tried to obtain one, but, no dice. Remember, I received only basic guidance on this rig, ensuring headaches (both for me, acts, and the audience) at the fest.

The Art Ensemble of Chicago with their arsenal (but consistent) of acoustic instruments were a breeze compared to what was coming....

Zu Festival Event—October 8, 1978

We had a small army of people (Thanks to Keith Macksoud, Jinji Willingham, Barbara Leeds, Jayne Bliss, Michael Lawrence and many others) set up the stage the night before to get ready for the Festival, which was to start at noon October 8, 1978 and last until midnight.

When I arrived early in the AM, it was a true rush to see the line of patrons snaking all around the block. My friend Tom Acuna came up from Maryland and was a huge help with the sound. Band setups were nightmarish, as there was no electronic communication between the stage and the house sound mixer. Sound check? Ha-ha-ha. It was fucking mayhem. There were so many people crammed into that theatre, it was faster for me to run out the front door, and go around the building to the loading dock & stage door to get on the same page with what was going on with the stage and make notes.

For EVERY act.

Not one act as I recall had prepared an input list or written down any other useful information beforehand, so all was done on the fly. Add to that, I hadn't a clue WHAT people were going to do after they plugged in, as I had heard NONE of them, excepting a little bit of Zu Band rehearsal, Peter Blegvad, and NY Gong at Gomelsky's place. Billy Swann sat in with Peter Blegvad and Chris Cutler and they played some of Peter's great tunes. I heard a couple snippets while they rehearsed at Gomelsky's place. Other than that, from my standpoint it was a true crap shoot. There were no proper sound checks.

Once the crowd got in, it was packed and total mayhem. The only constants on stage were the community bass rig and two drum sets. After several of the no wave bands played, there was sort of a debate on stage with Robert Christgau, Daevid Allen, John Paige, Chris Cutler, & Michael Bloom (I forget who else) regarding the merits of punk vs. progressive rock. The highlight for me was Daevid Allen standing on his head and farting into a microphone. That about summed it up.

Glenn Branca, Elliott Levin, and George Bishop played in various groups. There was some poetry, and this dude Dr. Space (Joe Lyons, I think) played a solo set on a handheld synth that resembled cross between a chrome bassoon and a glasspack muffler. I enjoyed some of the sets. Sitting near me at the sound board at various times were Robert Fripp, Debbie Harry, Robert Christgau, Hardy Fox, and the guy that would be godfather to my second son 11 years later, Jamil Guellal, who was then a DJ at WGTB in Washington DC.

I really liked ROBAL which featured the Hertzberg brothers, Rob and Alan from the band Manster on guitars, and Bill Laswell in bass. Manster had also recorded with Genya Ravan producing prior to the fest. Good stuff.

When The Muffins played our set, Tom Acuna and Colleen Scott took over the soundboard. My ears were also fucking toast by then after some eight hours listening to strange racket emanating from the stage.

After our set, we then did our encore with Yochk'o Seffer, playing the arrangement of his tune Inkosz, which I don't think has ever been used elsewhere. We worked it out at our house during the time he was rehearsing his Neffesh Music trio with Dave Kasler on bass, and the great French drummer Francois Lazeau (later in Magma). Francois also played the 2nd drum set when we did Inkosz, so we had two drummers on that tune. We had The Muffins, with Yochk'o Seffer, another sax player, I think his name was Eulalie Ruynat, Dave Kasler on bass and Francois.

On that one tune, we had two extra saxes, two bassists and two drummers. An eight-piece band.

A big noise.

Neffesh Music then turned in a fine set considering how little rehearsal they had at our house. Fred Frith did a cool solo guitar set. Peter Blegvad, Fred Frith, Chris Cutler and Billy Swann played some of Peter's tunes. Very late, maybe midnight, Daevid Allen and NY Gong hit the stage and did quite a long set going well after 1 AM. Theatre management cut the power around 2 AM. The crowd went apeshit and Daevid invited anyone that wanted to bang on stuff to get onstage.

So, of course with the sound down for the count, up I went and we had quite the drumming event going, and then the cops arrived and they shut off the lights and advised us all that the gig was up.

Almost thirty years later, The Muffins former manager, Bil Poole, visited us when we lived in Baltimore and gave me a bag of memorabilia from his days managing The Muffins.

Surprise.

In the bag was a Zu Festival T shirt, to this day, the only one I have ever seen.

Recording

A lot of this was recorded, I think, on Mike Bloom's TEAC four-track reel-to-reel. A few weeks later I received a cassette from Bill Laswell with our set. It was not well recorded or mixed. Several audience boots are floating around still. For thirty-plus years, Giorgio obstinately refused to let me (or anyone else) have the tapes. When I built a special computer for recording back in the early 2000s, he still would not let me have them, or send them to me so I could at least digitize them.

When he passed away in 2016, a lot of his stuff was headed for the landfill, and whoever was handling his estate did not care about the tape collection, and so the violinist and Soldier String Quartet leader Dave Soldier, who was close to Giorgio during his last days ended up with the tapes.

Dave has since baked the tapes, and digitized the fest, and now, thanks to him, bless'm, I finally have a lot of it...after some thirty-nine fucking years. None of the recordings are what one would call good, and a release is unlikely. Just getting permission from everyone would take donkey's years, and likely would be refused.

The Muffins and Random Radar received lots of snail mail

in those days. One cassette I still have, sent in by a guy named Tim Parr from Phoenix is "In a Manic Mode." Tim was later in the great group Pocket Orchestra. One of very few groups I can think of that was actually based in Arizona.

Not long after Zu, I started to get very strange "fan" mail from a chap (I think it was a chap) who called himself Thor Gildersleeves. He would ask things like "Did I have a cold at Zu?" "Is that bass drum really yours?" "Can you play like that even when you are sick?" Just weird stuff. He sent two or three of these oddball letters in late 1978. Wish I still had them.

BroKeN mUsic band

I, and the other Muffins met these folks, Stu MacNiven, (guitar, voc), Peter Hoepfner, (guitar), John Fletcher, (drums) Judy (MacNiven) Prantl and her then young daughter Stacey, I think at a show sometime in 1977. We became fast friends and hung out quite often. I developed a bit of a crush on Judy, who eventually married Stu. (they divorced many years ago).

They had a band called Broken Music. They lacked a bassist at the time, so Billy Swann often played with them. To boot, they were then living a mere four blocks from my parents home in a nice house on 42nd Street NW in the Friendship Heights area of Washington, DC. They always had the TV on, but with no sound. They had music in the direction of Faust, or Can, playing all the time. Holger Czukays' Canaxis 5 was on heavy rotation there as I recall. It was kinda cool.

When the Zu Festival happened in NYC in October 1978, we all hung out there as well, and Stacey, who was still a kid at the time ended up onstage as a Pothead Pixie with Daevid Allen and NY Gong. Later on in October of 1980, they secured a gig opening for the great Snakefinger (Phil Lithman, RIP)) at the old 9:30 club on F Street NW in Washington, DC.

For some reason, they asked me to learn their set and do the gig, and so Billy and I did that show with Stu and Peter. I have a rough, but cool recording of most of it. Stu telling the audience we were from Texas was pretty funny. Later, maybe around the time Billy joined The Urban Verbs, Stu, Peter, Billy and John formed still another band called 18 Brume that I don't think ever got out of The Muffins rehearsal room.

When Fred Frith's Massacre trio band with Bill Laswell, and Fred Maher came to play at Johns Hopkins in Baltimore, Billy Swann, Dave Newhouse, Peter Hoepfner, and I opened for them as Blowout. This was a great show, and I wish I had a better recording of that gig. I have an audience bootleg of it. Massacre were killin' too.

A Chapter about Broken Music by Judy (MacNiven) Prantl)

I was living in a large home on NW 42nd Street near the Sears home on Military Road with my seven-year-old daughter Stacey and room-mates Stuart MacNiven, Peter Hoepfner, Mark Mills and John Fletcher. Stuart introduced me to unfamiliar music that took me awhile to appreciate after growing up loving Motown and the Rolling Stones.

I have always loved people and remember meeting the Muffins in a field somewhere in Rockville, MD. Someone had the idea of mixing Pernod with Guinness in a large pitcher. I barely remember the music, but I do remember the starlit sky and an invitation to come to the Muffins house the next week.

Stu picked me up after work and I wore heels, panty hose, a pleated skirt and a red silk shirt. I walked into the living room and sat on a chair when Fred Frith walked through the room and our eyes met...that's another story. Paul emerged from his cave in the basement and Billy entered from the kitchen. Little did I know this was the beginning of a life-long bond that has lasted more than forty-five years.

Paul invited me to see his room and I didn't know if he was into black magik, drums, porn, comic books or whatever, but I was intrigued and we quickly became friends. Billy had a Keith Richards swagger and I adored him from the get-go. Stu had recently formed the extreme left-wing group Broken Music and he composed all the radical and still relevant lyrics. John played drums, with Mark on bass guitar and Pete on blistering guitar.

I worked, raised Stacey, fed the band and our ever-expanding family of musicians. No other woman wanted a bunch of smelly guys missing the toilet and leaving a trail of cigarette butts and coffee grinds all over. I loved our life and I loved when out of town musicians came and crashed on any inch of space in our home.

I was particularly fond of Bill Laswell and he always wore my favorite non-color; black. We drove to the Zu concert in 1978 NYC in a Veteran's Taxi Cab one of our pals drove. Stacey disappeared and I panicked. I finally got a door man to let me in to look for her. She was on stage with Chris Cutler with her eight year old hands on her hips reading him the riot act. Chris said in his very British accent, "You don't know me." Stacey replied, "I most certainly do. You're Chris Cutler and you play drums with Henry Cow."

I dragged her off the stage only to have someone in the aisle calling for her to come on stage and be a pot head pixie with Gong. We've grow up and gone through many changes but have always remained true to our love of music and love of true friends. I'll skip the Muffins reunion and jump ahead to RIO (Rock in Opposition 2009 in France) when I outfitted Paul and Billy and house sat for Paul. Precious memories few can say they have.

—Judy (MacNiven) Prantl

Michael Layne Heath, Muso and Journalist Remembers

When Paul asked me to contribute to this book, he apologetically prefaced his request by saying, "I know writing from memory is a bitch."

And he's right. I'm no Proust; I'm from Maryland. And maybe it's the Swiss cheese holes in my own brainpan, or just a general distrust of my recall: was that really Lol Coxhill having tea in the Muffins' living room? Did I *really* tag along with the guys when they picked Fred Frith up from the subway station? And was that really, REALLY Henry Kaiser with them, jamming on Captain Beefheart tunes in the basement? Nah, couldn't have been.

Nevertheless, I'll do what I can.

First Contact

It was probably on Georgetown University's progressive powerhouse WGTB-FM, amidst side-long Tangerine Dream cuts and the latest disc from David Bowie, where I first heard The Muffins. Something from *Manna/Mirage*, and most likely on the great John Paige's Abstraction Radio Hours program. Paige would play a big role in promoting the band, not only via his radio efforts but by helping keep their label, Random Radar Records, afloat both financially and in terms of collective morale boosting.

Looking back, DC Metro residents didn't know how lucky we had it in terms of radio. The range of quality radio in the 60's and 70's was quite remarkable: RnB/soul stations like WOL and WOOK, the more Top-40 oriented WINX (which for a time, around '73/'74, also broadcast a nightly hard rock showcase, *Heavy Metal Thunder,* hosted by Skip Nelson aka Groff, future ruler of Rockville, MD.'s premiere independent record store Yesterday And Today). And of course, that Triangle Towers titan of free-form rock radio that was WHFS-FM.

Thing is, they did their part to hip their listeners, long before any other American FM rock station, to the likes of Springsteen, Little Feat and local boy Nils Lofgren. Yet as the Seventies wore on, the collective DJ staff of 'HFS seemed to drop the proverbial ball when it came to more 'out there' sounds with only glancing commercial potential—'progressive rock', if you will.

Which is where college radio came in: specifically, stations like American University's WAMU-FM and, most importantly, the aforementioned 'GTB.

As near as I remember, the first time I saw The Muffins was a gig at Montgomery Jr. College in Rockville, Maryland, aka 'Princeton on the Pike,' sometime in 1978. They were sharing a bill with local mad synthesizer genius Rupert 'Ozone Music' Chappelle: poised behind a bank of analog music machines, dressed in chainmail, corkscrew hair and beard for days.

It didn't really click for me at first, but I was intrigued all the same. The Muffins seemed to have their (not so random) radar attuned to a wide global array of musical sources—reaching as far afield as ancient to future Chicago, the desert Dada of inland California, pastoral Canterbury and ivy-walled Cambridge—filtered and processed through their own homegrown, suburban Maryland sensibility.

Plus they were a treat to watch: no-nonsense Tom Scott; rock-idol-handsome Billy Swann posing and throwing shapes; Paul Sears sitting above his drum kit like his hero Christian Vander of Magma, master of all percussion he surveys; and Dave Newhouse behind the keyboards, overseeing and conducting with a snap of his head, and occasionally (as on a Tom Scott set piece *Horsebones*), blowing mad honking skronk hell out of a baritone sax.

Little House they used to Live In

Shortly thereafter, I started to get friendly with some of the guys in The Muffins, and gradually insinuated myself into their scene, specifically the activity centered around the small, unassuming suburban home on Portree Drive in Rockville, where Dave, Billy and Paul lived (Tom being more domesticated, living with his wife Colleen in their own home nearby, which also housed the home studio Catch A Buzz where much Muffins work and those of others recorded).

I could always count on stopping by Portree—I was a neighbor of theirs for a few years—and finding myself within quite the hub of much social and creative activity. Friends and cohorts came and went, brainstorming plots to take the music world by storm over industrial-strength coffee around the kitchen table.

And music, always music, whether coming from people's bedrooms, the main stereo rig in the living room, or down in the basement: your classic rehearsal/jam space soundproofed with quilts and egg cartons.

After awhile, I even managed to take on a volunteer job as Random Radar's 'press officer,' which basically meant going through the reams of college radio playlists sent to the band and looking for any RRR album getting airplay.

Being a young and inquisitive music-head, I was up for whatever music each of the guys was into, whether it was soul, reggae, classical music or more arcane progressive jazz and rock sounds. I was also very much in thrall of the Post-Punk and New Wave music gaining traction here and abroad at the time, and brought a lot of it around to blast in their living room.

Thus, there was a fruitful and palate-expanding sort of musical exchange ongoing amongst us: the guys turned me on to Henry Cow, Etron Fou le Loublan and all the Krautrock stuff, while I reciprocated with PiL, early pre-pop Scritti Politti and the Stooges' *Funhouse*.

Work

Tom Scott may have once half-jokingly claimed during a local radio interview that The Muffins were "Artistes," yet there was nothing pretentious or precious about the way they went about creating and supporting their music.

They all had day jobs of one form or another, and I respected and admired the fact that their work ethic, both individually and as a band, was very solid.

One conversation Billy and I had really brought this home for me in a big way. We were hanging out at the Portree house, and he told me the news that they were about to go into the studio to record what became the *185* album, with Fred Frith producing.

"Wow," I remember casually saying, "I bet that's gonna be fun." Billy got very serious and replied, "It's *not* fun. It costs *money* to do what we do."

That's always stuck with me.

Like-Mindeds

Although the progressive rock scene in DC/MD/VA during the late '70s was pretty small, The Muffins did have their share of local contemporaries whom they worked and performed with, some even putting out records on Random Radar. There was Mars Everywhere, featuring Ernie Falcone, Greg Yaskovich and the late Barney Jones, whose brand of space rock was even further out then the Muffins'. The band However was a more melodic, song-oriented progressive combo, with a brilliant songwriter and front man in Peter Prince.

Balloons for the Dog, (Paul also played shows with this group) meanwhile, was fronted by *two* guys: this Danny Elfman-prototype Pierrot/mime character, and a supremely buff Vietnam vet who was Bryan Ferry inhabiting the body of California's future Governator.

Then there was Broken Music: expats from Oklahoma whose singer, Stuart MacNiven, was every bit the equal (as far as a unique vocal style) of David Thomas of Pere Ubu, and whose guitar player Peter Hoepfner played through probably the first chorus/flanger pedal I'd ever heard.

Venues

While The Muffins did play their share of mainstream rock club dates at places like the Psychedelly, the 9:30 Club (Paul and Billy did a Broken Music show there with Snakefinger headlining) and Columbia Station, most of their gigs took place in venues more off the beaten path.

The Washington Ethical Society was the site of many a

Muffins performance; one particularly memorable gig for me involved a horn battle, in which the Muffins (along with fellow musos like Steve Feigenbaum and the Mars Everywhere gents) faced off against each other, four at one end of the hall, four at the other, stirring up a full-on free jazz cacophony.

The college circuit was also fertile ground for The Muffins to ply their trade, always drawing sizable audiences at local halls of academia like American and Catholic Universities in D.C., or Johns Hopkins in Baltimore. There was even the occasional out-of-town college gig, where I would tag along as their putative roadie (albeit maybe the world's worst). One I remember vividly was at Frostburg State College in upstate Maryland. It was held in either the student lounge or cafeteria, but I mainly recall it for the fact that your reporter got up between Muffins sets with a guitar, and played and sang Bowie and Peter Hammill songs.

Then there was a road trip to play a gig up at Penn State. That I remember for two reasons: one, for band and crew waiting the better part of an hour at a local Pizza Hut to be served (I reckon old prejudices die hard in your smaller burgs); and two, for the all-night trip back to Rockville, during which Dave Newhouse told me the most groan-worthy dirty joke imaginable, one that involved four pennies.

The End, But Not Quite

Looking back, I don't really see that The Muffins 'broke up' in the early '80s so much as organically dissipated. People get older, goals change and evolve, familial ties get stronger…and honestly, who wants to have roommates in your thirties? But I am glad I was able to maintain ties with them since then, mainly with Dave and Paul.

And when the Muffins did choose to reconvene in the early Oughties, (1998 actually) it was evident from the work they produced—be it albums like *Double Negative*, *Loveletter #2* (their collaborations with the great Marshall Allen) and *Mother Tongue*, their *Live At Orion Studios* video (mind the effects, guys), or more recent offshoot projects like Manna/Mirage and 4S'd—that their creative spark and drive was and remains undiminished by time. And, again, I'm glad.

Playlist

To end this, I thought I'd assemble a short list of some records I associate with The Muffins, their extended chosen family, and our times together. All on vinyl. (And many up on YouTube.)

Even now, these vividly, colorfully bring back those days long passed we were fortunate to spend amongst ourselves.

Anything by Beefheart and Zappa
Ornette Coleman—*Dancing In Your Head*
The Contortions on *No New York*
Henry Cow/Slapp Happy—*Desperate Straights*
NEU. '75
Egg—'A Visit to Newport Hospital'
The Art Bears—*Hopes And Fears*
Balloons for the Dog—*Assassination Candidate/Tuna Tonight*
Mott the Hoople—'Thunderbuck Ram'
The Stooges—*Funhouse*
Iggy Pop—The Idiot, How Do ya Fix a Broken Part, Get Up and Get Out
Scritti Politti—Rough Trade EP's, esp. *Skank Bloc Bologna*
Soft Machine—'Moon in June' (BBC Top Gear version)
Thomas Leer—'Private Plane'
The Psychedelic Furs—*Talk Talk Talk*
The Beach Boys—*Pet Sounds*
PragVEC—EP with 'Bits' and 'Existentialist'
The dB's—first two LP's
Prince Buster—'10 Commandments', 'Train to Girlstown'
Fred Frith w/The Muffins—*Dancing in the Street*
Michael Bass—*Parchesi Pie*
King Crimson—*Red*
Magma—'De Futura'

Angels and Demons that Play

Snakefinger— *Kill The Great Raven, Here Come The Bums*
Roy Harper—'Tom Tiddler's Ground'
Planet Gong—'Opium for the People'
Sex Pistols—*God Save the Queen/DidYou NoWrong*
Jobs for America (Rupert Chappelle), 'Wonderbread'
Throbbing Gristle—*D.O.A.*
Alternative TV—*Vibing Up the Senile Man*
Gang of Four—*Entertainment*
Peter Hammill—*The Future Now*
—Michael Layne Heath

About Michael Heath

Michael Heath is a music journalist, poet and musician. He has written for many international magazines and online music sites, including XLR8R, Maximum Rock And Roll, Shredding Paper, Tangents UK, Perfect Sound Forever, Popmatters, & New Noise and Record Collector News. He has also written a number of poetry chapbooks published by Kendra Steiner Editions of San Antonio, Texas. Michael lives and works in San Francisco.

During the late 1970s into 1980 the local music scene in DC was undergoing a paradigm shift, and this was NOT in favor of The Muffins. The punk scene was emerging, and even came with its own fashion. Every music trend, I think, needs this in order to survive. Razor blade earrings, ratty clothes, etc.

Anyone who could go "twang" on an instrument and looked like this was suddenly hip. In our area, these people often hid their parents Mercedes, if you get my drift. Also, a guy named Foster MacKenzie, who called himself Root Boy Slim, seemed to come out of nowhere and was suddenly playing everywhere. To me, he sounded a bit like a cross between Captain Beefheart and Tom Waits. He had somehow acquired some of the best players in town, and called them the Sex Change Band, and had developed an outrageous and funny stage show performing songs like *Christmas at K-Mart, Boogie 'til You Puke* , and *You Broke My*

129

Moodring. My sax player Mark Gilbert from Chainsaw Jazz was in this band for awhile.

He somehow secured a Warner Bros contract, and recorded with Gary Katz, who also produced Steely Dan. After some success, he fell into quite ill health and died young at 48. I also read he was schizophrenic.

A sad story: My dear friend Momo called me up in 1992 I think this was, from a bar and wanted to know if she could drop by with a pal. I asked who the pal was and she says after a little silence…Root. So, they cabbed to my place. Root was drunk, I think. He asked for a beer, and by the time I got that, he has already passed out on my couch. Thirty minutes go by, and we could not get him up. Great, I think. I'm getting worried by now. Loud Beefheart through the stereo next to his head did the trick. He quaffed a beer, we talked for a bit, then he called a cab and left.

Last time I saw him. Some months later, he passed away. Sad. A very talented guy.

Jamil Guellal Remembers—Friend, Journalist, 1970s WGTB DJ in Washington, DC

Paul Sears saved my butt big time one day when the manager of MAGMA, Georges Leton, asked me if I was willing to organize a small tour for Yochk'o Seffer (Magma, Zao, Neffesh Music) in the USA. Of course, I wholeheartedly agreed, and got them a gig at the famous BLUES ALLEY and at the ONE STEP DOWN in Washington, DC. When the day came to greet them at the train station, I saw Yochk'o, Georges, and the drummer François Laizeau. As we are having coffee at the station, I decide to inquire about the bass player, interjecting that he must have had a pretty serious stomach upset to stay that long in a bathroom, to which Georges replies that actually he did not come. Mind you, this was supposed to be a trio. I suddenly panicked as the gigs were supposed to start four days later. I called the only person that could take us out of this jam maybe—and that was Paul

Sears.

Paul laughed like a hyena, and called me back four hours later telling me he got us a bass player from the Marine Corps Band named Dave Kasler. The gentleman arrived with both an upright bass and an electric one, turned to Yochk'o and asked him which of the two instruments, he'd like him to use. This really impressed Yochk'o . In two days, the band was ready, couldn't believe it, thanks to Paul Sears.

Another interesting fact with Paul is that his family house always welcomed musicians from all types of musical backgrounds and Paul loved to organize jams, so it could be "prog" styles, to "hard rock", to " jazz", and even "blues psychedelia"; and it showed his versatility as a drummer and his open mindedness. One night, to my immense pleasure, who do I see arriving at Paul's house? The one and only Steve Jolliffe of Steamhammer and Tangerine Dream.

We spent countless nights at his house in D.C. listening to all the jams happening there. Later on, Paul moved to Baltimore, where plenty more guests came to visit and jam, but it was too far for me to have the pleasure to attend, a loss for me.

—Jamil Guellal

Paul: How I met Jamil in the 1970s

I was riding towards Wheaton or Rockville, MD, and had WGTB on the radio. I could hear French. Then this guy would come on translating every couple of minutes saying "Now Christian Vander is laughing as his dog tries to bite my face."

Something crazy like that.

Then more French conversation. Then the guy would come back on and translate again. I thought, who in god's name IS this dude, airing an interview, in French, with Christian Vander of all people? I MUST meet this guy. This was Jamil on his radio show called Mixages. We did finally meet, at a concert likely and he and wife Momo have been very good (and family) friends through thick and thin ever since. We were neighbors for a couple of years in Washington, DC. He is godfather to my younger son, Niall.

1979 New York Gong

Early that next year after the 1978 Zu Festival, Giorgio rang me and told me Daevid Allen wanted me to play in the new U.S. Gong band for a tour along with Kramer on trombone, Bill Laswell on bass, Mike Beinhorn on keys/synth, and Rob Hertzberg on guitar.

I was still in The Muffins, and we were active, but they said okay. There was a rehearsal/gathering at Gomelsky's. I Amtrak trained up there and brought a cassette deck.

I had asked if Daevid wanted me to learn Gong repertoire, and the answer was no.

We'll wing it.

So, here we are, Daevid's handpicked from the Zu fest Gong band at Gomelsky's place. Daevid gave us really vague instructions, like "play six—six with holes."

Stuff like that.

So, we jammed all evening and I recorded some of it. It was my deck, so I took the only recording ever of this band home with me. In my opinion, none of it is really worthy of sharing, and to this day I have only allowed two copies out, and that was for Don Falcone, who produced and played on Daevid's last proper record, as did I, and Daevid's son Orlando.

Daevid asked me where I lived that evening. When I told him Rockville, MD, he said "You're kidding, right?" and laughed. Since there was no firm plan for rehearsals and so on, I bailed, as did guitarist Rob Hertzberg. New York is an expensive place to just hang out in with no plan. All these other guys lived nearby. Later, they brought in the great drummer Stu Martin, to replace me, and he did the tour.

I forget who played guitar besides Daevid. Might have been Cliff Cultreri. I MC'D at one big fest type gig in Baltimore at Shriver Hall at Johns Hopkins, and caught another gig at the

Bayou in Wash DC. I think Stu Martin's young son was his roadie. He did not appear to be a happy kid.

Second Album, The Muffins, Air Fiction 1979

By 1979, we thought we needed another record out. This time we decided to use a lot more improvisation and some live recordings.

We combed through our growing archive and picked live recordings from The Psychedelly in Bethesda, MD where we had played a few times, and Dave wrote a quickie in our studio, and we had a bunch of our friends sing chorus on it. We went with an all black cardboard cover with nothing on it that is textured sort of like faux leather. None more black.

This was *years* before Spinal Tap.

I like this record more now, nearly forty years later, than I did when it was released. It is the only one in our catalog that has not been released on CD. Mastering engineer Pete Hellfrich left us messages on the Air Fiction vinyl end spirals. If you have the vinyl, you can see "light waves" on side B, and "first step" on side A. Around this time we were playing a lot of shows in the DC area, and one was at the Childe Harold, a two-floor venue near DuPont Circle in Washington, DC.

Roxy Music, Bruce Springsteen, Captain Beefheart, Danny and Fat Boys and Emmylou Harris all played there at one time. Owner Bill Heard, an heir to the John Deere fortune, quite a randy and hard drinking guy, was loaded as he often was and actually hit on me at the downstairs bar thinking I was a gal. This seriously lowered the bar for women there.

At that gig, for some reason, we were throwing things at each other while playing. Billy bopped me on stage with a rubber doll or something. I fixed him. Right before he was to play an intro, I tossed a U-haul blanket over his head. It was the only gig where we got THAT silly.

1979, France, Czechoslovakia, England Trip

I don't rightly remember the circumstances of how Ken Newman and I were at Giorgio Gomelsky's place in NYC on W 24th Street in 1979, or what led to this, but Giorgio and Ken had already decided that I was going to France to play with Magma, and Ken was going to pay for it.

Holy crap.

We were also going to Prague to see an Art Bears show, and then to England to stay at the Henry Cow shop/house in the Clapham Common area in London. "Have a good Magma" Fred Frith said to me after a gig in Baltimore with Massacre and Blowout. Back then, one could not just "go to Prague" on a whim like you can now, as it was then an eastern Bloc country, and obtaining a visa was a requirement. Ken and I had to go to an interview, personally, with the Czech Consulate in Washington, DC to obtain visas. They questioned why we were going there to see a British rock group, so we had to run down our whole itinerary. France was the first destination.

There, I found out that *merci* by itself when you are offered something means "no thanks." Ken and I were at some swank restaurant on a patio in Paris and the waiter kept coming by with plates of hors d'oeuvres, and I would say *merci* and reach out...ZIP the guy walked away. After two or three unsuccessful attempts to obtain some of these scrummy victuals Ken started laughing, and informed me that if you DO want the stuff, you must say *oui* before the *merci*.

Thankfully, Ken was fluent in French. All I knew was how to order Jambon, a ham sandwich. (Thanks for the cheat sheet Jamil.) I ate a lot of those. I secured a passport and off we went via Baltimore to Luxembourg, and then train and Paris metro, to stay at the home of Georges Leton, then manager of Magma. The first problem was that Leton was then in the USA, at the Muffins house no less and had neglected to inform his girlfriend that we were coming to his place to stay, which was in a suburb of Paris called Antony.

She was about to send us away when Georges younger brother Willi came to the door and to the rescue.

All good.

The second problem was when we arrived, there was briefly no Magma. I did get to play with some Urban Sax folks, and Ken, in Paris.

The third problem was that after we trained all the way to Prague, the Art Bears show in Prague had been postponed until after our visas expired. That fucking sucked. On a positive side, this was when trains in Europe were fun to ride. In second class, you could get a cabin for four with windows & luggage space. The trains were slow, 40-50 MPH or so, and one could actually walk out on a deck with railing and leisurely watch the European countryside go by. It was a beautiful trip through France and Germany on the way.

While in Prague, we stayed with the avant-garde artist Milan Knizak and his wife. Ken also connected with The Plastic People of The Universe, and I think, got some tapes from them to take to England. I remember we went to the U.S. consulate in Prague for some reason, and rang the doorbell. What came through the intercom after we identified ourselves was truly surreal. "What in HAIL are you two boahs doin over HEAH anyway?" Guy from down south in the USA. He was a nice enough guy. So, we trained back to the Leton house near Paris.

One late night after dinner and drinks with Willi Leton, we came home to find the very tall door on the street that opened into the Leton's and neighbor's yard was locked. No problem said Willi, as we can go down the street, climb on the post office roof, get onto a back wall and boom, be home as the back doors of the house were unlocked. All went well until, as I could not see in the dark, I walked right off the not too tall post office roof, bounced off a police car and was unhurt. The police jumped out of the car FAST...then had a good laugh.

Of course I did not have my passport on me, a mistake I have never repeated. If Willi had not been there, I might still be in jail. After a couple of weeks on this trip, Ken had made plans to go to England a few days ahead of me, in case other Magma related stuff panned out. It didn't.

I would follow him across the channel a few days later. Meanwhile, Willi Leton had showed me how to use (and jump the gate, which he did, but I refused to do) the fantastic Paris metro, so I visited Pere-Lachaise, the famous cemetery where Edith Piaf, Jim Morrison, Chopin, Oscar Wilde, and other notables are buried, and also went to Eglise de Sainte-Trinite the same day, the famous church where Oliver Messiaen often played and also designed the pipe organ.

My dad had asked me to pass on his regards if possible, and

I lucked out...he was actually there, with his wife. One or two others were there. Very cordial ten-minute or so visit with the great composer. So, then I trained to Calais, lucked out and got the faster French transport across the English Channel to Dover.

There were two.

The French one resembled a plane without wings and the English one was much bigger, box shaped, and thus, slower. Long before the Chunnel. So, I get to England, took a train to the Great City and then took the tube to Clapham Common, then sort of a dodgy place. To get a good idea of how large London is...when I saw the signs indicating we were entering London on the trip from Dover, I started to get ready. A couple of guys sitting near me laughed and one said, "You must be a yank. Sit down, it's at least another hour + + to the station". So I get to Clapham Common via tube and find the Henry Cow Shop at 5 Silverthorne Road.

There were record covers by The Residents stuck to the windows, so I knew I had the right place. There were nice gold stick-on letters on the front that might have said "Barber Shop", but read "Henry Cow." I ended up sleeping on a door that was hung by chains from the rafters. Pretty cool use of space. Good music in the local clubs though.

Saw the great band Punishment of Luxury someplace and hooked up with The Human Condition, a project of Jah Wobble at some house in Bethnal Green section of London. The Henry Cow/Art Bears folks were all in Europe, so I never saw them there, either.

Other folks that I didn't know were staying at the Henry Cow shop, but they were cool with our being there. So, time came to go home via Laker Airways. They flew only standby, only cash, one-way, and only between NYC and Gatwick Airport in London. Remember those guys? They invented discount international air travel.

A day or so before we left, the Tory riots had begun, and most of London and Gatwick airport were insane with potential danger and violence. I can't thank Ken Newman enough for the experience, and footing the whole bill, even though lots of stuff did not work out well. I was upset with Gomelsky for ages because of the utter lack of communication and planning.

1980, and Gravity LP, with Fred Frith and the Muffins Third Album <185>

Out of the blue, well known guitarist and composer that was in Henry Cow and Art Bears, Fred Frith, asked The Muffins to be on his debut LP for Ralph Records, Gravity. We ended up doing one side. Fred came to our Catch-a-Buzz studio at Tom Scott's house and we recorded some arrangements of Fred's and improvisations.

Mixed in was *Dancing in the Street*, the tune that was a huge hit in the 1960s for Martha and the Vandellas, and written by Marvin Gaye, William "Mickey" Stevenson and Ivy Jo Hunter. This remains a favorite of mine.

Not too long after the LP came out, I was visiting Skip Groff's great Yesterday and Today record store in Rockville, MD, and Skip says "Hi, Paul, GREAT new 45 by the way." I asked what the fuck he was talking about, and he showed me the 45 RPM vinyl single that was released from the Gravity LP.

The first time I heard that *Dancing in the Street* B/W *What a Dilemma* was a single. Fred never told us that I recall. This 45 pops up on eBay all the time, along with the BUY OR DIE EP that we are also on with Fred.

Fred recycled a Gravity drum track of mine for his next Ralph Record called Cheap at Half The Price. It was ex-Muffin Mike Zentner that told me. It's a cool album. Around then, Mike Z. was making a record, Present Time that included Fred, and wanted me on it. When I heard the material, I felt it was not me, so I didn't play on it.

I remember going to the Ritz in NYC in 1981 or so, and I ran into Iggy Pop (Jim Osterberg) who was sitting upstairs all alone and so I ambled over, said hi, and bought him a beer. They played *Dancing in the Street* through the PA while I was sitting with Iggy. That was cool. Iggy and I were having a nice casual chin wag when some ass ran up to us and rudely stuck a camera in his face, so he split. I was pissed. I had originally went there to meet Fred Frith and Brian Eno, but for some reason they did not make it. Material was playing with Sonny Sharrock that evening, and they just KILLED. Great gig. I spoke with them afterwards for a bit. A fun night. Getting ahead of myself here....

The Muffins also used to play, as did many other local acts, at The Washington Ethical Society on upper 16th street in NW DC. Tom and Dave were still working together at Chuck Levin's Washington Music Center. In the horn shop at Chuck's, there was a nice old herald valve trumpet (the really long ones) and a tenor trombone hanging on the wall. I thought it would be neat to use these at an upcoming Ethical Society gig, and so those guys let me borrow them for that show. I was more successful with the bone, not having anywhere near the proper tight embouchre for a trumpet. Our good friend Doug Elliott was also going to guest on trombone that gig.

At this gig, I came out from behind my drums and had a comical sort of trombone sword fight with Doug. It was pretty funny, and I think we have a recording of that gig someplace in our huge archive, which is well over 100 CDs worth of concerts and out-takes. We are considering compiling and releasing a box set of just some of those unreleased goodies.

During 1980, we had the perfect storm for recording our third LP. Fred Frith, with whom we guested on his wonderful aforementioned 1st Ralph Records LP "Gravity", had relocated to NYC, and offered to produce us. His first, I believe, outside project. Dave had written some more aggressive music, as had Tom by then, and we did a short east coast tour, ending up in Boston at the Modern Theatre.

A day or two before that show, we played at Big Mothers at Brown University in Providence Rhode Island. Taking advantage of the fact that no one there knew what we looked like, we decided to start that gig by switching instruments for a laugh. I think Nick Didkovsky, today a pal who built the great Doctor Nerve band in NYC was at that show.

Tom or Dave played drums, Billy was on sax and keys and me on guitar. We went out and did a wacky, noisy improvisation for a few minutes and managed to get applause. We thanked them, went to our usual axes and did the planned show. Then on to Mutant Music at The Modern. Sun Ra and others played this series of shows, which were organized by Mike Bloom, then a journalist in Boston and pal of The Muffins. He was also a bassist later on for the group Cul De Sac.

This was at the Modern Theatre, which was in a then dodgy neighborhood on Washington Street known in those days as The Combat Zone. It turned out to be van theft zone—the van we had borrowed from our friends, the band Grits, was unfortunately stolen during the night before load-out by our crew occurred, so we thankfully did not lose any gear. We neglected to tell the road team, boss and sound man Brian Rapp and another guy where we were staying, so they could not reach us with this bad news. Fortunately, Brian had relatives in nearby Lynn, MA and was able to borrow $500 from them to rent a truck and get home with all our stuff. A mess. We then had to pay back Brian's family and give whatever cash we had left to Grits. We had actually made it home by train before we found out what had happened. Rick Barse from Grits, called the next day. He asked if I had heard from Brian. I said I hadn't. He asked me if I was sitting down, and then informed me about the van.

But, as a result of that tour, the band was running on sixteen cylinders and we were at our pinnacle as far as being a tight band. Scary tight at the time. Good friends of ours, David Golub and Michael Bloom (who had set up the aforementioned Boston show) lent us some cash so that we could go into a professional studio to record <185> with Fred Frith as producer.

After looking at several studios, we ended up at Track

Recorders in Silver Spring, MD. This occurred during late
September of 1980. There was a Little Tavern burger shop right
outside, so food was easy. Besides being popular with locals,
Linda Ronstadt, Emmylou Harris, Lowell George, Gloria
Gaynor, The Clovers and Danny Gatton all recorded there. Parts
of two posthumous Jimi Hendrix records, Crash Landing and
Midnight Lightning had been overdubbed and mixed there.

Track had an early 1970s 24 x 16 Neve mixer, great
selection of microphones, sixteen-track 3M 2" tape machines,
and Scully and/or Ampex 15/30IPS quarter-inch half-track
mastering decks.

WGAY, the easy listening station was nearby and
occasionally leaked into the electronics. As I recall, we got all the
recording done in two days and mixed and assembled in about
three days.

One memorable session was doing the tune Antidote to
Drydock, where Tom had been playing a rather insane alto sax solo
that had become a part of the tune. Same one for ages. After
recording this over the top solo part, Fred said to Tom, betcha
can't do THAT again. Tom merely shrugged and in fact did it
again, (surprising the hell out of Fred and engineer Bill
McCullough—whose jaws dropped) doubling the track, and it is
so freaking close, one cannot hear that it is doubled.

Tom had been playing that same solo for months. Another
day at the office with these bad cats.

While mixing, Fred wanted something that had likely never
been done at this studio. Listen to my drums in the middle of
Under Dali's Wing. Cool, huh? Fred had Bill flip the 2" master
tapes so they were reversed, and then added reverb to just the
drums. When the tapes were flipped back to normal, you hear
the reverb BEFORE the drum hits. Nice effect. I remember
mixing that tune one day when just Fred, Bill, and I were there.
Six hands on the mixer.

One day while we were there mixing, a couple of guys
from the Nighthawks band, a DC blues institution came into the

control room one day while we were mixing. They stood in the back, and their eyes said "dayum." They did not stay too long when they heard the decidedly unblues racket The Muffins made coming out of the huge studio monitors.

One day during a session, Bill McCullough, even suggested getting Fred to produce a Root Boy Slim Record. Too bad that did not pan out. Fred wanted to use an Eventide harmonizer with our stuff and Track Recorders did not have one, so we rented one of the original 1st generation Eventide Clockworks devices from another studio. These were among the world's first digital effects processors, and were very expensive then, close to $2,000 1970s dollars.

When done, George Daoust and I drove the 30-IPS stereo master up to NYC to Fred, who also finalized assembly and supervised the vinyl mastering at Frankford Wayne labs. Fred had done a lot of creative work with the Harmonizer, directing, and mixing/editing different sections together that we had played at different times. A few fans commented that it did not "sound like The Muffins." I didn't care; I love this record. Frank Zappa did all kinds of stuff to his records, even modifying live recordings, and no one complained.

This record remains today my favorite of all our work. When Steve Feigenbaum (Cuneiform Records—Wayside Music boss) wanted to release it on CD back in the 1990s, he wanted the basic live tracks as an added feature on the CD. So, since I had the mulitrack master tapes (still do) we went into Hit and Run studios (Track had since closed) and remixed just the basic tracks.

That is why there are two versions of <185> on the CD. My own preference is the original stereo mix. A valuable lesson I learned from Fred Frith involves eggs.

Yes, eggs.

One morning before heading to Track to mix <185>, I made some eggs. I was not much of a cook in those days, and when I went to flip them over, Fred put down his Boyards ciggie (only time I ever saw him smoke) said NO!, rushed in to the kitchen, and then showed me the trick of splashing a little water in the pan and covering them quickly to steam them. Eggs Frith have been on the breakfast menu at my house since 1980.

Here's a funny. A reviewer of <185> mixed up our Tom (Frasier) Scott with the LA Express Tom (Wright) Scott. The review went sort of like, " We have never heard of these people, but this is one of the more interesting things we have heard from him lately."

Ha!

Russ Strahan—Friend, Pentagram and 9353 Guitarist Remembers

Way back in the day when I was skipping classes at Rockville High, I used to hang out in Bauer, on the outskirts of Rockville, Maryland. This is where I met many a head who loved all different kinds of music. Being a musician myself, I ran onto some similar hippie types who happened to have an acoustic guitar. As usual, I sat with them and mentioned that I myself was a guitar player. The guy handed me his axe and I started jamming on some tunes I knew.

This is where I first met the two Chris's. (Hinkins and Bransome, the latter became a roadie for The Muffins), one who lived in the apartment building right near where we sat. We began discussing bands we liked and found we had some similar tastes. They invited me to come up and hang out with them. This was the beginning of a long friendship in which I would spend lots of time listening to a lot of cool music with fellow fans of WGTB, a radio station broadcast from Georgetown University that played some of the coolest stuff I have ever been blessed to hear.

One day the two Chris's asked me if I would like to go over and meet this band that they were friends with. I of course said yes and we were on our way to a place of unforgettable magic and mystery. We walked several miles, this is how we got everywhere back then, and eventually arrived at the house of The Muffins.

Strange as the name sounded to me I would soon meet the members of the group and be delighted by some of the coolest and most far out sounds a budding young musician could wish to hear. Although I was fascinated by all in the band, I gravitated towards Paul and Billy. Paul, who seemed the most accessible and Billy because he was a mountain with Ethil the tree growing on his...okay, back to reality.

Of course, I tended toward Billy as he was the string player, as am I. I would soon start coming over periodically to hang out for a rehearsal or before one of their shows. It was at these sessions that I would go into Paul's digs and partake of various and sundries while being exposed to some of the wildest things I'd heard on record to this date. It was Paul who introduced me to Magma, The Residents, Frank Zappa and so many others. I will be forever grateful that I spent those times being exposed to so many artists I may never have heard thanks to Mr. Sears and his funtastic Muffins.

Many years would pass and I would become a musician both recording and touring. I got a job at a staging and sound company where I would meet several other musicians, two in particular Mark Stanley and Mark Smoot who were both still in touch with Paul. I decided to search for the members online and was blessed yet again to find all of them still alive and well. Dave Newhouse was kind enough to send me a couple of discs including the newest which I am pleased to say the guys have only gotten better with the years.

—Russ Strahan

Sometime in 1979 or 80, Random Radar Records and our president John Paige got involved with putting on a DEVO gig at Georgetown University. It was a great gig. I forget how this happened, but a small pile of DEVO's disposable tear-away yellow stage costumes ended up at our Rockville house.

One day I was sitting there in the living room with a gal named Mary Staples, who was renting a room from us, and Steve Feigenbaum. Mary, I think, needed to run to the grocery store a few blocks away. I suggested to them that THEY put on the DEVO costumes and go shopping. They did. I think I got a couple of cool photos of them in the cereal section or something. Steve, I think, has these pix somewhere, and I have been bugging him for ages to dig these out...Steve?

Around this time, close to summer 1980, the great guitarist Henry Kaiser came to the area, and played with three Muffins for a bit. We booked two gigs, one at DC Space in downtown Washington, DC, and one at Richmond Artists Workshop in Richmond, VA that was handled by Danny Finney, then of the Orthotonics.

Both shows were roughly the same format: Henry's solo guitar set, then he was joined by Billy Swann on bass, Chris Biondo on guitar and me on drums. We would do some improvs, and then play some tunes that we rehearsed at The Muffins house. We played the tune *HOH!* from a great record called Monster Island that Henry did with Owen Maercks, *Alice in Blunderland* and *Veterans Day Poppy* by Captain Beefheart.

At the DC Space gig, Dave Newhouse joined us on soprano sax for *Alice in Blunderland*. He turned in a fine Beefheart impersonation. Henry had a small Dumble amp, called a Steel String Singer with 1 x 12" speaker, and it was an ear-opener how loud and great this thing sounded. He also had two Lexicon, I think, digital delays. First I had heard of these sought after Dumble amps.

Henry has a few of them. Look them up. Try not to fall out of your chair when you see the $ these things command. We Amtrak trained down to the Richmond gig. Danny picked us up and we went to RAW to set up. Upon arrival, to our absolute horror, we realized that we left BOTH of Henry's gorgeous and expensive guitars at the train station. So, we hauled ass back there, by then a good twenty-thirty minutes had gone by, and both guitars were still sitting outside, next to the bench where we were sitting waiting for our ride. Amazing. Both gigs were great. I have a good recording of the DC show, but unfortunately, not the Richmond show.

Late in 1980 I recall, The Muffins ended up doing a one-off show at Symphony Space on Broadway. The Muffins got to play in a beautiful and huge Broadway concert hall. I forget who lined this up, but the headliner was the great jazz saxophonist Marion Brown. We were to play with him for a bit. He was making his debut on guitar of all things. He had played with John Coltrane on his landmark 1965 Ascension recording. The opener was Michael Lawrence Plus, whom we knew from the 1978 Zu Festival.

Mike played there with a couple of the bands. At this gig, Mike's band was to open, then The Muffins were to do a set, and then Marion joined us on guitar for an improv, then he played solo. Bill Laswell and some of the Material folks came to the show. Friends from Boston were also there.

On the way up there on the train, my gal at the time, Shawnbo, said "look at that," while we were stopped at 30th Street in Philadelphia. Sun Ra and the Arkestra were boarding the car right behind us. I went back and said hi. When I told him where we were going, he says "Broadway, huh? I hope Marion is okay these days." When I mentioned the guitar thing Sun Ra exclaimed in a cool drawl, "Marion? He don't play no git-tar."

Pretty funny.

Then Sun Ra bent my ear for a good part of the trip to NY of the trip, also extolling the virtues of the portamento on his new Korg Synth and then on life in general. Sun Ra was a lovely guy. I did not see him again until his last tour, not long before he passed away.

Later, Marshall Allen, (Marshall joined Sun Ra in 1958) and Knoel Scott from the Arkestra would work with The Muffins. Marshall would also appear with Thee Maximalists.

And now...Balloons for the Dog

One fine day during 1980, Fred Frith and Phil Minton stopped by The Muffins house to borrow a couple of microphones for a duo gig they were doing in Richmond, VA. They invited me along.

As I was getting ready to split, some of the guys from the band Balloons For the Dog dropped by to ask me if would do some shows with them, as their excellent drummer (Don Fontaine) had intermittent health issues that sometimes prevented him from playing, and would I please rehearse with them, learn their set and be on call? This was a great group with two vocalists, guitar, bass/keys guy and drums.

They had a single out on our Random Radar record label and were good friends. The single, with *Tuna Tonight* and *Assassination*

Candidate can still be found. I did not play on this. People asked me this question all the time back then. So, to make a long story longer, I ended up not going to Richmond with Fred and Phil, and spent time talking with Bill Kitsoulis, the Balloons great guitarist and his brother Steele, who was one of the singers.

He and his brother Bill are of Greek descent. Their material was all original, very well arranged loud rock music. So, for awhile I was gigging with them, as well as The Muffins. After an evening rehearsing with The Muffins, Steele would pick me up at 9 or 10 o'clock and I would go rehearse Balloon music in Silver Spring not far away until around midnight. They all had nicknames. Bill, the guitarist was Vasily Kite. Steele was Mantrod. I was nicknamed Cosmo McMoon.

Steele was a well-built, handsome and tall, muscular chap—the mums loved him. The other singer was a little animated guy named Georgy Jet. He had a unique primal high pitched scream in a tune called *White Pellets* that has to be heard to be appreciated. Interesting guy. He was a paralegal, and his gal/wife was chief engineer at a shop that built stock car racing engines.

By the time I was in the band, Tom Cox joined on bass, replacing a guy named Brian Bennett. Brian doubled on keys, and built a really cool clear swiveling Plexiglas stand that held his bass in playing position. When he would let go of the bass and switch to keys, on a dark stage, the bass appeared to hover in mid air all by itself. Nice effect. The band had a great show that alternated between the two singers. They also featured a real chainsaw to end their set, but not when I was with them. Sometimes one of them would sing from the wings, out of sight.

At one gig, the inevitable happened. Tom Lyle, (later on a punk guitar god in the popular band Government Issue) who had promoted many cool original shows at American University decided it would be cool to have Balloons open for The Muffins at AU. So, I played both shows. For a New York City show, our opener—oddly enough—was a well known, but not to us,

British intellectual ex politician and lecturer named Quentin Crisp. What a package. Older guy. White hair, red velvet suit complete with a red almost comic opera plumed chapeau. I had no clue who this guy was, and found out he was the infamous Naked Civil Servant.

Look him up.

I think every gay male within a 300-mile radius was at this thing. It was packed to the rafters. Elegant speaker. Absolutely rapt audience. I have never seen anything like this before or since. He was a nice enough guy, and had a photo taken with us. If I can find a copy of it, I will shove it up on my website.

And, to boot, the audience enjoyed our set as well. At a gig in the early 1980s at the new, larger, and improved Psychedelly location in Bethesda, MD Howard Stern turned up. He was in DC back then, and was in his perm stage, and being tall as he is, was easy to spot from the stage.

He was very polite as I recall.

The Muffins Disband and Paul Moves On

NOT TOO LONG after <185> failed to set our world on fire, outside life started happening.

Dave, Billy and I sometimes played with Broken Music and did a gig as Blowout (Billy, Dave and I with guitarist Pete Hoepfner) with Fred Frith's Massacre in Baltimore and that seemed to be it.

Tom wanted to spend time with his growing family and he and wife Colleen left. My dad had been diagnosed with stomach cancer, so I moved home in 1982.

Billy kept the house at 12117 Portree Drive in Rockville and not long after started his own family, and played with Washington, DCs own Urban Verbs.

They even toured Italy.

Billy also played with my old friend Nick Brown in his band The Primates. Tom Scott ran his Black Pond recording studio, and Dave Newhouse later launched a successful teaching career. Both Dave and I have played on many records since then, and Dave retired from teaching in 2018, and is playing more music now.

A Musical History by Tom Scott—My Very First Note

If I remember correctly, the very first note I ever played on saxophone was at Spring Hill Elementary School in a multi-use room right across the hall from the main office. Poor Ms. Swadley, the school Secretary, must have grown very weary of our early attempts. There was a constant drone, punctuated by blats and squeaks that slipped under the door into the hallway and office.

We were youthful and our exuberance oft times got the better of us. I don't remember our teacher's name; however, I remain in awe of the monumental task she dealt with five days a week. Introducing and inspiring a bunch of ten-year-olds to go home at the end of the school day and practice applying the concepts and techniques of the instruments they had chosen to learn...well, I don't think I could do that, or would ever want to give it a try.

So, Ms. I-can't-recall, thank you for your tireless efforts, and inspiration. The seed you planted took hold and grew and my life is the better for your efforts. I started lessons in the 5th grade and enjoyed the experience. It was slow going at first as we only received one lesson per week. There were five or six of us trying our hand at saxophone. The band instrument teacher had to teach each instrument as a section group and our task as students was to practice at home, learning our instrument and a few rudimentary compositions.

After months of sectional work, all the students were brought together as an ensemble. Geez, the sound we created. Out of tune, out of time, a dizzying cacophony of rancorous noise...it was amazing. Sure, we sounded like lumbering elephants, but damn, we were making music and we got better. Not by leaps and bounds mind you, but we learned that our teacher was our director, and if we all focused attention to her direction we would all end up at the last note at the same time.

Well, most of us any way.

As time progressed we lost a few members here and there. Not every student finds lasting joy in the practice and application of the art we call music. Many students did better than others and I think some drop out because of the competitive nature built into the schooling of music. The dreaded day came when we were told that we would be seated in our section; 1st chair, 2nd chair, 3rd chair, etc. etc.

I remember my stomach was full of butterflies. I didn't like this part of music.

Music was this thing of beauty, and the competitive aspect of chairs sullied its beauty. The terror that most of us felt as we proceeded through the chairs ranking process reduced many to a small heap of jumbled nerves incapable of playing at all. Personally, I suffered from a mental condition that would best be described as 'social ineptitude' and chairs really didn't help my condition.

I persevered, played my way through the required passage and low and behold…I got 1st chair. Anyone could challenge the chair above them to move up one chair in the chair ranking and challenge they did. There may have been a few close calls, and I did lose the 1st chair ranking once or twice, but for the most part I held onto 1st Chair and came to realize that as much as 'CHAIRS' was an evil, it was a necessary evil. I wanted to believe that there was order in the universe and I was where I belonged…at (or near) the top. Then I graduated 6th grade and moved up to J. F..Cooper Intermediate School

True Inspiration

Cooper Intermediate was for 7th & 8th Grade and the Band program was directed by Furman Riley. Mr. Riley was a truly gifted teacher and amazing Band Director. I didn't get first chair in 7th grade (at least not right away) but I did qualify for Concert Band, so a needed scoop of humility was introduced into my self-development.

It was during my 7th grade year that I started taking private lessons from Mr. Giovanelli on saxophone. Mr. Riley invited me to try out for Stage Band, an after-school activity that introduced me to Big Band Jazz music. The Intermediate and High School worked together to create a 'feeder system' for the Langley High School Music Program. The jazz concerts and competitive jazz festivals I was exposed too started during my time a Cooper Intermediate and many a great musician got their start due to the concerted efforts and organization of the band directors in the Fairfax County School System.

What I learned from Mr. Riley was that a musician from a Big Band Sax Section was referred to as a 'Reed Man.' A Reedman was expected to play saxophone, clarinet & flute. The first time I saw a sax section set down their saxes and pick up their corresponding wind instrument, well, I thought that was one of the coolest things I had ever seen.

Instead of a ripping sax sound, these folks created a lilting wind section of two flutes, two soprano clarinets and a bass clarinet. The trumpets and T-bones had mutes and the sound of the entire jazz ensemble had changed character. This was magic to me.

I told my Mom we need to go to the music store and purchase a clarinet. She took me out and did so, and I still play that same clarinet now. It is a wooden Signet clarinet with an Otto Link mouthpiece and I have never needed another. Like all things you keep using from your childhood it became part of me. It sounds just like I want, and that, as they say, is that.

As I taught myself clarinet it became evident that I needed direction and took a few lessons from a friend in the concert band to help develop the tone quality that was eluding my self-taught efforts. It wasn't long before I purchased a flute and started the long training to develop the proper embouchure for splitting a wind column on the head joints tone hole.

One very poignant memory I have from this time occurred at the beginning of the eight-grade school year.

During one of the first after school Stage Band rehearsals for the new school season, I met, a newbie to the music program, Kenny Hitchcock. Kenny, now entering his second year of study, had made amazing progress. The first Big Band chart was handed out and as Kenny reviewed the chart he asked me what the chord changes were in the tenor solo. I told him that they were the chords for his solo, kind of a road map to let you know what the harmonic changes would be, and that he would make-up the solo up as he went along, a new improvised solo every time we played the chart.

Kenny looked at me, with a heaping helping of stink eye, and called bullshit. When you think about it, the entire idea of improvisational Jazz is a bit hard to believe…making up a solo in the moment is one of the most challenging aspects of jazz and seems a bit miraculous.

The fact that eighth grade me was in no small part, a jokester, may have helped lead to Kenny's suspicion. Kenny, not one to succumb to Tom-Foolery, checked it out with Mr. Riley and was informed that it was as I had explained.

Geez, you try to help a brother out.

Over the next few school years Kenny became one of the finest jazz improvisers I have ever known. If you don't know his work you should check him out. I think you will find his music well worth your listen.

I didn't realize at the time, but the music that we shared would be very influential to who I was to become musically. The band director and students shared what they were listening too, we talked about it, and listen to it together. It filled us with possibilities and our eager young minds were absorbing everything we could as fast as we could. Then Mr. Riley announced that we would be making a record. Whoa, a Record.

Mr. Riley arranged to have a recording engineer come to the school and record the Concert Band and Stage Band. The masters from that were pressed into an album. We were all so very proud to have an album that had our name on it.

That was the kind of teacher Mr. Riley was, a very involved and dynamic director. As I said before, our Intermediate School was only seventh and eighth grade, and my time there went by so fast. When you are having fun, time really does pass quickly. I graduated JF Cooper and on to Langley HS.

The Temple

Langley High was a pinnacle in learning for me. It was a time of influence, core skill development and decision making. My new director was George Horan and I continued my private study with Mr. Giovanelli. When summer break came around my mother would sign me up for summer music programs at the College of William & Mary or the University of Miami. One of the major differences about Langley HS was that George Horan didn't do Marching Bands.

The vacuum that was created by that rule of thumb went a long way in changing the kind of musical experience I was to receive at Langley. The energy that would normally be channeled into Marching Band went a long way in creating an extraordinary jazz program—The Langley Jazz Lab. Jazz Lab was a big change from 'standard fare after school jazz programs. The Jazz Lab was a core class that met five days a week during school hours. It was a demanding class that required in school work and after school individual practice. The level of musicianship was amazing and I had to work hard to keep up with the pace.

In order to improve my flute and clarinet doubling work in the Jazz Lab, in my junior year, I joined the Wind Ensemble on Alto Clarinet and the Concert Band on Flute. This meant that I had three music classes and one non-music class. Langley HS had adopted the four-block daily schedule system early in the 70's so all curriculum was immersive.

When Jazz Lab competed it won, well, for the most part anyway, there was that one nationals competition down it Mobile, Alabama. Jazz Lab came in second place to a show band that was so well choreographed we just didn't stack up.

Whenever I see a band that has a good tight sound and well-choreographed moves, I'm always reminded of that band in Mobile, Alabama, bless their first-place hearts. For the most part, we won, and every year you lost some of your most developed players to senior graduation and newbies from the 'feeder system' joined in. This constant rebuilding of the band helped me come to terms with the transient nature of musicians and helped me cope with the inevitable lost and rebuild cycle most bands experience.

When a newbie was having trouble with a part or section of a composition others members would find a way to help with the concept or if the problem was technique, suggest that the part be 'woodshed'. The expectation was that we would all rise to the level needed to bring the ensemble to a superior level of play.

Some years as we approached the end of the school year we would record and press records. This was one of the influences from my school years that made Random Radar Records such a comfortable idea. In more than one way, the School Program was preparing me to understand the idea of record production. For private lessons Mr. Giovanelli really focused on melodic interpretation. He helped me develop a melodic sense that changed the way I heard and interpreted music. Although Mr. Giovanelli focused on classical music, his lessons affected my approach to jazz and improvisation as well. I started to look for the melodic development in all the music I listened to. It could be Classical, Jazz, Rock or Country…it didn't really matter what medium the composer used, if the music failed to develop melodically I would quickly lose interest. If the composer really stretched the limits of melodic development, then my interest would hold.

After school and on weekends some of us formed garage bands. For a while I played in a bar band call 'Cream & Coco', yes, I was too young to be in a bar, but no one ever asked how old I was. We did copy tunes and played in dive bars and private parties, although fun at one level it was not what I wanted and so I left the band. Some of the students in Jazz Lab got together to form progressive rock bands, Tom Grignon, Peter Princiotto, Tim Tanner, Bobby Reed and a few others formed several ensembles; Black Orchid, Ancient Moon Orchestra (better known, I think, as Ancient Moon). These folks were writing their own music and I was truly inspired by their efforts.

It was Tim Tanner that suggested that I give composition a try.

Thank you, Tim.

I worked on my first composition and when I got stuck received help to finish the piece from Peter Princiotto. My first composition *Egress Gnome Odd* was okay. It was a linear piece and the melodic development was weak at best and if one was being completely honest it didn't really hold together very well. Results aside, I loved the process, albeit a slow and painstaking process on paper. Composition suited me and gave me a sense of accomplishment.

I didn't have much left-over time for composition, with all my other school responsibilities, so composing time fell to the side only to be taken up at a later date. One of the things that ruined my desire to play in all of these bands with my friends was doing copy tunes from other successful bands. I wanted to do original pieces if I was going to work in a band. So, I quit working with all of these bands and focused on my school study.

What are your Plans?

Mr. Giovanelli was more than a teacher, he was a mentor—always pushing for more from me than I accomplished. I felt bad sometimes that I didn't progress to his expectations. I wanted to do more but the amount of time that teenage me had to expend was spread thin; school, family, afterschool job (I worked at the CIA Langley Base as kitchen help) and girlfriend all required time and so practice became shorter rather than longer.

Then came the day that Mr. Giovanelli announced that he

was moving away and that he had arranged for me to receive lessons from a new private instructor, Jimmy Schaffer. Jimmy was a more relaxed instructor in his approach, and I never felt quite as pushed to stretch my efforts by Mr. Schaffer, so I was caught by surprise when he asked the question. It was during my senior year mid-lesson Mr. Schaffer asked, 'What are your plans'...

I didn't have a reply. He pushed further and asked if I intended on going to college or university. Notice: He didn't ask if I was going to study music at college or university... YIKES. I responded that I didn't feel compelled to further my education. Mr. Schaffer explained that having playing experience on Sax, Clarinet, and Flute made me a good candidate for an apprenticeship as a wind instrument repair technician.

I told Mr. Schaffer that I was interested and so he set up an interview with Glen Hansen, the Wind Instrument Shop Manager at Washington Music Center in Kensington, MD. I did the interview, and boom, my apprenticeship was arranged, I was going to be a professional. After graduation I would start my training and most importantly I was getting paid to learn. I was excited about this—the term 'apprenticeship' rang of old world education. Masters and journeyman carefully guiding and shaping the youth of today to become the Master Craftsman of tomorrow.

The entire process was fantastic.

Glen Hansen checked out my playing skills on sax, clarinet, and flute and decided to send me home with a loaned oboe and bassoon. The idea was that while I was apprenticing at work to repair sax, clarinet, and flute, I would be studying oboe and bassoon at home preparing for the next phase of my apprenticeship. The level of expertise required on the two new instruments was that of a chromatic scale and basic embouchure.

That was lucky because the amount of effort that it took to play that old oboe made me feel like I was going to bust a blood vessel. The results that I got from the bassoon could only be likened to a 'farting bedpost.' After a year of using the loaned oboe I returned it and purchased my own oboe. I still was a very poor oboe player but the back pressure needed to obtain an oboe sound was much easier with the new horn and that made my oboe practice time immensely more endurable.

Six years into my apprenticeship I reached the level of journeyman and as folks retired and/or left to work elsewhere I rose to the position of shop manager.

Hi, My Name is Billy Swann

One day while working at the instrument repair shop, this fellow walks in the door and asks for Tom Scott. When I walk to the front of the shop he said 'Hi, my name is Billy Swann."

Billy explains that he had asked Paul Rinne, a graduate sax player from the Jazz Lab, if he was interested in joining a band doing all original compositions. Paul wasn't interested but told Billy that he should contact me.

Billy comes across as a trustworthy and sensible sort of fellow, so I decide to take him up on his offer to get together and listen to some of the compositions that they have been working on. When the appointed day comes I leave work and travel over to 402 East Diamond Avenue, The Muffin Band House and meet with Billy Swann, Mike Zentner and Dave Newhouse.

I listen to their tapes and we talk a bit. The recordings I listen to are kind of 'off' in a good way. What vocals there were—and there were not many—kind of came across as tongue in cheek and some of the violin work was a bit underwhelming, but all in all, it was for lack of a better word 'captivating.'

It reminded me in some ways of European Jazz, but the melodic sensibility was very American for lack of a better term. The compositions were linear and zigzagged around more than what I was use too, but that abnormality really resonated with me.

I decided right then and there that I could bring something to this ensemble, even though, from what I could foresee, our chance of commercial success was slim to nil. At the very least, from what I had just listened to, I could see a path less taken, and definitely worthwhile.

If we dug our heels in and worked hard, we could make our mark.

The Quintet

I joined the band and that made it a quintet. Right away, it became obvious that the drummer, Mike Appareti, was conflicted about the material we were doing. Maybe conflicted is too strong a word, it was hard for me to put my finger on what I was sensing. Without going too far into the deep end of the pool over why each and every drummer we burned through left, let us just say that, shortly after I joined the band Mike Appareti headed off to find greener pastures. Truth of the matter is that I have very few memories of that time.

Mike seemed to me to be a 'fish out of water.' I was not caught by surprise when he decided to leave. This is as good a time as any, during this vignette, to point out that during the entire history of The Muffins, a least the part I was involved with, no member of the band was ever fired, kicked-out or asked to leave the band. The Muffins were bathed in acceptance and supportive cooperation. If at any time one of us became stressed, or out of balance, the rest of the band members helped guide that individual back into the fold. We became a band of brothers, we disagreed on some matters for sure, but as a rule, we always invested enough care and thought into our dealings to bring everyone back into harmony. When an individual made the decision to leave we honored their contribution and wished them well in their future endeavors.

Mike Bass was a natural choice to become the next in the parade of drummers that we worked with. Mike and Dave worked together at 'Petey Pop Studios' on a variety of projects that featured music infused with dialog that edged very close to comedy. Mike was an accomplished percussionist, with a heaping helping of classical training. If you listen to Secret Signals 1 & 2 (CDs re-released by Newhouse Music) you can hear some of Mike's playing, composition, and arrangements The Muffins performed.

This era of the band, as I remember, marks the beginning of the group search for a new sound. Some of the compositions during this period show real bright spots others have less cohesion, need further development, or are ready to be circle filed.

The Muffins were never so emotionally involved with a composition as to be unwilling to 'circle file' or retire a piece. During this time the band toys with manipulating individual parts and compositional development, a means by which the entire ensemble, thru incremental steps, becomes the arranger for the compositions. Baby steps at first, but we are growing. Mike is more of a jazz drummer than a rocker, but overall, we were very happy with his contribution. Alas, the long rehearsal hours we spent in the band room were more than Mike had bargained for, and he decided to leave the band.

Stuart Abramowitz was the next to throw his lot in with ours. Stu brought a bit more rock feel in his style of playing. The Muffins continued to stride forward in compositional cohesion. The random course changes that our music took started to sound less like a bad edit and more like a natural human course change. This took hours of rehearsal time to accomplish, the toll of this brain strain and the energy it consumed, required a salve. That salve was improv…totally free and unfettered improvisation.

We made time to do improv so we wouldn't burn out on rehearsal. The goal of our rehearsal was to come to a place where the band was so comfortable with the abrupt changes our compositions involved that they sounded easy and natural. The listener might be thrown for a loop but we would pull them right back in. We got fairly tight during this spell, and our listenership increased, but not dramatically. Our music was hard to listen to, not impossible, but challenging. Some folks expect music to be comfortably in the background. The Muffins were not connecting with that segment of the populace. We demanded your full attention and then some.

Stu announced his retirement from The Muffins and sold his drums right off the stage after our last performance together. Michael Zentner decided that he was finished as well. A bit of a setback, but to be honest I was relatively unaffected by the loss of two members. Billy and Dave were hard hit due to the fact that we were back to square one.

For me it was just like Jazz Lab, a few folks graduated, you go on summer break, and in the fall, you start over with the replacements. This is how great bands are built. More importantly, I felt that most of the talent that was in the Quintet remained in the Trio. I let Billy and Dave know how I felt and encouraged them to venture forth with me as a trio.

The Trio

We really had to change gears to do the Trio. Most all of the music we were doing had to be dropped. New music and some copy tunes (Oh, Lord) were incorporated, and improv became a much bigger part of who we were.

If I remember correctly, we embraced a more edgy quality of performance during this time and the fan base that continued their support really did make a difference to help prove to Billy, Dave and myself that the three of us were still relevant. I would like to say more about this time, but my memories are few. It was like we were in automatic mode, carefree, do as you will.

And as Zen as that might be, it all became a flow of energy that didn't make a lot of recallable memories for me. There was one venue that I really enjoyed playing...the WAFU coffee house. WAFU (Washington Area Free University) was held in the back section of an old burned out church. It was plush and the acoustics were excellent. Something happened during this period that would change everything completely, Michael Zentner was out and about, reaching out to other musicians (likely for his next project) and spent some time talking with Paul Sears. Michael felt that Paul might be a good fit for The Muffins and suggested that he check us out. Paul came to see/meet with us and we decided to become a quartet. We never looked seriously for another guitar player to replace Michael. We had been a Quintet, and a Trio, so now we would be a Quartet.

There was something explosive about the Quartet. Paul had introduced a vitality that bordered on volatile. It was during the early days of the quartet that *Hobart Got Burned* was born from an improv. *Monkey with the Golden Eyes* was a written pieced that connected to *Hobart* by means of an improv, so in this, totally free improv became entrenched in a composition.

The Muffins sound was evolving once again and it occurred to me that the quartet would never stop evolving. Some of the tunes Dave wrote during this period had horn solo after horn solo, so while we practiced I slowly evolved solos into parts that were repeatable. Some were more flexible than others while some could have been committed to the chart as a written section.

In this, I was free to play beyond the limits of the composition and I could get back to one of my loves…Melodic Development. I spoke with Dave about the use of a central melody that comes back around to be restated by another instrument, a compositional tool that would help our efforts. While a landmark of our music was 'linear to the max' the return of a stated melody can do a lot to help hold a composition together.

The band was working on an extended Newhouse composition *The Adventures of Captain Boomerang* and the flute melody that started the piece was just beautiful. I suggested that we bring it back in a new voice. We restated the melody several more times in the piece and *Captain Boomerang* stands today for me, as one of the best melodically developed compositions The Muffins ever produced, although, in all fairness, its strength goes way beyond a few returned melodies. Dave put a lot of effort into that composition and the band did a lot to help hold the composition together and develop it further.

The band stabilized at this point. The ensemble coalesced around the music. The music became solid...no one quit, holy moly, no one quit.

So, what to do next...

Random Radar Records

How this idea developed into a full blown Record Company is beyond me. There were so many reasons why this idea should have fumbled, then failed in the early developmental phases. The thing of it is, it flourished, due in part to a very good idea to create a compilation sampler album of the artists the record company intended to promote.

The other sound business idea was to co-opt the efforts of artists that already had name recognition. Fred Frith, Lol Coxhill (they contributed tracks to the Random Radar Sampler LP-PS) were already recording artists and they gave RRR credibility. The record company was going to make a profit from its opening advertising efforts from distribution of the Sample.

In short, RRR had the right group of folks, at the right time and the right place. That this worked as well as it did, changed the life of more people than most of us could ever imagine. I was there from the very beginning and I never doubted that we could do this. After all, I had watched this process multiple times back in Intermediate and High School. For me it was simple, this is what musicians do.

Random Radar Records (RRR) was a full blown 501-C3 Non-Profit Corporation that really did make its mark. Brief but effective, RRR got The Muffins 'Manna Mirage' and <185> in front of the public.

Without RRR The Muffins would likely have be just another garage band that became a random blip on the radar screen of life. It is also a strong possibility that Wayside Music and Cuneiform Records would never have existed. Steven Feigenbaum saw an opportunity when RRR dissolved its corporation. The mailing list that RRR (in larger part via The Muffins—PS) had accumulated during its years of operation became a valuable tool to launch Wayside Music.

The success of Wayside Records paved the way for the birth of Cuneiform Records. Both companies 'could' have happen without RRR but the lessons learned in RRR by the artists that created and ran the company were transformative, and I don't think that it is likely that Steve would have ended up doing what he did without the RRR experience.

First Record, Manna/Mirage

The sampler did well enough that The Muffins were going to be able to make their first record. The budget for recording was always the responsibility of the artist with RRR releases. I was making a decent wage at the Washington Music Center working in the wind instrument repair shop and could best afford to purchase a better suited multi-track tape recorder.

We had been using Dave's Teac four-track machine and The Muffins were going to need more tracks to do justice to the new compositions. I purchased a Teac 80-8 with a DX-8 DBX noise reduction module. We decided to use our Peavey twelve-track mixer to serve as the recording and mixing console. The decision to use the Peavey really influenced how the end product sounded. The Peavey had a highly colored sound, and both the low-end & hi-end frequency curves were deficient, and we didn't use compression during the recording or mixing.

I want to make one thing perfectly clear. The end result of the recording for Manna/Mirage was not a sonic masterpiece. We did the best we could with what we had and we compromised with each other for recording technique, EQ, FX, Balance and Mastering. We worked together making mix notes and took dozens of shots at the real-time final mix before we called it DONE. No automation, just well-choreographed mix notes done old school. Four guys huddled around a mixing console performing a complex range of changes as the tape rolls...one missed cue and the mix had to go back to start over. Believe you me, old school sucked, in my humble opinion.

You got so involved with the dance of the mix that you weren't really listening critically. That being said, the notion that the record was not well mastered by the cutting lab is nonsense. Peter Helffrich mastered the record, doing the best he could with what we gave him, and when he finished with Manna/Mirage he made a point of playing for me a well mastered track he had recorded in an A/B comparison to Manna/Mirage that sonically opened my eyes, or maybe it was my ears.

It changed how I approached recording forever. My new vision did put me at odds with my fellow band members. It became apparent that we would need a producer for the next album. We had done the shared vision thing and done it to the best of our ability, but the result of Manna/Mirage and the growth we were all experiencing necessitated change. Enter Fred Frith.

<185>

Dave Newhouse was trying to change what his compositions 'were' during this juncture. Contact with members of Henry Cow had an influence how Dave was seeing where his compositions were headed. Personally, I think that Dave was attempting to embrace RIO and connect to a perceived larger audience. Dave's efforts brought about a new group of compositions, oh, and there were some vocals. Billy Swann was handling the vocals and Dave was creating the lyrics. This was fun stuff to play for me; fast moving, angular, discordant, resolute, and to be painfully honest, an insurmountable listeners challenge to a very large segment of the population on planet earth.

We went into Track Recorders totally prepared to record. The tunes were tight, we had mastered our parts and we were excited to work with Fred Frith. The thing I really liked was that Fred's vision as a producer came across. He took command and the raw tracks were laid down fast and furious.

I remember at one-point Fred sent me out to double track a line that was particularly difficult. (Tom's alto sax solo in *Antidote to Drydock*—PS) I presume he meant to capture a tight doubling, so I played the line dead on as it should be played without the first track in my headphones. In the control booth both lines were playing so tightly synced that Fred made some exclamation, like 'amazing'... hey, all I can say is that we knew our parts, and we could play them however many times you needed.

Time to Go

The aftermath of <185> was very anticlimactic. It was not well received in reviews and I found myself agreeing with the reviews. Punk was becoming the relevant music form of the day. The Muffins were becoming a question mark for me. I was feeling that we were not relevant or important musically in my life. I just didn't see what was next, or more importantly, what I foresaw coming next was to be avoided.

I had started a family and I wanted to spend my time after work with them. I explained to my brothers in the band that I was done. I thanked them for everything we had shared and left to start the next adventure. Running my very own 24-track recording studio. Black Pond Recording Studios became my daily job. I left musical instrument repair behind and never went back. The musicians that I recorded and mixed let me develop my Peter Helffrich-inspired soundscape.

I might still be producing music today if not for an early onset of midlife crisis. I put Chris Biondo in charge of my studio and headed off to the far north of Alberta, Canada to study with a Cree medicine woman. I know, I know...I can imagine what you are thinking. Tom Scott had lost his ever-loving mind. And by most standards you would be correct. Just continue reading on and I'm sure you will agree that I came back to my senses before it was too late.

Before we continue though, I have got to say I'm happy that I had the Alberta, Canada experience, I was introduced to a culture very different from my own it was an important transformation in my life and gave me focus. The life of a modern Medicine woman is very full and the problems that she faced every day would fill a book. A book...not this book.

So, I found myself studying to become a medicine man. That was all good and well during the summer but when it started to turn cold and the locals accused my family of failing to put enough weight on during the summer, I pressed for an explanation. They said the layer of fat was needed to deal with the winter conditions. I pressed even further and they explained that your piss freezes before it hits the ground in the dead of winter, and the sun rises barely above the horizon four hours a day, night being twenty hours long.

WTF?

I packed up the children and wife and headed back to the good old US of A. My second apprenticeship in life was terminated early. The family spent some time touring the U.S., the studio was doing well, Chris was successfully building a clientele, and I received a comfortably large check every month as owner.

In the years that followed I got divorced, remarried, sold Back Pond Studio and was enjoying my other life passion, professional woodworking. Life was good and I was feeling like I belonged where I was. Then one day (in 1998—PS) I got a call...it was Paul Sears on the other end of the line and he said 'I got an idea...'

A reunion....

It seemed like a completely innocent thing to do.

We get together and play for a day.

No Biggy. Right?

What I forgot is that there would be new music, the lure of

creation, just like the Siren's Song drawing the sailor's ship towards the rocks, or the pre-addict that thinks he will only do Heroin once. You forget why you left the band it in the first place and you dive right back in, feet first or head-over heels, it makes no difference. I was right back where I started from.

The Muffins Phase II

Phase II seemed like the most normal thing in the world. Gone was the angular music. The new collection of music that was to become 'Bandwidth' was more 'melodic Canterbury' than 'RIO'. It was both fun to play and more importantly it was an enjoyable listen. I had sold my 24-track recording studio to Chris Biondo years before so that was never an option, and some of our earlier attempts at digital recording at another studio were not good enough, so we asked Carl Merson to undertake the project at 'Beware of Dog Studio.'

I watched Carl working with the new digital equipment and made mental notes for what would need to be purchased to set up my new Digital Studio. Digital to tape was phasing out and digital to hard drive better known as Digital Audio Workstation (DAW) was becoming the norm for the home recordist.

Steven Feigenbaum with Cuneiform Records put 'Bandwidth" out in 2002 and we were back. One huge exception to our efforts was we didn't go at it in the rehearsal room ten hours a week. We couldn't, our homes were geographically spread over hundreds of miles. What we could do was summer retreats to prep for performances and learn new music. If you listen to our post reformation performances you will hear a band that isn't as tight as it was in the old days. We were doing the best we could with what we had, same as before. We hit the ground running for 'Double Negative', released 2004, on Cuneiform Records, and I composed about half the pieces so the outcome was a 17 track CD with a double album play time.

Paul and I produced this project together with Paul handling the outreach to guest artists while I handled the Editing and Mixing. We worked with Sun Ra Arkestra saxophonists Marshall Allen and Knoel Scott. You can tell when you listen to 'Double Negative' we are experimenting with new sounds. The album covers a lot of ground, maybe a bit too much. Double albums take a lot of material to make and there were a couple cuts that didn't really fit. *They Come on Unknown Nights* was on the chopping block; the second half of the track just wasn't working. I dug as deep as I could into my bag of tricks to help the second half of that tune fit the first half. Eventually we decided that it was good enough to earn its place in the lineup. In hind sight, I think that was a mistake.

Six years passed before we had enough material for the next CD. Notably 'Palindrome' had a mere eight tracks, but they were strong and Billy composed track #3 *Fishing in America*, a lazily evocative piece that I absolutely love. When Steve with Cuneiform Records reviewed 'Palindrome' for release he decided he wasn't interested with the CD as it was. The power brokers that call the shots for digital sales prefer a CD to have ten or more tunes. With email communication and a few noses being out of joint, the band consensus was to pursue other labels and Musea proposed a contract.

We released 'Palindrome' in 2010 on a French label, Musea Records. Dave had been pushing for us to return to our RRR practices of self-promotion using a digital age model. I had done some follow-up reading after Dave's original inspiration and I came to understand that the digital age model performs best for touring bands who capitalized their operation with merchandising revenue.

Dave's self-promotion idea was looking like the only rational path left to us, albeit sans touring capital. What Dave (or anyone else—PS) could never have been expected to see coming was the CD markets slow decline, as file-sharing on Torrent web sites made it easier for would-be fans to procure music at no personal cost, the result of which was going to hurt CD sales.

SIDE NOTE; I want to say at this point, we are eternally

grateful to all of our fans who continued to purchase CDs from us and our distributors. Your investment in our music kept us going. It was the summer of 2008 and all of the Muffins came to the Mountain to do a recording session. This was an impromptu session with no rehearsed pieces of music. We lay down nearly twenty beats, created in the moment, then recorded as soon as the beat came together. This went quickly as there were no melodies being created and I could serve as engineer. At the time the sessions were being referred to as 'Love Letters 3'.

Not much happened with the 'Love Letters 3' beats right away. Mike Potter captured a more usable multi-track version at ProgDay 2010 of one of the beats titled *Going Softly*. We used to start our performances during this time period with this tune, a slow, comfortable improv piece that allowed the band to get our 'heads on straight' and 'sea legs' under us at the start of a performance.

Dave and I continued work apart from one another on melodic development of the beats from the 2008 recording session that spoke to us, composing melodies and recording them one after another, and as the beats came together we gave each beat a name, save one, named *Beat 10*, which was the 10th beat we recorded back in the summer of 2008. We did add a couple of rhythm tracks to the collection during the summer of 2011.

Then I started mixing and mastering the CD, a process that I had been doing by myself at 'The Mountain' since 'Double Negative' in 2003 when I had finished selecting and purchased a full suite of mixing and mastering Software. I would create a set of mixes and send CD's out to the Band members for feedback. I would incorporate the feedback I received into the next mix. We would continue the process of mix and feedback until we felt the CD was DONE.

Somewhere during the process of recording 'Mother Tongue' I made the point that Love Letters 1 & 2 hadn't done well for us, and that repeating the same action over and over and expecting a different result was, in fact, a defining aspect of insanity. My point was taken and the CD title 'Love Letters 3' was circle filed. We came up with the new name 'Mother Tongue' released in 2012 on my label Hobart Films & Records.

I started composition on the next CD right away. We had been talking about doing a big band Muffin style CD for years. I started composing and was making good headway. Dave was talking about starting work on <186>, but I'm not big on repeating the past so I would just hold my tongue any time Dave mentioned angular discordant music.

As the project developed it became clear that Dave was having trouble with the Big Band concept. By the time Dave spoke with me about the reservations he was having with the project, we were well past the midpoint recording wise, I let him know that I had more than enough compositions completed to finish the CD without him needing to struggle with the compositional aspect. I had spent years playing in Big Bands, Dave had not. I wasn't surprised that he was having compositional issues. Dave didn't have any formal training in composition and Big Bands required some. No direct playing experience, and no formal training left Dave in a very challenging place.

In my mind it wasn't an issue if Dave didn't compose for the Big Band CD. The Muffins were a collective and we had survived and reunited because we were flexible. Dave decided to continue with his compositions for the Big Band. Problem solved, right? The next issue Dave brought up was that his compositions and my compositions didn't sound like a cohesive album. To my thinking this was the same issue and Dave was coming at it from another angle. I realized that we had reached an impasse. I receive a letter from Dave dated 3/23/2015. Hmm, a letter…

A Letter Dated 3/23/2015

The letter explained that Dave was pulling his compositions

from the project to release as a solo album, and he expected me to do the same. This was an unilateral decision, and for me the end of the reunion. Dave wanted me to give it time and so I did, but eventually I let Dave know that our work recording new music together was over. I would still play Muffins performances, but the days of Dave Newhouse and Tom Scott creating new music in 'The Muffins' had come to an end. Done and Done. I've given this decision plenty of time; months, and now years, and I remain resolute. It is over.

4S'd Man or Muffin

The thing is, Billy and Paul wanted to continue with the Big Band project, so I checked in with Mark Stanley who had been recording the guitar parts for the big band CD to see if he wanted to continue the project if Dave was out. Mark answered that he was in. So strangely enough the project continued on— never even missed a beat.

I purchased a tenor and a bari sax and replaced all of Dave's sax parts with the exception of the first thirty-seven seconds of the fifth track called *Busy Hands*. This stands as the last recording that The Muffins ever made. It is a beautiful intro to the rest of the song with Dave on bass clarinet, me on alto clarinet, Paul on drums, Billy on bass, and Mark on guitar.

We needed a name for this new ensemble and as I looked at the band roster I noticed that every band member last name started with 'S', four people with 'S' last names. 4S'd immediately jumped to mind. I liked it because 4S'd sounds like the word Forest. Even the four backup-vocal chicks last names all started with 'S' so they became the 4S'd-ettes. The cover-art idea coalesced around the 4S'd name, the Forest Gnome image came from a Pretty Baby Naturals bar of soap. I was taking my morning shower, looked up to locate the bar of soap, and there staring back at me from the surface of the soap was a forest gnome.

After my shower I used my cellphone to take a picture. My

youngest daughter, Tara Scott, applied her college education in the arts to the project, and worked with the forest gnome image idea I described. Boom, new band, new music, new art concept, and we were working our way to releasing our very first CD. Paul built a studio next to his home in Arizona, & worked with engineer Joshua Medina to create about half the drum tracks.

When Paul moved from Apache Junction to Superior Arizona, Joshua was too far away to assist as engineer, so for reasons of practicality, Paul took over and self-engineered the rest of the tracks. Paul's willingness to really learn the compositions and create truly inspired drum tracks shows in the music and I am so very pleased that he pushed for us to continue with the project. I had about half of Billy's parts recorded as The Muffins Project, but still needed to record the compositions that I added after The Muffins dissolution.

I checked in with Billy to see if it would be better if I brought The Mountain-Mobile Recording Studio to him in Orangeburg South Carolina and he jumped at the idea. For years, Billy has made the eight-hour drive up to Virginia to work on Muffin projects, and I thought 4S'd could do better by him. Billy's work on 'Man or Muffin' is for me a culmination of a lifetime of musical creation.

Mark Stanley worked from his studio in Gaithersburg Maryland. We used file sharing and email to do the project. This method of email communication and file sharing works really well for folks with their own studio and Mark used markers in the completed guitar files he sent to me that corresponded to markers in the master tracks. This helped make sure that the timing of the parts was dead on. It had been years since I had worked with a guitarist and Mark was very patient with me as we corrected range mistakes in my written guitar parts. Mark's interpretation and creative input helped make up for my lack of guitar compositional skills. I was very lucky to have Mark on this project. His guitar work is superb.

The mixing of the Big Band was a lot harder than I thought

it was going to be. The ensemble size peaked at a four-piece rhythm section, five saxes, four trombones, four trumpets, twelve-piece string section, and a four-voice chorus. An ensemble this size with my writing style creates a lot of midrange movement. The Big Band and the density of my compositions in places created a wall of sound and the wall of sound was occurring in places where it shouldn't.

Although I had played in Big Bands for years, I didn't have any Big Band ensemble mixing experience. I corresponded with Jason Moss from 'Behind the Speakers' about the midrange build up centered around 5K and received some very helpful guidance concerning EQ cuts and midrange compression. I also took one of his online classes for mixing low end to help get Paul's kick drum and Billy's bass sub tones out of each others' way.

The most important thing to my ears was keeping the transient attacks from all of the players so that the very dense sections of arrangements didn't lose the midrange melodic movement. Jason also recommended that I have the mastering done by another set of ears. I had always mastered The Muffins final mixes so this was a big letting-go for me. When the master came back from The SoundLAB I breathed a sigh of relief. Tom Scheponik had mastered 'Man or Muffin' in the Blue Room and although it had a little less deep bass than when I mastered it in my studio, it was a very good mastering job.

The master had plenty of punch, exceptional transient presents, shimmering highs and a solid low end. I could hear into the ensemble and pick out every instrument. Job Done. The only thing that I find challenging about finishing a project is I'm never sure about what comes next, this time it feels a lot like wait and see.

—Thomas F. Scott

Vice Versa, a Fun Duo with Sanford Scheller Post the Muffins

I met a guy named Sanford Scheller in 1982 or 3, who had been on the scene for some years and played guitar and keyboards. He was keen to do something, so we hung out and began improvising and jamming in the basement I started in. After my dad passed away, Sanford became my best buddy and moved into our house.

Sanford and I had played a bit by then, but not much. Not long after, I was contacted by old friend Tina Bovis who wanted The Muffins for a new music festival at the Marble Bar in Baltimore. She and Ken Newman had booked The Muffins, Frith/Cutler and many other acts in the Baltimore area over the years. We played there too sometimes with a cool band called Neige.

The Muffins had split in 1981, and at that time were not a deliverable act, so I suggested Sanford and I as "Vice Versa". Tina said okay.

Sanford said "WHAT...?? ARE YOU FUCKING NUTS??"...and then agreed to do the gig.

We had barely played together. It was pretty insane as we had only played together for a minute, and knew how to play a couple of brief systems of Sanford's as a duo, and so most of what we did ended up as cool batshit improvisation. Sanford is a great improviser. This show was loud.

Marble Bar had great sound with monitors on each corner of the stage facing whoever was on stage. The stage was in the middle of a large room, so the audience could walk around the whole thing. The place had a seventy-five-foot long actual marble bar, which is where the only seats were.

Sanford even played guitar with his foot while playing keys. A crowd pleaser.

We were the headliner that night and went over pretty well given the singed flavor of the other acts. Baltimore News 3 (I

think) TV filmed some of our set, and I was interviewed after
wards while sitting on a pool table. The TV station wanted
absurdly large $$$$ for a copy, so we never did get one.

Family Stuff

My dad passed away in 1983. There was a memorial concert for
him that year at the Shrine of The Most Blessed Sacrament near
Chevy Chase Circle in Washington, DC. He worked there as
choirmaster and organist for over twenty years, and designed
their new Wilhelm Zimmer pipe organ in the mid 1970s. Over
500 folks showed for this memorial.

My dear friend Caroline Forsyth sang in the choir. There
was a harpist. The guest star was my dad's old friend and then
world reknowned organist Herman Berlinski, who fired up the
old Sforzando (pedal to the metal in pipe organese) and really
blew the dust out of that organ, even playing with his elbows and
whole arm.

That woke 'em up, I tellya.

I recorded this whole concert on pal Bruce Cornwell's
Otari four-track machine with some old RCA ribbon
microphones and got a pretty good recording. Bruce then did
great job editing this concert, and we made a small number of
cassettes available for those that wanted a memento. When I was
a young child back in the early 1950s, my dad went to Europe as
part of the Marshall Plan, and consulted on the rebuilding of
damaged pipe organs from WWII. Some projects included the
organ at the *Heiliggeistkirche* Cathedral in Heidelberg, Germany, a
couple in France, and the huge organ at St. Paul's in London, and
that one is one of very few that has full length sixty-four-foot
pipes. (some 64's are actually folded 32').

Dad also consulted on the instruments at The Kennedy
Center in DC. He also understood the intricate workings of very
old, what are called tracker-touch organs, that predate
electricity. The linkages going from the keys down into the floor,
across the room and up into to the swell box to the pipes are

entirely mechanical, very sensitive and a real pain to maintain. The air came from bellows and pumps operated by people back then.

Another thing about pipe organs is that they are often afterthoughts and get crammed in wherever there is space. Ideally, an organ designer will be in cahoots with the architect in order to maximize acoustics. Many organ pipes that you can see are often placebo and decorative, with the sound-producing ones hidden behind them. A clue to this is when you see a huge, usually gold color pipe attached to a thin piece of filigree wood, you can be reasonably sure it is a placebo pipe and there for appearance. Real pipes of course have air lines and mechanical linkages attached. My first part time job as a teen was via my dad working with Newcomer organ co. in Washington, DC, that maintained organs all over the Washington area.

I was an assistant tuner. My dad did bookkeeping and consulting for them. Service contracts for organs are not uncommon, nor are they cheap. A good pipe organ is a serious investment and can cost way north of $400K. I was warned that one must avoid touching the actual pipes when working on them, as the oil, moisture, and temperature from your hands can have deleterious effects on them.

A funny story: When I was about 10, (1963) my dad insisted that I sit next to him on the organ bench at Blessed Sacrament for Christmas mass. Full Monty men and boys choir. The place was packed to the chandeliers with churchgoers. Right in the middle of a hymn, I slipped off the organ bench, fell on the keys, and took a couple of steps descending on the bass pedals on my way to get off the organ, of course using the lower manual keys for balance. A show stopper. EVERYONE turned around to see what the HELL was going on, and I thought my mom who was sitting close by was going to wet her pants trying not to laugh. That was my only public appearance on pipe organ, never to be repeated.

My sister developed rather early and soon I was having to

fight off many of my pals that were attracted to her at still a young age. She was four years younger than I. While still fairly young, she started dating Nils Lofgren, the then local guitarist (Grin—Neil Young—Springsteen). I shot hoops with Nils at the Fort Reno Park where Grin was to play that night. I think that's where and when they met. 1970 or 71. They saw each other off and on all the way up to Nil's first Springsteen gig. He left a nice Stratocaster guitar at our house for ages.

Damn, he remembered and came for it one day. I have great recordings of Grin from The Emergency Club in DC at what I think was a New Years Eve gig. Grin were on fire that night. What a great show. They did Smokestack Lightning right. I remember working an Alice Cooper show when Nils's band Grin was opening. Back stage, Neal Smith, the Alice Cooper drummer gave my sister the sunglasses (or an identical pair) he wore on the cover of Love It to Death. I advised her to put them away, but no, and she of course quickly lost them.

She had disastrous relationships right and left going up until her young adult years and developed a downer habit. At another gig, Marc Bolan hit on her backstage. May have been at a Humble Pie gig I worked on sound crew for at Alexandria Roller Rink. She actually married a great guy who owned an art gallery on the top floor of the Atlantis Building on F Street in Washington, DC, where the original 9:30 club was and loved her, but that was not good enough and she was very unhappy. Her ongoing calamities cost her lifelong friends and had my parents very upset. She refused help from everyone.

Late in 1986, my dear sister committed suicide in my mom's basement. She had as unstable of an adult life as one could possibly have. It was very sad. This depressed my mom to no end, and undoubtedly contributed to her early death in 1991. At that time, very suddenly and unexpectedly, I had whole lot of other shitty stuff foisted upon me the same week she died to deal with, hitting me from several sides.

Ever feel like four walls are closing in on you

simultaneously?

That was me at that time.

I was also dealing daily with all the estate details (probate and so on) related to my mom's death, by myself, and no support whatsoever from any quarter.

Lovely.

VERY depressing.

Hello more booze than usual.

Thankfully, our family lawyer had retired and advised me how to save some $, and do probate pro se', which I did myself with his guidance without a hitch. Being the only living relative, only entity in the will, and executor, this was easier than most probate cases. But, I still had to do it, and go through it unaided.

About that: I was advised by the retired lawyer to just waltz into the Washington Law Reporter in DC, pretend I knew what I was doing and ask for a Probate Pack. This contains all the forms that were required for Probate. They eyed me kinda funny, but sold it to me for ten or fifteen bucks.

Then, back at home and via speakerphone, the family lawyer advised me on exactly what this instrument had to say. Thankfully, my mom's old IBM typewriter still worked. I then went to the DC courthouse on Indiana Avenue and filed the probate stuff. After the sixty days or whatever it was, I went to close the case. Remember, I am doing all this pro se'.

So, I end up in a waiting room at the DC courthouse waiting for an available judge and courtroom with a bunch of well-heeled, suited-up central casting lawyers, some of whom are gleefully socking dead folks' estates for big hourly bucks while sucking down coffee and smoking.

I was dressed as usual, half-assed, disheveled, wannabe rock star casual. And still in my perpetual foul mood. A lawyer approached me, stuck out his hand and said something like "Have we met? I'm Smith from Dewey Cheatem and Howe; what firm are you with?" or something similar. I told him I was there pro se' to close a simple clear cut probate case.

SILENCE.

No one else came near me in that room for the next hour. When my case was finally called, the judge was a young black gal. She has my case file in her hands and and says "what's your story? What do you want to do here today? I said, simple; close the case.

I thought she was going to sail over the bench and kiss me. She bitched a bit about all the lawyers in the waiting room wasting her time, and ripping peoples estates off for large $, and I was signed off and out of there in five minutes. Case closed. I noticed that the deeds and records building was right across the street. I needed to deed the house in my name.

I went in and asked the clerk for a deed form. She said take this to your attorney, and have them complete and mail it. I asked her for a pen, and rewrote the deed right there on the counter by hand, and handed it back to her and said "Here, FILE IT. I'm the executor and boss of this case right here."

She was flummoxed.

Done, and done.

However, nothing else was going well.

My personal life was a fucking mess for quite a while. I still have some scars. Makes me go fakakta in the kop just thinking about it. Sometimes I would like to forget parts of most of a decade from 1991 until I started playing again with 9353, and again with The Muffins. There are some mugs I never want to see again with my blinkers. I got through some very serious shit, but barely and totally alone.

Some of the bullshit went on for quite awhile. I was orphaned, seriously disillusioned, living alone, and had no adult family anywhere to rely on for support in 1991.

A tough time.

I was like that cartoon strip The Angriest Dog in the World that depicted the same snarling dog at the end of a chain every week. That was me for ages. Lemony Snicket would have loved me at that time. Done with that.

I Forget To Remember To Forget
　—Elvis

Today, the only blood relatives I have are my older son's beautiful family and my grandson in England. I now also have my great wife's family of cool inlaws. Great, refreshing, supportive folks.

That's that. I am happy.

And now...

Not Music

I WOULD BE a dishonest guy if I did not take this rare opportunity to share SOME nonmusical thoughts and my own opinions in writing, and not on social media. What a sewer THAT seems to be turning into.

So, here goes.

Folks that know me well know I do not practice any religion. I totally believe in freedom of religion and subsequently, totally believe in freedom FROM religion. I don't think religion has any business, period, in government. I kinda like the rule of unbiased law, period.

Our country was thankfully not founded on ANY religion. I recommend reading the book *Salvation for Sale* by Gerard Thomas Straub. Our founding fathers seemed to have some sense.

George Washington Says...

*If I could conceive that the general government might ever be
so administered as to render the liberty of conscience
insecure, I beg you will be persuaded, that no one would be
more zealous than myself to establish effectual barriers
against the horrors of spiritual tyranny, and every species of
religious persecution.*

John Adams Says...

As the Government of the United States of America is not, in any sense, founded on the Christian religion.

Thomas Jefferson Says...

I contemplate with sovereign reverence, that act of the whole American people which declared that their legislature should make no law respecting an establishment of religion, or prohibit the free exercise thereof, thus building a wall of separation between church and state.

And, he says...

I am for freedom of religion and against all maneuvers to bring about a legal ascendancy of one sect over another.

Yes.

Gerard Straub actually worked with the delusional predatory creep Pat Robertson that had, get this, "presidential aspirations" and Straub learned how to tell the difference between the brown smelly stuff and chocolate. People can worship whoever, and however they want. I just refuse to discuss this subject. I have had preachy types in the past go totally apeshit when I refuse to discuss the subject with them, because I would not let them draw a bead on me, and then lump me into one of their convenient categories so they can tune their jeezo rap to my attitude. I just can't give them that satisfaction. I don't fit your profiles, folks.

It's my business only.

Refusing to discuss this makes some people go utterly nuts. I do know some great folks that are religious, but thankfully, NOT preachy. I believe in the concept of the individual, and the concept of personal privacy. What's left of these that is, thank you. When I see the words "act of god" within a contract I object to it. A grey area. Until this god is a subpoenable signatory on the document, get it out. Who determines this? This is usually an easy-out clause for grabastic insurance companies. Most of the time, they are referring to predictable and known *meteorological* events.

My view of government also differs from the average bear. I do not consider myself to be a liberal, or conservative. I am not a dem or a pub. No Brooks Brothers suits or love beads here. So, what does a crusty old contrarian like me do? I try to be a realist that pays attention to history and facts, and an individual.

The very concept of individuality is being trampled on from many sides. My views seem to run contrary to conventional wisdom. I pay attention to results, not words, or sham partisan "party politics." In my opinion, the problems facing the citizenry in USA are driven by hitherto nameless special interests that drive efforts on Capitol Hill. Not the white house, which seems to be a effective distraction from what REALLY affects us. Our "friends" on Capitol Hill. Neither party has worked for the average US citizen for a long time. We need to departy.

Read up on evil hill lobbyists. Large bribes called "contributions."

Touching, eh?

There lies a lot of it. Important is that all bills became due and many of the same folks around Evil Hill give money to both parties. They don't give a rat's ass who wins as long as they get what they want. They don't care about most of the people in this country at all, because they truly are a completely separate society. These people could care less about health care, health insurance, Social Security, public education, or public transportation because they don't use any of it. Politics is a codeword for the consummation or continuation of old boy capitol hill and state/local business deals. That's very likely why there are no term limits on the hill. Think about that. THEY handle our $.

When you hear phrases on the news alluding to "studies

planned, task forces, & committees appointed", that there's code for a whole lot of lawyers are going to drag out whatever issues there are and sock us for a shit ton of OUR $.

You betcha.

Our guvvy is Woodstock for lawyers. Private sector as well. Obfu$cate. It pays well.

Why does anyone think WHY we have so much crime, so many lawyers, an abused appeals system, purposely crowded courts, and for profit prisons, etc. etc? It's a business. Anyone voting for bills that support the for-profit prison system needs to be run the hell out of town. Who do you think pays for this shit? If I was emperor, prisoners, especially violent ones would be working twelve-hour shifts fixing potholes.

However, if this happened, crime would surely go down and lawyers will bleat and ululate loudly 'cause the gravy's gone from recycling crims through the corrupt courts. Less jail space too. Let the first shift crawl into the 2nd shifts stink. They lied to you and I when we were kids.

CRIME PAYS.

My own parents hinted to me that we have been handed a sham via the two-party system when I was a teenager. They were absolutely right. We have a political party purports to want "smaller government." "Lower Taxes." What a sense of humor. Come. Let's have a laugh.

That same small-guvvy party foisted a whole new department (DHS) on top of what they just refuse to admit is a horribly broken system. For $. I grew up in Washington, DC. I got to the point where if I heard one more dem or pub utter the phrase "Let's take back America", I was going to puke. They already took America. Sold it.

Then there's that pesky Constitution. Well intended, but, the meaning of everything in it is subject to a variety of interpretations. Remember, constitutional law is taught in colleges. Who knows what it means in real life? If you have a related cause or case, on ANY related issue, try taking it to a court. Hope you have deep pockets, because you will spend many LARGE dollars to pay people to interpret whatever piece of it that you think is relevant to your case. Good luck.

Let's argue.

Divide and conquer has worked very well. United we stand and divided we fall. Anyone get it? Much better to have a divided country. A distraction. Guvvy would be terrified of a truly united voter base that is on to them, and is aimed at changing the way things are. That's the last thing they want to see. Personally, I think Washington, DC needs both an exorcism AND a wire brush enema. Get rid of these blithering *pithecanthropoid bimbos.* Start anew, and jettison the Edsels. The emperor never HAD clothes. Never will.

Taxes

I'm all for abolishing personal income tax. That has been too much of a gravy train for far too long. Guvvy simply extorts too much of OUR money. We have out of control incredible guvvy bloat. That fact is unarguable. Think of the savings the IRS alone would realize by eliminating income tax. If folks HAVE more money, they will SPEND more money. Let's have higher sales and luxury taxes. Rich folks sure like to spend money.

The underground economy spends lots of money too. Let those guys make a glowing debut as taxpayers. Let guvvy survive by improving the economy via business growth and sales by prudent stewardship, rather than raping the individual taxpayer and small business like they do now. Let's let the small government party ruling la machine now in 2018 live up to their rhetoric and lobby to CUT government, and spending. Don't hold your breath. Part of the lie. Remember those guys? What humor.

Abolish taxes, period, on personal savings, and investment accounts such as 401K, and annuities. The tax laws are a mess. Our own laws ALLOW businesses to hide money offshore. Do not blame the businesses. Fix the fucking laws. It's Capitol Hill where the problems lie. The entire U.S. tax code needs to be jettisoned, re-written, and simplified. Who, short of an experienced tax attorney can decipher any of that mumbo pocus? My point exactly. This code currently is purposely a disaster by design. Raise hell with your representatives to make this an issue. How many times will we let them tax the same dollar? Your earnings are taxed. Then you scrimp and save, and they wanna tax those dollars AGAIN? No.

Reminds me of a story. I call it soda bottle economics. When we were kids, we would collect soda bottles and cash them in at the local Highs store. It did not take us long to realize that they just put the bottles out back on racks waiting for the vendors to retrieve them. Nothing stopped us from just sniping those same bottles, carrying them around front and cashing them in again. This was a GREAT source of income to pad that measly old allowance when you are a mere twelve-year-old. When my dad wondered how I had managed to accumulate a staggering ten 1965 bucks on my own, I copped to what we were doing and told him.

He roared with laughter, and told me "you've learned how things work", but that it was wrong, and to not do this anymore. I see a correlation between that and our system.

Took me a long time.

Get this, the Dept of Defense, the largest Hoover of OUR $ has NEVER been properly audited. How many billions is it that they can't even account for and they want more $? The HILL is the problem. Both "sides" of that money laundering machine. What do you think they do all day on Capitol Hill? If you think they are there to us help taxpayers, you are living in an utter fantasy. It is a money laundering machine. Does anyone really think ultra rich white guys in any elected office give a rat's ass about the common man? Often spouting religion as some sort of camouflage, or influence? What??

Belief in that hooey, folks, is the chimpanzee part of the brain at work.

Get re-wired.

It's bad enough without dragging religion into it. Mumbo jumbo often gets confused with hocus pocus. Pay attention to what they do, not what they say on the campaign trail or on propaganda laden TV. While we aren't looking (we always prefer entertainment by the less important and endless clownery provided by the executive office) the Hill has been quietly raiding things like Medicare and "entitlement" Social Security to pay for corporate and rich guy "tax cuts". Cut the unaudited DoD...stop these Hill bastards, NOW. Social Security is NOT an entitlement.

Things Are More Like They Are Now Than They've Ever Been Before.
—Dwight Eisenhower (and the title of a record I played on)

Dwight Eisenhower warned us about these DoD thieves and vandals back in 1961. Here an excerpt:

> *In the councils of government, we must guard against the acquisition of unwarranted influence, whether sought or unsought, by the military-industrial complex. The potential for the disastrous rise of misplaced power exists, and will persist.*

Ever notice when "the guvvy" take from us, it's nearly an immediate affect on our wallet in THEIR, or their pal's favor. When they say they're gonna help...takes just long enough for everyone to forget. People seem to have very short memory, don't pay attention to history, don't have even a basic grasp on economics, or any grasp on where taxes really go. Twitter mentality is just that. For twits.

I don't have to name names to get my points across. Not important. The whole SYSTEM is the problem. I blame most of the mundane, and way too small USA voting bloc for tolerating this shit for this long. EVERYONE that can, should vote. Should be mandatory. Many are plain asleep at the switch. Or watching TV. Most people just plain don't think, nor do any research on who they vote for anymore.

That, and the fact that Frank Zappa was right. Paraphrasing here...stupidity is now more abundant than hydrogen, and that stupidity has replaced hydrogen as the basic building block in the universe. Break the mold and THINK, folks. Our existing system is a Potemkin Village, in the truest sense of the term. We will only succeed when EVERYONE is on the same page, and has the same opportunities here in the USA. I will not go into a diatribe about how different things are in other countries, but I encourage all to study up on things they do that we can certainly learn from. Remember, they have centuries of experience.

We 1960s war protesters are a dismal failure. The same horrible stuff goes on today at even greater expense. Where are the protests? Is everyone so used to lies and mass media bullshit that they don't care?

Young people today (and millions of older ones) are too fucking dumbed down and preoccupied with social networks, gaming, and TV to give much of a damn about anything important. I remember the huge protests in the 1960s.

Where are you now, kids? Nice to see some of them out at gun violence protests.

PAY ATTENTION.

This is YOUR future. Do some research. Read up on recent history. Do not listen to the TV. People seem to have forgotten how much power voters have. We need to use it. How did women get the right to vote? ENOUGH of them finally demanded it. Don't keep doing the same stuff over and over, and expect change. History is proof that it just does not work that way. Force change by voting. Use the phone and Internet to demand term limits on Capitol Hill. That, in my opinion, is the BIG PROBLEM here in the U.S. END the "career politician." The correct term is "career opportunist and $ launderer."

Angels and Demons that Play

No one ever went broke underestimating the intelligence of the American people.
—attributed to both H. L. Mencken and P.T. Barnum.

We have met the enemy and he is us.
—Pogo

Kill your TV.
   Okay, let's get back to some music.

More Music

DURING THE EARLY 1980s, I had no real band, other than playing occasionally with Sanford Scheller as Vice Versa. Right before I met him, I forget who I was with, but a gal I knew suggested we go see a local, cool guitarist named Pete Kennedy. My friend knew Pete, and suggested I play with him. I ended up jamming onstage, in a small club somewhere, I think on Wisconsin Avenue in DC.

Also on stage, there was a little guy tuning a Les Paul with his back to me. He turned around. It was freaking Steve Stills. I don't know if this was an expected visit or what, but there he was. Nice guy. We played two or three loose bluesy things, and then he thanked Pete, and left the stage.

Made my evening.

Braille Party Band—mid 1980s

I was out for lunch with Sanford Scheller in 1983 or 4 at an Italian sandwich shop called Strombolis in Bethesda, Maryland one day, and overheard a conversation in the next booth. This was Lou Gigger (guitar) and Matt Reidl (bass) from the cool DC band Braille Party discussing an upcoming gig at DC Space and that they did not have a drummer for. I had seen them before. Whore that I am, I introduced myself and offered my services.

We ended up rehearsing their set at my place, and we did the gig a week or so later. Sadly, I no longer have the video that my then gal, Bethe, shot. We had a tight version of Prince's tune *Let's Work*. Sadly, Lou was killed in a car accident a short time later.

1980s Fuck Art, Let's Dance

There was a cool band called Shock Opera that was around for awhile. The main guys were Jon Brayton (gtr-voc) and Eddie Arnold (gtr). Billy Swann played with them for awhile after The Muffins went away in 1981.

We were friends.

Sometime in 1984, or 5 I ended up jamming a bit with Ed and Jon, and a guitarist named Kim Garcia. They wanted to do some cool covers. We got together a cool set that included classics like Alice Cooper's *My Body* along with songs like *Mustang Sally*, *Little Bit O Soul*, *C'Mon Everybody*, *Little Wing*, *Matchbox*, *I Saw Her Standing There*, and others.

We called it Fuck Art, Let's Dance, or FALD for short. I remember playing at an outdoor party where the stage was actually the 2nd floor of a roofless abandoned house that somehow still had electricity. Kind of dangerous, but we did it anyway. We had a silly habit of tossing a rubber chicken at each other on occasion during tunes. Our singer had a crutch. This was Jon, first time out front sans guitar, and so he needed a crutch. So he obtained, just that, an actual crutch, and he even stuck some stuff that looked like frets and strings on it.

Old Friend Jon Brayton aka MYSTR Treefrog has this to say about a FALD show...

All I know is that it was blistering D.C. heat and we were playing some Parks and Recreations gig in N.E. D.C. with a Go-Go Band named the Back Street Cruisers and some total hair metal band named Lazarus—it was me, Eddie Arnold, Kim Garcia and Paul—and we decided, on the spot, to name the band Fuck Art Lets Dance, because Eddie had a way of babbling genius shit when he was plastered. The Go-Go band basically had one song that they managed to play for a solid two hours.

When we finally played it was about to storm, insects were sticking to our skin, I was delirious and out of sorts—so every time I looked like I might either growl something obscene or forget the words this goddamned yellow rubber chicken would come flying through the air and hit me in the side of my face—which had the miraculous effect of giving me total recall and helping my digestion…Paul, that friggin' gnome, had perfect aim.

And more than one chicken.

—MYSTR Treefrog

A Fun, but Short-Lived Cover Band, Purple Helmets

For awhile in the 1980s, I was running into Pedro Sera Leyva often in the neighborhood. He is a fantastic guitar player that was with Evan Johns and the H Bombs, and a group, I think, that may have been called The Choir Boys.

He always called me "little buddy".

I guess I resembled Gilligan. He, bassist Jim Cavanaugh (Danny Gatton, Sleepy LaBeef) and my neighbor, singer guitarist Bruce Cornwell saw each other often, and decided to try to play some Yardbirds material. We were all fans. Pedro also happens to be a scholar in this area.

So, The Purple Helmets commenced casual rehearsals in Bruce's basement which was right across the street from me, and was where Danny Gatton rehearsed for awhile. I thought we were sounding pretty good, and that was the only tribute band I ever tried. Unfortunately, everyone was busy with other projects and we never gigged.

Pity.

During December of 1984, Dave Newhouse and I went into Track Recorders in DC and spent a couple of days recording. It was his idea, and he financed this. Just us two. We ended up calling it "DROP". He suggested I play drums, bass, and guitar. I did not have a bass then, or a guitar.

A neighbor and friend, Randy Haines, lent me a Telecaster, and I borrowed back my old original 1970 Rickenbacker 4001, (that I stupidly sold to a local collector who refused to sell it back to me) and showed up with all my gear. Dave played mostly woodwinds. No pre-ordained arrangements. We just went in and hit. Then owner and engineer at Track, Mark Greenhouse, was very surprised when told…just roll tape. He was like…"what are you guys going to do?"…We were like…"dunno yet"…he said…okay… It was a blast and we got a few ideas down and came back for overdubs. I am hoping the stereo mixes are okay enough to release someday in some form...with Dave's blessing.

Not long after, I thought it time for another band. Sanford was still around and living in my house, so with he on keys, we recruited a great bassist, Greg Lijons, and a guitarist named Greg Faust (studied with Stan Whitaker of Happy The Man) and started a quasi funk fusion band called Rate It X.

Hotshot guitarist Johnny Tsakanikis (later in Power Trio from Hell on Warners) played with us too, briefly. Greg Lijons— who was black—had a contact at the then well known Ibex club in DC, which catered to black audiences, and (to our amazement) got us a gig in the ground floor lounge.

This place had three levels. It was on the corner of 16th Street and Missouri Avenue, NW. Bottom was a bar/lounge with a smallish stage and PA, the middle floor was the much larger Marvin Gaye Room, which did larger shows, and on the top floor a disco complete with a large mirrored twinkling light ball.

To my surprise, we went over quite well in the lounge, and the manager dug the show and offered us a gig in The Marvin Gaye Room. A great gig, and I have a rough recording and photos. An old guitarist and singer cat named Doctor Love opened the show. To this day, I am convinced we were the only predominately white band to ever play there, let alone more than once.

The place got kind of rough a few years later and closed.

Pity.

Great place to play.

NEXT, Chainsaw Jazz

By 1988, I had gone through some personal stuff, along the birth of my first son, Adrian, that kept me from focusing productively on music. During that time I went to see old friend Teresa Gunn's always great band somewhere in DC. She had a bassist that just knocked me out. Wild looking, Chuck Taylor shoes, really animated, and whipping the bejesus out of an Alembic bass.

I thought; gotta have this guy.

Mark Smoot.

We spoke during a break. Fan of The Muffins. Gotcha. So, I up and done stole his ass. (Sorry Teresa) He and I hibernated for a couple of weeks to see if we could work together, and decided to do a group. We put ads in the DC City Paper. Got Mark Gilbert on sax/woodwinds, (played with more people than I have room for...RIP) and after some hysterical comicy (wow there are a lot of guitarists) guitar auditions, we ended up with a teenager on guitar, Christian Nagle.

Best of the batch.

Great player, nice crunchy tone that was more chainsaw than jazz and was into improvisation. So we had us a bitchin' quartet. Mark Smoot and Chris writing with Mark Gilbert's and my input. We called this band NEXT. Mark Gilbert suggested this guy he knew, Ed Maguire, who played electric mandolin and violin. Fine bassist/composer/arranger as well. I resisted the very idea of violin and mandolin in this band, given our aggressive sound. Gilbert knew something we did not. He finally wore us down talking about this Ed dude.

So, we finally invited Ed Maguire over. What a package. Short yuppie hairdo. Bermuda shorts. Loafers. Golf shirt. Cadillac. He is also a big guy. We asked: What do YOU do? He plugged into the PA and played an absolutely INSANE Jimi Hendrix electric mandolin solo using a digital delay. Our jaws dropped.

SOLD.

He was in. He had also studied with the late great Jaco Pastorius. He got a mention and is referred to as BIG ED in Bill Milkowski's great JACO book. Our first show was at the huge RIVERFEST on the Washington, DC Potomac river waterfront. Some genius put us on right after a gospel group. What a noise that was. It was a million degrees that June day with the usual 97%+ humidity in that area during summers.

Right before we played, I followed the lines from the stage

out into the audience out of curiosity, and lo and behold, at the front of house mixer was Tommy Linthicum, with whom I had worked with on sound crew as a teenager. He had also worked with the Canadian rock band Rush for many years. When I was a kid, I told him he would do sound for me someday...he laughed.

It happened. 18 years later.

Ed Maguire referred to our music as "Chainsaw Jazz" at that gig, and so right after that show we switched the name from NEXT to Chainsaw Jazz. After a few smaller gigs in Washington DC at places like BBQ Iguana, and DC Space, (a show my mom attended not long before she passed away; last show she saw) Grog and Tankard, (where I had to pry my sax man Mark away from the strip club next door at call time) we decided to record a CD. Mark Smoot had an Otari 1/2" eight-track deck and outboard equipment, so we did our record which became DISCONCERTO at his house out in the MD boonies on Ednor Road.

My late son, Niall, was born on June 21, 1989, while we were recording the tune Iranasaurus Tex. We also had a very bad windstorm in Washington, DC that week and a BIG tree fell on my house. It caused little damage, but this storm effectively shut down the neighborhood, and it took a week and an out of state crew from PA to remove the tree from our property. Thankfully it was a city tree, so it was on them. If a tree that fell was on your property, it was your problem. Hundreds of old trees in our hood went down. Place was a mess for weeks. Eleven days with no power, but oddly, we had phone service. I got to meet neighbors I had never met, 'cause word got around that our phone worked.

So, that particular tune, Iranasaurus Tex was done in parts. DISCONCERTO was the last record I was to play on that was an all analog recording. Towards the end of 1992, Chris left, and Mark Stanley came on board (met through friend Teo Graca) to record on the last two tunes, *MadWhiskey Bitch*, and *Cytoplasm*.

Old pal Steve Feigenbaum agreed to release

DISCONCERTO, and it came out in the early 1990s, catalogue # Rune 46 on Cuneiform Records. The cartoonist/artist Marty Murphy did great graphics for the CD cover. Somewhere are good live recordings that may even be releasable. We'll see if we can find masters someday. Some videos are on my YouTube channel.

Oh, yeah, Ed Maguire started with the band nicknames. He was Night Train, I became Cool Breeze, Chris became Pop Boy, Mark was Mooncricket, and later Mark Stanley became Sparky. What a hoot. At one gig, Night Train actually arrived with small bottles of Night Train and Cool Breeze. Vile concoctions these, but funny!

Around that same time, a DC friend of ours was pals with, and introduced us to Bo Diddley's nephew, Ricky Jolivet, who gigged as Bo Diddley Jr. and his wife Gloria, who had been a backup singer for Bo Diddley. Jolivet had one of Bo's signature rectangular red Gretsch guitars.

They had secured a paid New Years Eve gig, 1990-91 I think, for an American University student party to be held at a huge rental house on Wisconsin Avenue just above Georgetown & Calvert Street.

They needed a drummer and a guitarist. Mark Smoot ended up on guitar and I played drums. This was one crazed drunken affair. At quarter to midnight the hosts shut down the two open bars, and then broke out about 250 bottles of champagne. By 2 AM there were people staggering around just shitfaced with a bottle in each hand, "wanna pawtay?" and bodies asleep and otherwise just flopped all over this house.

Cabbed home, and came back for gear the next day. A friend that had been working at a DC cable station just up and left a big pro video camera there. Shoulder held camera. I knew the guy, so I took the camera that next day and returned it to him, AFTER I copied the hilarious video of the party he made. The lighting is horrid, but the video is pretty funny.

Clinton Inauguration Gig

Not long after Chainsaw Jazz recorded DISCONCERTO, the group sadly disbanded. Our woodwind player, Mark Gilbert, had also been playing with a Latin jazz band called Locura. One of them had an in with the Washington, DC guvvy, and finagled a slot for Locura to play at the first Clinton inaugural celebration in January of 1993. They needed a drummer for this gig, and Mark asked me.

One doesn't get asked to play at an inaugural too often, so I rolled with it. We had one or two rehearsals. We were stationed at a prime spot just outside the beautiful and now gone old Post Office Building at 1100 Pennsylvania Avenue. Glad I was playing drums, as it was a cold day. I had an official vehicle access and NO TOW parking pass on the windshield of my one ton Dodge van, and it was a trip to have the cops clearing traffic and making a path...for little old me, for once.

Since my van lacked windows, the not so Secret Service inspected it before I could go where I needed to park and unload behind all the barricades. We had two U.S. Army MPs with M-16 rifles assigned to our station, and one of them would always accompany whoever needed to visit a restroom.

We played for about two hours, and then the parade came by with the Clintons. Since I'm guessing that because we had saxophones, the prezzy Clinton limo drove right up to us and checked us out for a hot minute, and then went on. We did not know then that Bill played sax.

He was probably checking to see how Mark Gilbert could even play sax in that damn thirty-degree weather. After that was done and I packed up, I went into the Post Office building to check out the party going on, but it was a freaking madhouse, so I split.

That was a fun day.

Decline, Fall and Rejuvenation

The mid 1990s became a personal horror show that I brought upon myself. I was going nowhere with my life, so I sold the house (bad memories there, and it needed a whole lot of work) my mom left me in 1994, (It would be eight years before I owned real estate again) and moved in with the gal that would become my first wife (for a scant few years) later on.

I had also befriended some folks that were not at all friends and developed some stupid, unhealthy, unsavory and expensive habits. Plus a lot of drinking. (I had not been an angel throughout the 1980s into the 1990s) I let down 9353, with whom I had been planning records and gigs, REALLY pissed off and lost/disappointed a lifelong friend, and distanced myself from many others.

I sometimes thought I would not live much longer. Serious self loathing and depression were setting in. Eventually, my gal left me. I was very unhappy. I eventually brought myself out of that fog all by myself sans any semblance of a support system.

I had no gal, no family to rely on, (all my adult relatives were gone) no real friends around, and a short time later, through sheer force of will, I cleaned up my act and came back later with a vengeance and no doubt surprised a few folks that by then had certainly written off my sorry ass.

During 1996, Bruce Hellington jump started 9353 again as a trio with he on guitar, Susan Hwang on keys, myself (much more clear-headed) on drums and with no vocals this time. This configuration had quite a unique, sometimes almost carnivalesque vibe. This version played shows in DC area, Baltimore, and Philadelphia. Here we go....

9353 Band

Back in the 1980s, there was this band, 9353, that sounded like no other group around at that time. Really great choon writers. They were happening at the time the DC punk scene was taking off, and played to many of the same audiences, but this band was very different and towered over all the punks, in my opinion.

Quite stylized, and original, with a singer that had unbelievable range. I saw them at DC Space, and at the old 9:30 Club where they often played. I played briefly with a trio called Guilt Combo, (a 9353 connection) that played a cool show with Government Issue, who were looming large in the punk scene then.

Guilt Combo was Phil Duarte on guitar/vocal, Bernie Wandel, late of the Henry Rollins band on bass, and myself. Later on, Bernie would play with 9353. Sometime around 1986, my friend John Fletcher, who was also a drummer, asked me to help him move with my van.

I was a very popular guy when people needed to move.

John was moving out of Bruce Hellington's, who was the 9353 singer with an apartment on 16th Street in downtown Washington, DC.

This was the first time I had met anyone in 9353. We seemed to get along just peachy. A few years after that, Bernie Wandel joined 9353 on bass. In those days, these guys were playing all over the area, and I was glad for Bernie. While he was in the group, they made a tremendous record, Insult to Injury, Magically Delicious.

One of the coolest records by ANY group from the DC area.

Still spin that sucker, and their previous discs. Some years go by, and 9353 disbands. Somehow, I ran into, or talked with Bruce in 1994 or 5, and told him how much I dug that Delicious disc. They were drummerless, so we discussed working together. We proceeded with Bruce's brother Will on bass and guitar, and a guy named John Snoderly on guitar. We rehearsed for awhile at Bruce's home, then in Berwyn Heights, near the University of Maryland.

Neither John, nor Will lasted very long, and we ended up moving the band to DC with guitarist Mike Taylor and Bruce's old friend from the band Specimen Fred, Tom Crawford, (hey…Tommy) on bass. Tom had some cool grooves down, and we recorded some tracks at Mike Taylor's, but these were never finished. This was entirely MY fault.

Around this time, I had by then developed the aforementioned stupid, unhealthy and expensive habits and just disappeared from 9353 and from most everyone else. Took me awhile to get myself sorted out. A couple of years later, 9353 rebooted as a trio with the now NON singing Bruce on guitar, Susan Hwang on keys, and, as I said, a much healthier, and clearer headed me on drums.

We did about a dozen gigs, and did some recording, and then, lo and behold, The Muffins rebooted in 1998. Susie also went to Korea for awhile. She is of Korean heritage. That was it for my 9353 adventure during that decade. The Muffins had our first rehearsals for the July 1998 reformation in the 9353 studio on Newton Street in DC.

We tried recording to ADAT there, but most of that did not come off well. 9353 again rebooted in 2007, with original bassist Vance Bockis, and over a few month period we had Mark Nickens on guitar, then Ted Feldman and also Mark Stanley, who was in Chainsaw Jazz. (Mark would also join The Muffins for our last show in 2016.)

We had a great time playing some of 9353's 1980s and 1990s tunes, and also playing some music from the great HARLINGTOX Angel Divine CD Bruce made with Dave Grohl. My fave Grohl. We headlined at the 9:30 Club twice within a four-month period in 2007, VERY unusual for a DC-based band to headline there, let alone twice in the same year. I don't think any of that great HARLINGTOX stuff has ever been done live, but for our versions.

More on this groovy 9353 band coming up…take it away, Bruce.

Bruce Hellington of 9353 Remembers

Hello people. I'm happy to be here today and to be part of this book by my drummer friend, Paul Sears. I feel like I could still easily write an entire small book about the memories of the times I shared with him.

Since these are the recollections of the 57 year old version of myself, post head radiation, any similarity of those named by name to anyone in real life is purely not coincidental and are for entertainment purposes only. So you know what you have to do. I knew you'd understand.

The other day, I was discussing with Paul my earliest memory of him. It came in the form of a local free paper article about The Muffins. Some of you historian types might know the answer to this as neither Paul or myself can recall the name of which paper it was. We agree that it was most likely either The Unicorn Times, The Washington Tribune or The City Paper.

It was the summer of 1980, I think but it could've been the summer of 1979? Probably 1980. I lived in a group house in Arlington, VA. One day this article about The Muffins was being discussed by the members of this particular house. We were locked in a serious debate. Looking back on this now I have to seriously laugh at what I thought and fought about with my peers on that day. I was absolutely convinced this drummer in this picture, in this paper, had submitted a photo of Alex Harvey to be used as the photo of The Muffins drummer, Paul Sears, instead of himself. People hadn't done this kind of thing very much and it wasn't a popular thing to do yet. Very funny. I remember thinking—if I ever meet that guy we will at least have the love of Alex to discuss.

The Muffins had a serious underground following in DC. It extended out into the suburbs too—way beyond what was normal, like into Europe. They had a community buzz with a similar yet smaller and of a more select level that oddly reminded me more of The Nighthawks type of a following than any of the upcoming punk legends of our time did.

WGTB is how I first heard The Muffins. What that one radio station did for this city will forever be impossible to fully tally or understand. For me WGTB was the final catalyst needed to sow the seeds of everything musical in my life outside of my own family DNA. It all came from this radio station and oddly all within one year. I was an impressionable teen. I also had some experience looking for the real stuff.

The first ten years of my life as a consumer of rock n roll were spent in the suburbs. Self educating was a priority in those years for me from 1968 on. Returning to DC in 1978 was when WGTB changed my life. Only for that one year until they were shut off in January 1979. I can't say enough about what it was to have true community radio on that level.

I knew who Jimm Altman was from high school but it was on WGTB that I first heard his music. Same with The Muffins and many, many others. WGTB exposed their work to us in an honest here-it-is manner that we've never had again in the DC scene. It is my observation that what happened to our scene after we lost WGTB could not have happened had it stayed. The honest exposure of the city's bands recordings kept a decent and mostly agreed on value system in place. Based on the word on the street concerning the accepted merits of actual recorded works.

After that was gone it was weird.

WHFS made some effort to absorb some of the loss but couldn't ever be nearly as effective with having to make so many opposing forces happy in their programming. All was soon lost to a strange world of an almost secret social bully lobbying promo efforts that created a popularity take over that I do not believe could have happened if the actual listening of our local music hadn't been removed from the equation.

That sounds harsh, but that is my observation on what really interrupted the growth of The Muffins local rise in size. The same thing happened to many others too. I say all this as a complete and fairly innocent eyewitness bystander. 9353 didn't exist yet. The death of WGTB came before my time. Six months before I ever held a microphone in my hand or knew I was ever going to. Losing this one radio station really was the biggest tragedy of the Washington music scene. The 1980's would've never ended up the way it did without this one sad milestone shaping things.

Anyway that is where I first heard Paul play drums. On the radio.

I did not meet Paul Sears till the spring of 1986. It was at my apartment at 1616 16th Street through our mutual friend, who was my departing roommate at the time, named Fletcher. I didn't realize till after the fact he had been invited over to be sort of a peacekeeping referee. Paul was in rare form (which was common in those days) having just recently gone through the family tragedy with losing his sister. Everything seemed to backfire because we instantly became friends instead.

I gave him a vintage Pee Wee Herman type bicycle that was abandoned there. Paul always had a thing about vintage bikes and especially about tandems too. Once I saw an awesome tandem selling for nothing. I called a blind friend knowing how much he needed it. He declined. Oh, well, I called Paul, who was there in an hour. So that was the first time I ever met Paul. Like the first time I ever heard him, it was at home.

I had several social encounters with Paul in the next following nine years, most of which, to be honest are somewhat of a blur. Nature of the situation. I remember hearing from him in 1995, after 9353's fourth release. When he passed word that he wished he had played on it. Is that a fact? Well, Buddy, 9353 has had nothing but drummer trouble for the last ten years and you're a legend in these here parts so it is game on.

I knew that was actually a serious game-changing moment for 9353 but I had no idea how much so. I had no idea what was about to happen at all with Paul becoming the 9353 drummer but I certainly knew something was about to happen. I had no idea Chainsaw Jazz had disbanded or that Paul was available or ever interested.

As it turned out, everything was about to head into serious uncharted waters for 9353—further in a direction never pondered before. To say Paul was a sport about it would be a serious understatement. Nine out of any ten other drummers would have run for the door. I know this for a fact because more than ten did run for the door.

Paul came on board shortly after 9353's Magically Delicious disc came out and it was on that material mixed with about nine standards from our first couple albums that he joined 9353 to play drums and joined under the assumption that we were going to be continuing to play live monthly as much as we were, which at that time was a lot.

We hadn't even played for a month with me as the lead singer and with my brother William playing flawless guitar renditions of our early stuff as well as the 4th (now 5th) 9353 disc that he did originally play on. Then we hit a huge stalemate of ability vs. intent, none of which Paul was anything other than sportingly patient with.

Talk about a rug yank.

I honestly thought I was bidding him farewell when I told him that I had could not surpass the creative trauma brick wall the last and current lineup was suffering. Something had to be done as we were steering away from where we needed to go and had drifted too far into a audience-disappointing cover band version of our former selves etc. Blah-blah-blah. Once again, nothing that Paul was responsible for to the slightest degree. Like I said, I expected Paul to express proper condolences and excuse himself from further future whatever-the-hell-I-was-going-to-do-about-it suffering.

Oh, hell no. The complex Paul was loving this. I was so surprised when I could see in his face that he was down for the full-morbid ride wherever it was going and this surprised me as much as his willingness to join 9353 in the first place.

I wrote it off at the moment to how much he was probably enjoying not being the cause of any of his current band disasters. He wasn't squeamish in the slightest. You could say Paul had been around a bit at this point. I loved hearing him talk about gigs he played when he was only 15-16 and I was 7. This was not something I ever had in a drummer before—someone with a serious musical past whose very involvement lent credibility to 9353's continuing.

I knew his interest in 9353 was a very good thing for all of us. Whoever "us" was going to be. Paul had seen a thing or two and like I said I was convinced he was just pretty amused to see exactly where this would go and was happy to not be the problem in the cause of any of this. When I say Paul was not squeamish, I really mean it. In all fairness to the other ten wimps who ran before him, we really were getting pretty fucking scary at this point according to most anyone capable of observing anything.

By the mid 90's, we weren't the cute guys we were in the early 80's anymore at all. Prior to Paul joining and periodically thereafter, the only other original 9353 member to still share the stage and record with us was Vance Bockis, our beloved bassist. Our original drummer had returned for disc #4 but only as a pianist. The very nature of how things had worked with Vance was fairly refined at the point that Paul joined. Vance was always in other bands and was also an incredible study of what the human body can endure.

That said, we had a very realistic viewpoint of all the considerations of when and how we get to have him with us. This involved many coordinated elements to have a successful outcome. It was mostly always discussed openly without a lot of hostility involved. Vance was not well for 24 years. We worked him in whenever and however we could, and we usually approached each upcoming thing by seeing if he wanted to be and could be involved in whatever it was. It was a system that continued to upgrade and refine itself through the practical perimeters life gave us to work with.

This explains why at the end of the Magically Delicious's line-ups time and this aforementioned brick wall was hit. I truly did try to make this new upcoming moment one that would include Vance because he and Paul are like the rhythm section no one can look at with their naked eyeballs and with their ears open at the same time. They both have had a reputation for antics that defy most anything any others can come up with. Putting them together was a responsibility on my shoulders to all of rock and roll humanity within an earshot of our little world.

As one girl we know said "OMG Vance Bockis and Paul Sears in the same band at the same time will tear a hole in the sky." That was the a moment I was grateful enough to live long enough to finally be a part of, though it wasn't possible for it to be the case from that moment forward for awhile.

I must say, this was despite all of Vance's obstacles at that time which were many. The true reason Vance and I and Paul weren't able to set the city on fire in the mid-90's comes down to me. I knew we were in serious creative trouble. I couldn't twist any of these fantastic guitarists into the writing partner I needed to go on past our 13th year.

This brick wall was real. Our original guitarist was still missing in action and remained committed to being totally worthless to 9353. Choices weren't many. I told Paul that I had started writing songs on guitar with Susan Hwang playing keyboards and I was very happy about where it was going, He said he was still in.

This was a big thing for me.

Putting down the microphone and picking up a guitar and becoming the main songwriter for 9353 when I was just a beginner and they both were practically virtuoso level players meant I had some serious work to do. I knew I had to have a brilliant sound to start with no possible exception. I went with a Custom Les Paul through a vintage 66 blackface Fender Bandmaster using a Marshall 30 into a vintage blackface Fender

Princeton Reverb as the pre-amps. It really was all that. I also knew I had to develop a solid playing stamina within a range I could maintain some control.

Easier said than done. Fortunately, I rose to the occasion—within reason.

I am not sure there is any other experience any other musician has had in the last fifty years being in a band with Paul drumming and them being a complete axe newbie? How could such a thing ever occur? I'm pretty sure I just described one of the only possible ways. So there it was. The strangest chapter to date for 9353. Proceeding as a three piece. Paul drumming, Susan playing keyboards and me on guitar. Vance was there briefly on bass, but he didn't dig my playing level or the vibe of where it was going. This music definitely had both my limitations and a serious vibe to it. As one of Paul's co-workers at Greenpeace said when they saw us play live once. "This sounds like 1890's Black Sabbath carnival waltz music."

I couldn't have been happier with where it was going musically. I remember not having any luck with bass players in general at this time. We asked a couple to leave cause it sounded worse with them on board than without them. A good part of that in all fairness was the space being a three piece gave us.

A big sound was born.

I had been through many line ups with 9353 as well as four other bands before 9353 began and I had always been a vocalist who co wrote songs with a guitarist. Just like in the original line-up's case, most of our songs were written without any discussion at all, in an exact length of time and didn't change a bit from the very first time they were ever played. Paul and his fearlessness and patience was a big part of another wonderful chapter of pure musical magic for 9353. I'm eternally grateful for his instinctive gamble on what would come next. This chapter of things changed my life forever.

It wasn't all fun and games. We had problems. I remember once we even had a fight. Today I can think of nothing sadder and dumber than things coming to that. I love Paul. We had problems and some of them quite similar in nature, so we did for the most part find our way through the shit to the more important issues worth preserving without much personal scarring of each other. We were both capable of pulling some serious stunts you might say.

I remember this house where we were recording prior to our studio getting finished and they were very scared of Paul. One guy was sure Paul was going to turn on the garden hose and feed it into the house when they weren't home one day. Like how I leave out the 'why'? Haha. Here's where it gets blurry again. I seem to recall something about a temporary bass player's car getting stolen out front ended that line-up I think? I know a sordid mess of what? What am I actually saying here?

Exactly.

We (Bruce and Susan) then got the house on Newton Street. in the Mount Pleasant neighborhood of DC where everything changed and some serious musical things started to happen. I couldn't get Vance involved in too much more of what we were doing in the 90's but he always said he did like the work we did.

Paul and Susan and I did a lot of recording—starting as soon as our studio was done in November 96. We played only eleven shows I can recall which ended at the end of September 97 when Susan left for Korea. I don't recall much else after this in DC happening in the 90's?

Another very dark era began for us and it had to run its course—which eventually it did.

Fast forward to 2007. Vance has done the impossible. He has gotten clean after a year inside a treatment facility. He wants to do 9353 again and so do I. Both Paul and I had both gotten married by this point (Paul for the 2nd time). He was living in the Brooklyn area of Baltimore. Here's another example of our strangeness. We hadn't been in touch for awhile. He had two dogs, named Sydney and Phoebe. I have a dog and a cat which are oddly also named Sydney and Phoebe. I didn't name either one either. Too weird.

It is at this house of Paul's that we put it back together again in 2007. Susan was not available still living in Brooklyn NY and was in a touring band at that point so I did the logical thing. I picked up the microphone again and handed off the guitar to more capable hands, First it was Mark Nickens for one show. Mark Stanley also played one show but most of it fell on a former 9353 guitarist from 1993, Teddy Feldman.

It was around this time I first ever heard the term "Progpunk" applied to 9353. I do not know if it had ever been applied to any band before us. I honestly don't know if it ever was? Or if 9353 was the first? I do know this. It's quite safe to say that this honorable title wouldn't have been given to 9353 without Paul.

By 2008 it was the former guitarist from 1994, Andrew Simmons who took over the guitar job till his death the following year. Paul left 9353 just before this. He moved out west and did even more great work. My wife Kathleen became the 9353 drummer in 2010. Vance died in September 2012. Our work is not completed given our intentions. Both Susan and Paul play on the next record as well as some of the greatest not yet released 9353 there is. Susan's current band in Brooklyn is Lusterlit. Paul is playing with so many legendary household names it will blow your mind. I recently had the awesome experience of buying the final album by Daevid Allen and not knowing Paul played on it till I had it in my hands.

Very exciting stuff.

Hopefully we aren't done by a long shot. Maybe I am and they aren't? Who knows? My guitar journey started again in 2010. I've done more recording since then than ever before. I had to wait a couple years on throat cancer to come and go to resume singing.

Glad that my cancer over for now, hopefully forever. Whether we have another chapter or not? Whichever it is will be of a much more peaceful flexible nature than what we've known. I think I've managed to give a lot of info here without incriminating anyone in anything harmful.

Did I succeed at telling stories without telling any actual stories? I'm grateful to contribute to this Paul Sears' book. He is truly one of a kind—like the best of our peers, he is action figure worthy. If I had to describe him to someone who knew nothing I'd say, He's like a mixture of part Tony, Williams part Paul Whaley (Blue Cheer drummer), part the ice cream kid on the cover of Live Europe 72. Give him too much Mountain Dew and he could put a jazz twist to a Philthy Animal Taylor beat.

He's an outrageous, loud, fearless dresser and no color combos will offend. As a drummer he absolutely hates being compared to either Keith Moon or Neil Peart.

I have my theories.

Ha.

With age, he has definitely gotten increasingly more pleasant to work with. I hope one day someone can say that about me. He has always had a well-developed sense of humor. I've also always like the way he hones in on the most outrageous detail any story has left out. We share that way of thinking about a lot of things in the world. That is a less appreciated conversational art form seen less and less these days.

Paul has also come up with some great one-liners of wisdom I will always fondly remember. About fellow musicians "Don't ever scratch under the surface with any of these guys if you don't have to, the show will go on longer if you don't." Now tell me kids if that isn't a brilliant reminder how to extend the rock. Matter of fact, Paul, I think you need to get your pocketbook of wisdom one-liners book together after this one. I know it would be a good read. Same drums fifty years later. You know something about what you're doing.

Thank you, Paul, for so many reasons. I love you.

—Bruce Hellington

Paul Sears

Ted White, aka Dr. Progresso, Remembers DC Music Scene and WGTB

The seventies were a great time for progressive rock in the Washington, D.C. area, not least because of one radio station. That station was WGTB-FM, at 90.1, hosted by Georgetown University, a Jesuit institution. It was an odd match.

Georgetown had a radio station, but no curriculum associated with broadcasting. The station was an orphan within the university, with almost no budget of its own. The entire staff, with three exceptions, was volunteer and unpaid. But that staff of deejays, some 70-strong, was made up of people connected to the local music scene who were highly knowledgeable and enthusiastic about the music they played, and they helped build a strong music community.

The staff was also politically leftist (some in the "news collective" extremely so) and pro abortion rights. This set up an ongoing conflict with the Catholic university, which led to the station being taken off the air for several months in the mid-seventies with the purging of its staff before it went back on air. The music didn't change, but the political expression was muted.

I was a regular listener to the station, and joined it, as "Dr. Progresso," in 1977. My specialty was imported Italian "Pop Italiano." or Italian progressive rock. I was also writing a column on rock imports for a monthly D.C. paper, The Unicorn Times.

Little did we know what was in store for us. Each year WGTB held a pledge drive; listener contributions kept the station alive. We all came in to man the phones during the pledge drive. But, unknown to us, our General Manager (one of the few salaried employees) had been tasked by the university with sabotaging the pledge drive—and sabotaging the station. He and the Chief Engineer (another salaried employee, although he was also a late-night deejay) conspired to hamper maintenance and upkeep, allowing equipment to fail.

Luckily, among our staff of volunteers were several chief

214

engineers of commercial stations, and they did the necessary work—often during their on-air shifts—to keep the station up and running. Late in the station's life, toward the end of 1978, several of us broke into a locked file cabinet in the General Manager's office and found a stash of hundreds of uncashed checks sent in to honor pledges made during the final pledge drive—proof of the General Manager's sabotage efforts.

But, by then, it was too late. A new university president announced the shutdown of the station and the return of its license to the FCC. He was the son of thirties broadcasters and apparently hated radio. He'd done the same thing while president of Fordham University.

We circulated petitions, which I collected, which had over 100,000 signatures, opposing the shut down. They had no effect. In early 1979, WGTB went off the air for good.

There were—and are—no "open" slots on the FM dial in the D.C. area. Every one was and is taken. At the lower end (or left-hand side) of the FM dial are the non-commercial stations. At 90.1, WGTB was close to WAMU, American University's station at 88.5. WAMU was the polar opposite of WGTB. Its studios had the latest equipment and most of its staff was salaried. A bit higher on the dial was WPFW, a Pacifica station devoted to jazz and politics. That station used cinder blocks to hold up ancient donated equipment, and had an all-volunteer staff.

WGTB's slot—90.1—was taken over by WDCU, a brand new station hosted by the University of the District of Columbia. It featured mostly jazz. When WAMU dumped its jazz programming, some of its jazz deejays, like Rusty Hassan, moved to WDCU. But the D.C. government, during a period of belt-tightening, decided WDCU had to go, and shut that station down.

Who got 90.1? None other than CSPAN, the cable network which broadcasts from the floors of Congress. You can now hear the audio from their cable broadcasts on your radio. What a waste.

The area had one commercial station which played some progressive rock, WHFS-FM. It has had a checkered history and has changed both studio locations and its spot on the radio dial more than once, its owner selling the station and then starting it again. It had one "celebrated" deejay, Cerphe ("Surf"), who, when I encountered him at a Gentle Giant concert late in that band's career, asked me to "explain" the band to him. The Unicorn Times ceased publication in mid-1979. It didn't bring the entire music scene crashing down—but it felt that way to some of us.

When the Cellar Door, in Georgetown, closed, that was another apparent nail in the coffin. For a time ex-WGTB staffers tried to rally together to create new music scenes.

We organized concerts.

I put on several at Georgetown's Key Theatre (which, lacking a real stage, was a less than ideal venue).

We organized a big concert in a Northeast warehouse (in what is now NoMa). But there was no center. Factions split up. We all went our own ways.

Thus perished the progressive music (DC area) scene of the seventies.

—Ted White

About Ted White

Ted White is a professional writer/editor, former radio deejay, and musician who plays wind synthesizer and keyboards in the improvisational band Conduit.

And On...

Back in the mid 90s, I was sitting in my house with Leon Tsilis, a neighbor and friend that used to work with MCA Records, (and is tight pals with Wishbone Ash) and watching the Zappa Baby Snakes video, when the hilarious Punky's Whips section came on, a funny thing happened.

Leon thought Punky Meadows, who is a DC area guy and used to be with the Casablanca Records band Angel had passed away.

In those days, those guys did not know, but I knew that Punky (whose given name was Edwin Lionel Meadows, he now goes by 'Ed') was then a local DJ. Leon said he was sorry to hear about Punky. I countered with "what do you mean?" Leon was sure that Punky had passed. I said naww, he ain't dead. I knew something he didn't. Punky was then a DJ at the Crazy Horse on M street in Georgetown, DC.

I told Leon that I could actually take him to Punky. He refused to believe me. So, later that week, I took he, and another friend, neighbor, and Punky fan, Scott Bennett, to the Crazy Horse, walked in the door, and then I said "behold...there be Punky." He was of course up in the DJ booth. Not many people were there on this weeknight, so we hung out and spoke with Punky for quite awhile.

He's a good guy.

Punky cracked up when we told him that story, and we had a fun evening chatting with him. It was then that he told us that he was in on the whole Punky's Whips Zappa thing in the Baby Snakes Zappa video. Punky has since gotten back to playing guitar and is touring with his new band as I write this. More power to him. Punky's younger brother Robin worked as a roadie for years with Phil Lynott and Thin Lizzy, and his youngest brother Timmy played a little in the DC area, as I have mentioned.

During the late 1990s, two important events occurred. I married that same long time off and on gal, and while I was working with the trio (Susan Hwang on keys, Bruce Hellington on guitar, and I) version of 9353, the stars aligned, and The Muffins ACTUALLY reformed with all four of the so called "classic quartet": Billy Swann on bass and guitar, Dave Newhouse on woodwinds and keys and Tom Scott on woodwinds and keys.

I had by then, 1996-7, noticed a lot of stuff on the Internet about The Muffins. I was amazed. So, I bugged the guys…which eventually worked. Sadly, my first marriage did not last very long, but both groups, 9353, and The Muffins did. Bruce and Susan (9353) let us Muffin guys rehearse in their house on Newton Street in Mount Pleasant, DC for the first gig in 1998.

Were we ready for this?

Did we know what was about to happen?

Many more years of The Muffins was about to begin. The Muffins did "reunion shows" in 1998 in Washington, DC (July 16th) at Chief Ike's Mambo Room, and again in 1999 at Phantasmagoria in Wheaton, Maryland. Phantaz, as it was called, was a cool venue. Part record store, light fare restaurant/bar, and concert space. One could also buy what was required to brew one's own beer. Chief Ike's Mambo Room was in the movie *Enemy of the State*, but they called it Captain Ike's for the movie.

Both the 1998 and 1999 shows were packed, so we decided to again be active and start recording new material. Wife #1 was amazed that a couple flew over from Germany just to see the 1999 show at Phantaz.

She couldn't believe it.

Her weird husband's even weirder old band?

During 2000, I thought I'd look for out-of-town shows. Bruce Gallanter and his great Downtown Music Gallery in New York was mentioned, so I contacted him. He told me we really should be at The Knitting Factory, which was a very popular venue, then in the Tribeca neighborhood in NYC with one large and two smaller music spaces and bars.

I did not think we had a prayer of playing there, as that place was pretty popular and many of NYC's A-listers hung out there and sometimes played when they were not touring. We also had not played NYC since 1978. Bruce Gallanter told me that the guy that ran the Knit, Glenn Max, was a fan of ours. Later, Glenn ran London's South Bank Centre and was responsible for helping to reunite Van Der Graaf Generator in mid-2000s. I contacted Glenn. It took that one email for him to offer us a Saturday gig there in the Knit's big room, and in addition…would we like to represent the Knit in 2000 at the Villa Celimontana festival in Rome, Italy?

I think I reread that email ten times to make sure it was real. I called Glenn. It was. We had a great show at the Knit, (Nick Didkovsky from Dr. Nerve even showed up and was a roadie that evening, bless 'm) one difficult show (with keyboard and other problems) at The Metro Cafe' in DC, and then went to Italy to play two nights at this 33-day Italian festival. Some of the first Knit show performance and Villa Celimontana shows were released on The Muffins first post-reunion CD, Loveletter #1.

We played at WFMU in NJ, and at the Knit in NY on the same day, July 15th 2000. Two gigs in two states in one day. This is noted on the CD. Parts of WFMU show are on the Loveletter #1 CD, as well as an improv we did at the 9353 house in 1998. Thanks go to Stork at WFMU for hosting us that day.

The Loveletter #1 CD is scarce, but can still be found. It also has some of our older material played live.   We released it at Progday in 2001, and shortly after licensed the recording to Marquee, a great Japanese label.

The Japanese version is identical, but for a Japanese obi

strip, with some Japanese text included. Not long after Italy, we began work on a CD with all new stuff, with Carl Merson, a long time pal that had a studio in his house in Kensington, Maryland. Coincidentally, his house once belonged to Ernie Falcone, (was in Mars Everywhere, a Random Radar band) a muso and genius electrical engineer, whose cousin happens to be producer Don Falcone in California, with whom I work with nowadays on many projects. Let me tell you, the Internet has made things QUITE a bit simpler. When one set up a tour back the days of yore, $400 phone bills were common, and in general, all communication was much harder.

Today, I live by email which is my preferred means of discourse.

Racing on, The Muffins were to remain active until the mid-2010s. A big band CD was in the early stages when I moved to Arizona in 2010.

Between 2000 and 2010 we recorded a further six CDs, a DVD, and played festivals in the U.S., France and Italy.

Sometime during 2002 I tried without success to get The Muffins a spotlight on NPR, as several of our friends and colleagues had been featured. We had been playing in DC, NYC, and a big festival in Rome, so I thought…why not? I sent NPR in DC several CDs and other related PR material. To boot, we were a DC-area product. No response. Ever. Sometime in late October of 2002, (as I recall) I started to get calls from folks in towns on the east coast saying they heard our music on NPR.

I was mystified until I heard it myself. NPR was using music, uncredited, from our then new Bandwidth CD for news bumpers for stories on the DC Sniper.

Thanks NPR.

From 2001-12 The Muffins released:

Loveletter #1—The Muffins—2001, CD—USA, JP
Bandwidth—The Muffins—May 2002, CD—USA
LIVE AT ORION, DVD 2003

Double Negative—The Muffins—2004, CD—USA
Loveletter #2—The Muffins—2005, CD—USA
Palindrome—The Muffins—2010, CD—FR
Mother Tongue—The Muffins—2012, CD—USA

We played our last show (with Mark Stanley guesting on guitar) on May 16, 2015 for a video shoot. This was for Romantic Warriors III, the special features DVD. Dave Newhouse of late has been releasing his old cassette series called Secret Signals that are early recordings of The Muffins. Number 1, and 2 predate my arrival. The CDs sound great. There will be a Secret Signals 3 sometime, I think, that I'm on.

As referenced on both Tom Scott's and Dave Newhouse's websites, there were disagreements on the content of the aforementioned big band CD. Some of the planned music for that big band disc ended up on Dave's BLUE DOGS disc by Manna/Mirage, and on Tom Scott's 4S'd Man or Muffin disc.

Billy and I ended up playing on both on them. Both Dave and I were hoping that there would be these two separate CDs, and that The Muffins would still carry on. Sadly, the band The Muffins ceased to exist.

However, being the optimist I am regarding my Muffin brothers and being continually amazed that the first reformation EVER OCCURED in 1998, I would say YES to working together again as The Muffins. These guys are still the brothers I never had. I dearly miss all of the argy-bargy that goes on when we are all in the same room. Same four guys, off and on, for nearly forty freaking years. I love them and miss being around them. We have an enormous archive of well recorded shows, outtakes, and so on going back over thirty-five years. We have been discussing the potential, and practical realities of putting out a box set of some of these unreleased gems on CD/DVD.

So there.

End of story.

For now.

A Shout Out...

A shout out to Chester Hawkins. Chester is an old friend, and grew up to be a pro graphics guy.

He did all the artwork for these CDs by The Muffins...

Loveletter #1
Bandwith
Loveletter #2
Double Negative
Palindrome

He also generated several great concert posters for Thee Maximalists, which is the improvising project started by bassist Keith Macksoud and me.

He has played experimental music for ages under the name Blue Sausage Infant and under his own name. He collaborates with many other folks too, even playing a show with Thee Maximalists.

New Recordings, Learning Curve

WORKING WITH FRIENDGINEER Carl Merson on The Muffins Loveletter #1 in 2001, and almost simultaneously The Muffins Bandwidth CDs was my first exposure to the process of manipulating music recordings on a computer. For those two discs, the recording was done on multitrack digital audio tape machines (DAT) and then transferred to a computer for mixing and production.

Carl was using a software package that was/is used for making video/TV shows called Vegas. Vegas also has lots of audio tools. These machines, Digital Audio Workstations (DAW) are today commonplace. I think of them as akin to word processors, but for music files. Like word processors, they can have a bewildering assortment of options, and what are called "plug-ins" actually software effects and accessories that can be used. These include equalization, reverb, and many, many others.

It is important to have high quality analog outboard hardware for inputting to the computer in order to ensure that you obtain the best possible quality sound on the way to converting the signal to computer files.

The hardware will connect to an analog to digital converter (A/D) of some sort, of which there are many options available. High quality analog electronics have not drastically changed in a very long time. For instance, high quality microphones that are decades old are still great, and a high quality pre-amp is still pretty much the same thing it was forty years ago.

Hell, I have a very expensive microphone that has a tube in it. For music recording, the actual analog signal that you provide, be it vocals, woodwinds, guitars, etc. with good quality A/D conversion dictates the quality you end up with. From my experience, there is no difference in "sound" itself between the different DAW software packages; rather, it is dictated by the quality of the sound file itself. There are also things to be considered when recording like bit depth and clock speed to consider. You will see references to 24/96, 24/48, 16/44, etc. Read up on these things. All CDs, by the way, are the 16 bit /44.1 khz .WAV file format.

Here, a Huge Thanks to my Friend Carl Merson

Huge thanks and a too short paean to Carl, who remains a good friend and is one of the funniest guys on Earth. A very good recording engineer. He also did the near unpossible at the Knitting Factory in NYC. The Knitting Factory at the time still in Tribeca, had its own record label, and upstairs studio for recording live shows for their own Knitting Factory Records. When we played there for the first time in 2000, Carl decided to take a chance, roll the dice and bring along an eight-track TASCAM DA-88 digital tape deck and connections for it. He would also do our live sound.

While joking around with the house engineer, he was able to quickly (and rather surreptitiously I suspect…) patch this tape deck directly into the front of house mixing board and got a great recording. It is unusual to mix for a live show, and still obtain a decent multitrack recording from the live house soundboard. My hat is off to him…again. Four tunes from that July 15, 2000 Knit gig are also on the Loveletter #1 CD.

I am convinced that only Carl Merson could have pulled off the tape deck thing while keeping the house engineer distracted and guffawing. He was to remain as The Muffin's go-to recording engineer for our first four post-reunion CDs, Loveletter #1, Bandwidth, Double Negative, and Loveletter #2, The Ra Sessions. By then, around 2004, we had begun building our own DAWs and took over recording ourselves. He also worked with me on other projects in my basement Baltimore studio up until the move to Arizona in 2010.

For my own recording, I currently use for audio three Echo Mona A/D converters, which are no longer made, but are nonetheless very high quality. Each one has a dedicated sound card for A/D conversion that goes inside the workstation. So, I need a computer with three internal PCI slots.

Each Mona supports high quality condenser, and dynamic microphones, has phantom power for those condenser microphones, and universal inputs that enables one to plug either a microphone, or an instrument either directly into it, or use a preamp of some sort. My DAW is dedicated and runs Windows XP. It is very fast, efficient, and never sees the Internet.

Because of all the outboard stuff attached to it, it requires twelve electrical outlets. It is of paramount importance to keep all of your data files on external discs for two reasons.

1. The computer will have a very hard time running your operating system be it Apple, Linux, or Microsoft, your audio software, options, and reading and writing music data simultaneously to the system hard drive (C:), and this is never recommended. All DAW best practices are to always keep your data on external drives and, of course, back it up.

2. If your computer crashes, you won't lose all your work. In my case, ten-plus years of work are all stored on external discs. Many terabytes of work. I go a step further than many do, and keep a clone of

my system disc (C:) handy, in case the computer
does irreparably crash. If this happens, I can just
build another computer at fairly low cost, plug in
the clone drive and my preamps. Good to go.

I tried to use the Sony Vegas program years ago, and I personally
found the interface infuriating and hostile. In the manual I have,
the audio stuff is over a hundred pages before you even get to it.

Grrr.

It is designed mainly for video. Some folks swear by it. I
swore at it. There are many programs; Pro-Tools, Vegas, Cubase,
Logic, etc. I use a very simple one (DAW) called Reaper. My
friend John Landy, a great bassist here in Arizona, hipped me to
it. It works very well, is low cost for personal use, small
business, is compact, stable and sports an interface reminiscent
of an old school mixing desk.

It also supports the plethora of optional VST software plug-
ins that are available. For final stereo production after mixing, I
use a program called Soundforge. All this software took me
awhile of futzing about to learn it. All the hardware parts
involved in this effort, i.e. wiring, microphones and preamps,
and building the computer itself are a breeze for me.

It's using the DAW's audio software that was my problem.
While we were in Apache Junction, closer to Phoenix, from
2010-2016, engineer Josh Medina was a huge help. He recorded
me and others for many recordings during that period. Since we
are now living in Superior, I have been on my own for a couple
of years, and am surviving okay. Two things I will not use in my
studio are wireless anything, or anything battery powered.

Just my preferences.

I do a lot of work remotely. That is, folks send me music
files via FTP, or email, and after I learn the music, I record my
drum tracks and send them in using FTP. My mode of operation
is currently thus for remote projects:

Angels and Demons that Play

Drum Tracking Information

What I need at the very least:

MP3 or 16-bit 44.1 wav files, along with any notes. If it starts with a time signature, please provide at the start, a click count in. i.e. 1,2,3,4. If a click track or electronic percussion through the tune are provided, I need that separately. Please, no .AAF or any other proprietary import file tools. If you use Google Drive, make sure my email address has permission to access. Prefer MP3 or WAV via WeTransfer.

If Skype is helpful for discussion, let me know via email when is a good time. My address is: paul.sears66

What I routinely supply are, up to three takes: Separate, flat, no EQ or other effects, 8x mono 16 bit / 44.1K .WAV files. If your requirements differ, let me know. The drums are 1960s Maple Rogers with a chrome Dynasonic snare and fibreskin heads. All heads installed. They are loud. I am experimenting with a 1923 Ludwig chrome over brass snare drum at the moment for certain applications.

1. 20" bass drum (sometimes two as when I do use double bass I use two real drums) Telefunken M82 & or AKG D112
2. 14" Snare Telefunken M81 & or older SM57
3. 13" Rack tom AKG D140E
4. 16" floor tom
5. 18" floor tom AKG D112
6. Left overhead Neumann TLM102
7. Right overhead Neumann TLM102
8. One ambient room microphone ten feet away—facing 3" from plexiglas sheet on brick wall—AKG Solid Tube condenser mic (with a Telefunken 12AX7 preamp tube) large diaphragm condenser microphone. Adds some air to my overall drum sound, and an ever so slight delay.

I will also provide a rough flat mix using your original track for reference.

I am currently experimenting with alternate microphone placements.

Here, I thought I'd impart some practical, and perhaps useful, information. Over the years I have accumulated a ton of recorded archives that are on quarter-inch, quarter track tape reels at 7.5, and 15 IPS, and a lot of cassettes. I keep a working TEAC A-3440 reel-to-reel deck and a Nakamichi 500 cassette deck for the purpose of digitizing archives. When I have spare time, I run these into my DAW. This has to be done in sometimes painful real time. If you have a ninety-minute tape, it takes ninety minutes to transfer. I have been lucky with the stuff on reels, but cassettes can be problem.

Often older cassette tapes will exhibit a muffled, or incomprehensible warbling sound when an attempt (after successful pencil rewind procedure) to play on a known-good tape machine is made, causing one to just throw the cassette away. Not always a good idea. In many cases, the little pad doo-dad that presses the tape against the tape head is rotten, missing or the little metal band it is attached to is broken. Solution: surgery. Remove the little reels and install them in a brand new cassette case with new spring/pad. I have many successful patients, since digitized, on my shelf. Tedious at first. I now have this process down to just a few minutes with some great results. I have live shows going back thirty years that now sound like they were recorded yesterday.

No Comics

The Muffins in comics...NOT.

There have been a couple of cool cartoon graphics done of the Muffins in comic panel style over the years. Not long after we regenerated in 1998, I was contacted by a fellow that wanted to know if we were interested in presenting The Muffins in an actual comic book. I said sure, if my character has a ha-ha-ha chainsaw and drums. The guy said he would send me some of his work. He did, and these were very well produced comics that were Christian oriented and featured some like-minded Christian rock bands.

I dislike any kind of religion mixed up with rock music, thanked him, and politely declined the offer. One of the featured bands in one of these comics was a well known group whose singer was later charged with, and pleaded guilty to ordering a hit on his wife.

NEARfest

NEARfest was a great progressive rock festival at Lehigh University in Bethlehem, Pennsylvania for many years. They were very well-organized and financially viable in a great location demographically, and, along with the smaller NC based Progday fest, on the adventurous side. It was run for all but one year by two guys, Rob Laduca, and Chad Hutchinson. These two are definitely hundred-watt bulbs. Kevin Feeley, also a hundred-watt bulb came on as Production Manager in the 2000s. I miss working with these guys. In 2002 and 2003 it was at the Patriots Theatre at Trenton War Memorial, which was a somewhat larger venue than Zoellner Auditorium at Lehigh. They had acts as diverse as Alamaailman Vasarat, Magma, Present, Sleepytime Gorilla Museum, Univers Zero, FM, Enchant, Kenso, Gerard, Mike Keneally, and Bob Drake as well as older better known old school Italian groups like Banco, Balleto Di Bronzo (a personal fave) and Premiata Forneria Marconi.

NEARfest also was responsible for the reformation of both Happy the Man, and Nektar. Caravan played their first show in many years at NEARfest. My efforts to get The Muffins a gig there were not met with success.

Out of the blue, Rob Laduca REALLY liked a tune on our Double Negative CD, and put us on in 2005. Present, mostly from olde Europe were there in 2005 too, with who is now one of my best friends, New Yorker Keith Macksoud on bass, and pal and great player David Kerman on drums. Their set was a stunner, and the best act there in my opinion. The next year, Kevin Feeley asked me if I wanted to work there as a stage tech mostly supporting drummers.

I worked with Todd Guerrieri, (the best ever drum tech, period) who was senior drum tech there. He has much more experience doing that gig than I do. He took care of me the previous year when I played. I also did other stuff there, like helped schlep Keith Emerson's giant old Moog Synth (lovely guy he was—we had a nice one-on-one talk there), Mellotrons, Hammond organs, Leslies and whatever else was needed.

I worked that stage for several years up until the move to Arizona in late 2010. I remember in 2008, during Liquid Tension Experiment's set, whoever was on FOH sound had the bass so loud it shattered light bulbs in the ceiling over the first few rows. It looked like rain. Had to stop the show for cleanup. No injuries.

I remember a band called The Pineapple Thief well, because their drummer said to me as I recall, you have such bewildering drum options; you have played here, so please pick out a drum set and tune it as if it was yours.

Alrighty...only time THAT ever happened. He wanted a really simple setup. I was used to really picky people. One guy showed up with a tape measure and needed everything JUST SO. When Niacin played there with the great drummer Dennis Chambers, their road manager gave us an old school flip phone with a tiny one-inch photo of how Dennis set his drums up. So...we used that as a reference and got lucky, he was okay with our set-up. Dennis is a cool dude.

Rob and Chad had families and lives to live and stopped doing this fest after 2012. The festival is missed. A great many patrons now attend one called RosFest, which was also located in Pennsylvania, and is moving to Florida, which caters more to a traditional "prog rock" niche. George Roldan does a great job with that one. Very successful, and no doubt benefits from past

NEARfest patrons.

I wish him all the best with the move to Florida.

Progday

This is the longest running progressive rock festival in the USA, going every year since 1995. It is located near Chapel Hill, North Carolina on Storybook Farm in Carrboro. It happens on Labor Day weekend every year. Due, I think, to its remote location it draws only a few hundred every year. It remains solvent. Rabid music fans attend.

It has a large field, a canopied eating area, covered stage and being outside, never too loud. I had not even heard of this one until a guy named Geoff Logsdon contacted me in 2001 to see if The Muffins were interested. This is also an adventurous fest, having groups like Thinking Plague, Focus, Cabezas de Cera, Wishbone Ash, Hamster Theatre, Doctor Nerve, and Deus Ex Machina. Mats/Morgan also played there in 2004. One helluva show. Morgan Agren played the drums so intensely that he burst his right foot right through his shoe and broke his belt. At the hotel I saw him walking around holding his pants up, and so I took off my belt on the spot and gave it to him, and pointed him toward where he could go buy shoes.

The host hotel Near Chapel Hill has a swimming pool, with (trust me on this) legendary post-fest parties until the wee hours. One of the stage techs (not me) provided a totally nude, avant-garde semi-comedic strip tease dance/performance one year at the pool when a small crowd was there. My dear old friend Debi aka The Boid and I laughed so hard that evening neither one of us had a voice the next day. Some insanely funny shit. I KNOW someone got pix, but I have not to date seen them. I know who you are....

The Muffins played there in 2001, and 2002, and headlined in 2010. Sometime during 2002, Giorgio Gomelsky contacted me. He had friends in North Carolina and wanted to know if I could get he and his two galpals into the fest. Progday very graciously allowed these guests. Mind you, I could not bribe the guy to come see us when we were near him in NYC, but women were involved here.

While backstage with Carl Merson, my son Niall, and Giorgio, (who compered for The Muffins at the festival) a funny thing occurred. We had brought a dog, Sofi, aka Miss Perfect to the fest. Just as Happy the Man were about to start a tune, Sofi bolts for the stage, gets out there and startles the band. I saw her little freckled butt rounding the corner to the stage and went NOOoooo..to no avail. I could hear the audience...Who Let The Dogs Out? Pretty funny. Unfortunately it rained all that weekend, so the fest was held indoors that year at the backup venue, a large high school auditorium.

A consecutive repeat festival gig is VERY rare considering how many great bands there are, and how few gigs are available. The next year, after two years in a row with The Muffins, I played Progday 2003 with Clearlight. How? They were slated to play that year, as Cyrille Verdeaux, who is French, was in the USA, and had a new, California-based Clearlight. Their drummer, Shawn Guerin, a great drummer/singer/omposer and son of the great drummer John Guerin (Frank Zappa, Joni Mitchell, Thelonius Monk) committed suicide in July 2003 not long before the festival. Clearlight were going to cancel their appearance, but somebody at Progday suggested having me fill in. Clearlight did not know me from Adam. Progday simultaneously asked if I would consider this, and having been a fan of Clearlight for donkeys years said sure...an honor. Since I was a drive away from the fest rather than a flight might have had something to do with it too.

So...

They Fedexed me, Sunday delivery, the music the week before the fest. The plan was I would study that week and rehearse with them at University of North Carolina in Chapel Hill the night before our show. John Covach from the group Land Of Chocolate was then a music professor there at UNC, and hooked us up with a nice studio that included a grand piano, backline, PA, and drums. Bless 'm. So, when I arrived at the host hotel the Friday before, the Clearlight band was waiting for me in the driveway. Cyrille Verdeaux on piano and keys, Peter McCarthy guitar, Dan Shapiro, bass, Cory Wright on tenor sax and then…me.

The plan was I would chump along with Shawn Guerins already recorded drum trax. This is a hell of a lot harder than it sounds and was way more difficult for me than playing with another actual drummer. It sort of worked, but I will never, ever, play a show like that again.

Cyrille did have me do one tune without the drum trax in my headphones, which was great. Back to the previous night's rehearsal at UNC…there was a guy there with the Clearlight guys that was being real quiet and tinkering with a Theremin that was not plugged into anything. When I inquired about this mysterioso, Voila. It was Paul Whitehead, the great artist who did the early Genesis and Van Der Graaf Generator LP covers. I did not know that he was also a muso/performance artist type. After rehearsal, he asked me if I would improvise a bit with him as " The Borg" after the Clearlight set.

I said okay. I had no clue WHAT a Borg was. I am so lame. Next day, I forgot about that detail, as I was focused on just getting through the 1 hour + Clearlight set in one piece. It was shaky on my part, but the audience loved it, so…good. Then, right after Clearlight stopped, there is a tap from behind on my shoulder from Paul Whitehead asking if I was ready. I nearly pissed my pants. He was all done up in this plastic black Star Trek Borg rubber thingy outfit with tubes flopping around, a white mask, and a Purple wig. Not being a trekkie, I did not know what the fuck this Borg stuff was all about.

So, for the Borg set, Paul had a CD of loud industrial type noises that the sound engineer played through the PA, while I bashed about on drums, and Cory honked and snorked on tenor saxophone. Paul borrowed one of my large Chinese cymbals and danced about, playing the cymbal with a violin bow. What a racket this was. The audience did not what know what hit them.

Priceless memory.

Many years later, a fan sent me a video of this. If Paul is okay with it, it may well make it to YouTube. For the record, I have tons of concerts on video that I filmed, and I NEVER post anyone else's stuff on the Internet. Never have. Never will. In many cases, I send the master video tapes to the group, and THEY can post it. I would work again with Cyrille, but not for many years.

One year, while hanging at the pool with Gary Green (Gentle Giant) and my pal Tricky, and alcohol, I got lit, and started threatening to toss folks in the pool.

Gary Green said he would be upset if I did that to him. So, this silliness goes on for awhile and I sit down with Tricky (Pat Walsh—great guitarist from the band Buzzard, and at that time Tricky had more hair than anyone you have ever seen within our species) and drink yet more. My blinkers shortly went dark on the chaise lounge. Next thing I know, I am flying in the lounge chair through the air into the pool. I have pals Mike Ostrich and Chad Hutchinson to thank for that. I sure asked for it. A minute later after I get out, Gary Green strips to his skivvies, says "this is for you, Paul," and jumped in backwards. So…for years when I was there, Progday would auction off the Paul Sears pool toss to the highest bidder. Fun times, really.

I helped out with stage stuff there for years. One year, I got to meet the owner of Storybook Farm, where Progday is held. I asked this gal how Progday rated on the pain in the ass meter as a client. The place is huge, and they rent the field and stage out for many events. She replied that the biggest pain they had was a Catholic girl's high school. She said they would be picking up booze bottles, cigarette butts and various items of clothing for days.

My next question was…when is this event, and how do I get a ticket? Heh. Great fest, and I mentioned that The Muffins have played there three times; once as headliner. I also got to jam once with Mike Keneally, Bill Plummer, Bill Kopecky, and Glenn Phillips the great guitarist from the Hampton Grease Band. So, counting Clearlight, five times I have played on that stage.

Orion Sound Studios, Baltimore, Maryland

For some reason, it took me until 2001 or so to become aware of this great place in Baltimore that was run by an astronomer and ace audio engineer named Mike Potter, and a guy called simply…J. They had a lot of commercial warehouse space in the Morell Park area that had been set up as twenty-five or so band rehearsal studios, a recording studio, and a live music venue, that was kept separate and not part of the commercial side.

They made their money on the rentals (which had a waiting list) and the recording studio. Mike and J were huge music fans. IF they liked your music, you got to play there, set your price, and lo and behold, get all the door cash, plus whatever revenue from merch you sold. Unique in the business for sure. They could also record gigs to multitrack. They had a nice PA.

From word of mouth, and very little marketing, they had a regular core audience, plus what one brought in. Very many local progressive rock bands played there. One-hundred people would fill the place. If more showed up, they would sometimes open the loading dock door and people spilled into a fair sized parking lot. Even A-listers like Bill Bruford, Mike Keneally, Tony Levin, and David Sancious played there.

It had quite a social scene, with folks bringing food and beverages in for the shows. It was BYO heaven. If you wanted to sit, you brought a chair. There were couches, but they filled up quick. I got to play there many times with The Muffins, Thee Maximalists, Conduit, Don Preston and Bunk Gardner, Present, and Mike Keneally. There are tons of LIVE AT ORION concert CDS and vids out there, including the official Live at Orion by The Muffins.

It is the one single music venue I miss from my eight years,

2002-2010, in Baltimore. I was the default doorman for ages, managing the bank and paying bands. J got out of the business and lives in southern Arizona. We visit sometimes. Mike Potter sold Orion to new owners awhile back, and live shows have been few and far between. They seem to be ramping those back up again. I have often said Mike needs a statue there in Crabtown. He has done more for the progressive rock scene than anyone else in that area.

Thee Maximalists—Improvising Rock Band

During Progday 2002, I re-met the bassist Keith Macksoud, who was helping man the booth for Cuneiform Records/Wayside Music that year. (He had also helped on the Zu Fest stage in NYC back in 1978 and we met then briefly). He gave me a copy of the latest Present CD called High Infidelity that he had played on. Amazing bassist. Today, he's one of my best friends.

Later on in 2003 I invited him down to Baltimore (he did then and still lives north of NYC) to play a bit. Home run. We hit it off well, and played a lot with just the two of us. He had no problems driving down for a few days at a time. We did a lot for a duo and discussed the possibility of playing shows. Band name? RIO Speedwagon? We settled on The Maximalists. THEE was suggested by Mike Potter at Orion, so we kept that. So, for the first version, we invited the great guitarist Yanni Papadopolous from the Philly power trio Stinking Lizaveta over to my house in Baltimore to play.

It was cool, just as a trio, so we went ahead with our first gig at Orion Sound Studios. Totally improvised, and big fun. We decided that it would be fun to invite folks we admired to come do totally improvised gig with us. We did many, and to this day that band has never ever had a band practice. We did more shows with Dave Newhouse—woodwinds, keys, Mark Stanley—guitar, Werbinox-voice, my son Adrian—cello, Cyndee Lee Rule—violin, Sun Ra Arkestra's Marshall Allen—alto sax, EVI, Elliott Levin saxes, flute and voice, Vonorn, Theremin, Jim Rezek—

Mellotron and mini Moog.

At an Orion show, we were approached by Louisa Morgan, a fine vocalist that also played harmonica. She said, "I really like what you all are doing and think I can contribute." So, up she came for a bit, and then we did a show with her at Orion, and another in Philly with her at the North Star Bar thanks to the Red Masque who invited us. Hell, we even did a TV special at Radio Fairfax in VA. with a trio version consisting of just Dave Newhouse, Keith, and me.

Around the time Thee Maximalists got going in 2003, in parallel with The Muffins, my friends The Red Masque in Philadelphia were planning a show at the Sedgwick Theatre in Philadelphia in June of that year, and wanted The Muffins on the bill. The Red Masque had already done shows with both Present and Chris Cutler, so we said okay. Beautiful theatre, and The Red Masque drummer, Vonorn, shot some very interesting video of The Muffins. I will share some online when I run across it. During 2006, The Red Masque asked me to actually play with them at a show they had set up with a great group called Skeleton Breath at the New Jersey Proghouse venue in Dunellen, New Jersey. The Red Masque drummer was unable to make that show, so when I agreed to do it, they came down to Baltimore for a few days to rehearse their set at our Charm City studio in the basement of our house.

It so happened that a very good drummer and mutual friend, Dave Kerman, was coming to town from Switzerland, also was going to play. After Skeleton Breath played a great set, I played with The Red Masque through their set, and then Dave came up, and so we had two drummers for awhile. Dave then played their encore. A fun show. During 2014, The Red Masque vocalist, Lynnette Shelly who is also a well known artist became my paulsears.net webmaster, or, if you will, webmistress. She still is. She does great work.

Sometime after the mid 2000s, Jannick Top, the tremendous ex Magma and many others bassist and producer in

France contacted me regarding his new project, called Machina. His manager sent me a video of this excellent piece of work in hopes of securing festival shows in the U.S., and for me to learn the music in hopes of participating in any U.S. shows. I tried the usual suspects, but nothing panned out. It is a great piece, and did come out on audio CD a couple of years later. I don't think the DVD I have was ever released, but parts of it are online. He also introduced me to a great French singer named Cheyenne Doll, who was coming to the U.S. for awhile, but timing was wrong and I regret not being any help to her.

2009 and 2011 RIO Festivals in France

The Muffins were fortunate enough to secure a slot at the 2009 RIO Festival near Carmaux, France. Many of our friends attend this great fest. To get there, one flies into Blagnac airport in Toulouse, then it's a two-hour or so ride by car. It is held at Cap Découverte, at Le Garric, France. This is a private leisure facility with picnic grounds, a small hotel, restaurants, a skate park, trampolines, and a large music hall with two theatres, offices, and many smaller event rooms. A very nice place. From the hotel to Le Maison de la Musique hall is a five-minute walk on these private grounds. For the brave, there is a zip line that goes a good part of a mile down to the old mining pit near there that has water in it. The festival is run by a great team of people led by Michel Besset. He has a long history of supporting music, and managing Art Zoyd early on. He put out their first vinyl. At the time, 2009, he was working for the French government Adda Du Tarn, and put on hundreds of concerts and many festivals. That type of job does not, never has, and never will exist in the U.S.

A government that supports culture?

Go figure.

Also on the bill were our friends, Present, Guapo, Magma, and many others. We rode in a caravan from Blagnac airport in Toulouse to the festival near Carmaux. Deb and I ended up in a car with some of the Magma entourage; Stella (Vander) Linon, and Francis Linon. About an hour drive. The day before the fest, Michel Besset said there would be a VIP party at the festival the evening before the fest for the performers, along with local politicos, the local arts council, and other dignitaries. They take this stuff very seriously over there.

They came.

They brought lots of wine.

Excellent food was there. Presentations and speeches occurred. They thanked all the musos for bringing tourist business to the locale. After each act played their show, there were individual press conferences for each act onsite in another big room, complete with refreshments, interpreters, etc.

There were maybe fifteen or twenty music journalists there from all over the world. Our friend Aymeric Leroy acted as our interpreter. Aymeric is also a fine journalist, and author. We were already acquainted from his visits to the U.S. in previous years.

Many friends from the U.S. attend this fest regularly, and it's great to see familiar faces there. The only hitch was they had our show time misprinted in the schedule, but, word got around correcting this and we had a full theatre. Deb and I took a vacation to Carcassonne (inside the fortress) after the fest, and also visited with our pals Bob and Maggie in the tiny town of Caudeval.

We actually fell in love with the area, and looked at property there in and around the charming nearby town of Mirepoix. Small towns with low crime, lavender, sunflowers and vineyards for neighbors I can take.

Gorgeous part of the world.

A lovely gig, and vacation. We took the TGV bullet train from Albi to Carcassone. Like being in a small airplane. Not much fun. I miss the older, slower trains from 1970s Europe. The days of a private seating setup for four people with luggage space in second class and standing outside your train car, leaning on the railing, and leisurely watching the European countryside go by at

45MPH are long gone. I had experienced this blissful, serene style of travel from Paris to Prague and back in 1979.

RIO Festival 2011

I was invited back alone by the festival director Michel Besset as a Guest Emeritus in 2011. This entailed drinking wine, poster pasting, drinking wine, shaking hands, drinking wine, going on Radio Albiges in Albi with Michel, drinking wine, and helping Marique the stage manager out with the stage at the festival. She is a great stage manager.

It so happened that Adele Schmidt, and Jose Zegarra Holder of Zeitgeist were going to film the festival as part of their second progressive rock documentary, Romantic Warriors II, about the Rock in Opposition movement and its affect. Our good friend Mike Potter, from Orion Sound Studios in Baltimore, was along with them to do the audio recording. So, in order to do this, Mike was located up on the second floor of the concert hall where the radio uplink was.

They had to run a long (100' or so) twenty-four-channel snake cable from the Midas mixer onstage up the stairs and down the hall to the room where Mike was recording, which was, again, where the radio folks were. They rented a twenty-four-track splitter to install between the mixer and snake in order to facilitate the monitor sends from said mixer that was on stage left in the wing, and used for monitors.

Problem.

No spare body was available to actually do the custom line patching required before each act. Guess who got drafted for the task of re-patching that puppy for every act? Your humble narrator. We had, I think, nineteen instruments going when Present/Univers Zero/Aranis did their beautiful pieces with all three groups playing together. Because Mike Potter was upstairs on another floor we used Nextel type walkie talkies to communicate as to what instrument was going to what channel. It went like this: SQUAWK. Mike. I have the bass in #19, guitar in #20, and accordion in #3. SQUAWK. SQUAWK copy that Paul. SQUAWK. NEXT.

Sort of like that for two days. The film came out really well, and I got an engineering credit. I had been interviewed for the first Romantic Warriors film, A Progressive Music Saga, and they again wanted to interview me for this one. So, in this great and spacious venue, they had set up an interview room with lighting and so on. After the interview, we were talking shop, and Adele and Jose were lamenting about how no one from the great French band Etron Fou Leloublan was available to interview. I said, what? Sure there is. I told them that the Etron Fou sax player, Bruno Meillier, was in the vendor room at the fest selling CDs. So, they happily went and got their Etron Fou interview.

All good.

Here's a funny: the festival grounds at Cap Découverte also contain a skateboard park and picnic areas. The skating is supposed to occur in the skate park section. Some obnoxious group with several kids along were skating around on the sidewalks around the music hall and generally being a pain in the ass. They decided to have a rousing picnic right next to one of the loading doors for the Maison De La Musique concert hall. Perfect. When Present/Univers Zero and Aranis were rehearsing in the afternoon, and it got real intense, I just opened up that big door and blew the obnoxious picnic party away with loud devil music. They left real quick-like.

For this trip, I was staying with Michel and wife Rosine at their home in Carmaux. We had planned a few days to relax after the festival, and Michel suggested that we go fishing of all things. Since I had never in my life been fishing, I said sure. He spent a lot of time on and around water, and knew the area very well. While we were on the way, I asked what we were going to use for bait. He just smiled, and suggested we stop at a Tabac for smokes. This particular Tabac also sold bait.

He took me fly fishing at Vallee du Viaur, next to Aveyron, where the famous feral child, Victor of Aveyron was found in the year 1800. I had read a book about him in high school. Michel knew where the fish were, too. I caught a very small one. He also took me to the small town of Najac, where we parked and walked across this hilly town and climbed the beautiful old fortress ruin, Chateau de Najac. There is a 900-year-old vineyard right next to it.

A great trip.

Years later, Michel and Rosine came to the U.S. and spent a couple of weeks with us in Arizona. I should also mention that both Michel and Rosine are fine chefs. In France, Rosine whipped up both Cassoulet and roast duck for me on several occasions. My faves over there. Here in Arizona, Michel cooked a fine Italian dinner that took him more than five hours working in the kitchen.

Later 2000s—Don and Bunk Show

I had already met Don Preston, the composer and piano/keyboard/synthesizer maestro that was in The Mothers of Invention when he was touring with his Akashic Ensemble and/or Project Object with great guitarist and tour demon extraordinaire Andre' Cholmondeley.

This was in 2008 or 9.

I bugged Don for awhile about playing together, without success. A little while later he contacted me, as he was shortly to be touring as a duet with Bunk Gardner, the great sax player that was in The Mothers of Invention with him, as The Don and Bunk Show, and he wanted to borrow my Kurzweil SP 88 for a small tour on the east coast. They (Don and Bunk) ended up not only doing that, but used our house in Baltimore for rehearsals, and as a base. One day, Don yells up from the basement, "Hey Paul, can you solo in 7/8?" I respond that 7/8 is a natural feel for me. So he says, "get down here."

I would be an idiot to pass up an opportunity to play with these heroes from my teenhood. So, they play part of *Pound for a Brown* by Frank Zappa, a 7/8 tune, and I trade four-bar solos with them for awhile and always come back on 1. For some reason, this impressed Don. We then played a weird blues version of *Any Way the Wind Blows* and a couple other things. Don says..."wanna do the tour with us?"

I could not at that time, and they suggested that I play their last gig, at Orion Sound Studios in Baltimore with them. So...off they went, leaving me a song list of Frank Zappa music to learn. Big problem. Lacking guitar and drums, their take on FZ music is excellent, but unique and not entirely faithful to the records. So, the only rehearsal we had was sound check at Orion. It was a rough gig. Maybe half the time what I played actually came off. I did, however enjoy singing parts of *Help I'm a Rock*, *Who Are the Brain Police*, and *It Can't Happen Here*. I did not know that Bunk Gardner was actually Italian, (Guarnera was his original name) and he cooked us a great Italian meal one night. Damn good time, and maybe someday we can play again...with actual rehearsals.

Move to Arizona

During 2009, while still living in Baltimore, festival gigs for The Muffins were on the wane, so I decided to create my own brand as drummer available to collaborate with like-minded folks and put up a website. Pal Mike Ostrich built one for me. So, I worked with Mick Wynn from the group Diseased Within and a few other people. Still recorded with The Muffins. Oddly, collaboration opportunities escalated when I moved to Arizona.

Arizona??? Huh?? How did THAT happen?? If you had told me in 2009 I would be living in Arizona in towns I never knew existed, I would have said you were nuts. Arizona? Well, our plan A, actually, was to move to southern France. We vacationed there in 2009 after The Muffins played at the RIO Festival near Carmaux, and fell in love with areas around the Midi-Pyrenees, Carcassone, and in particular a little town called Mirepoix that happens to be close to where friends of ours live.

I can handle small towns with low crime, sunflowers,

vineyards, and lavender for neighbors. Michel Besset also took us on a nice auto tour around the area. Well. Buy a house, no problem. Going there to live is not a walk in the park paperwork wise, and not practical to move all the stuff we own. Quarantine dogs. We definitely wanted out of the eastern U.S.

So...

I have friends in Arizona that had been bugging me for years to come out here, and my wife had lived there years ago. I had been out here a few times. I like the weather. So, here we are. Now, the real estate market, to our advantage, was in the toilet out here in 2010, and it was a buyer's market for sure. My wife Deb found the proverbial smoking deal on a 1900' house with an 800' outbuilding (with shaded patios and a basketball court) which became Garage Mahal, my first real operating studio. Huge space upgrade from Baltimore.

Problem

I had the luxury of having engineer Carl Merson around for many years, and he was not moving with us. Like almost ten years! I had built a nice Digital Audio Workstation (DAW), but did not really know how to use it. I needed a specialized engineer with DAW software experience. The hardware side is not an issue for me.

I put an ad on Craigslist, and the next day I was amazed to have about fifteen responses. I had no clue there were schools out here that taught this stuff. So, I interviewed three folks and settled on a young guy named Josh Medina, who seemed to have a grasp on what I needed and actually liked some of the material.

I could not have done better.

Josh, who became my part time engineer and friend, was also a huge help with construction suggestions and the layout of the new place—he also set up my six security cameras. It was full Monty with a control room, and the playing area was room-within-a-room approach, not attached to the building, and built by old pal Jesse Davidson, a very good friend (and builder)—our relationship dates back to the 1980s.

Carl Merson, The Muffins engineer in Maryland even contributed some nice microphoness. Since leaving Maryland, I have had the opportunity to play on a great many records and all since 2010 have been done in Arizona.

In 2014 I had a new website built, this time by popular Philadelphia artist and muso friend Lynnette Shelley. While in Apache Junction Arizona, we bought a second small house during 2012 (ostensibly for my wife to have an art space) in a little town about thirty miles east—named Superior. Its small population numbers about 2,700, and to boot, several movies have been filmed in Superior. Best known recent ones are U-Turn, and The Prophecy.

During 2016 we decided to actually move to Superior. Fun little town with Porter's Cafe right in the middle of the historic district, two great art galleries, SunFlour market with great coffee/sammys, and even a small film company called Fishgate Productions. Deb and I have been involved in film projects with them. Most of downtown is a mere few minutes' walk. It took ages to find a suitable house, but, we finally found one a half mile from the one we already own with large attached garage suitable for my studio.

Not being in a separate building is a blessing because the studio is seldom exposed to the atmosphere here, which is VERY dusty. Dust is the sworn enemy of everything in a recording studio.

Once, my engineer Josh suspected one of my preamps went south. I knew better. Disassemble the recording computer and blow out all the internal connections with a can of air. That did it. Have not had that problem since moving to the new place. I would love to have an actual band here, but here there is a dearth of muso folks here that get what I have done, and do.

There was a bartender here named Katy that was into music and she brought me two Ralph Records 45s that I played on with Fred Frith back in the 80s for me to autograph. That was a trip. My friend Joe that I met here knew who The Muffins are/were. Two people.

2011

My friends John and Jesse Davidson told me right after I moved here, that I absolutely must play with this bassist and stickist gal, Linda Cushma, who had a band, Oxygene 8 with guitarist Frank D'Angelo. Somehow, when they needed a drummer, I forget exactly how, but a session was set up for us at the home of a local promoter that was tight with them.

We had a good play, and it looked like we were going to soon be a tight little trio. Sadly, Linda decided she wanted to not play bass anymore and add a bassplayer to the band to free her up to sing and maybe play guitar. So, we added a bassist, and unfortunately, differences in direction caused this ensemble to self immolate, and eventually became another short lived band sans both Linda and I. I was hoping to do some recording with Linda, but that never happened. Frank and I have been working sporadically on music, and something may come of that. Linda did play some great bass/stick later on the Clearlight Impressionist Symphony CD. I have not heard from her in years, and don't know what she is doing. Great player she is.

Fathers and Son Projects, Andy West and Lobotomatic

Not long after we moved to Apache Junction, a fellow named Anthony Garone contacted me and asked if I knew Andy West, the great bassist who was in the Dixie Dregs and Crazy Backwards Alphabet. I said yes, I'm a fan, but don't know him personally. He said, well, I do, and we'd like to play with you, or words to that affect.

Anthony and Andy worked together in the tech business doing software at that time. We set up a time to play at my place, and along for this was Anthony's dad Tony Garone, who had seen The Muffins in NYC. Small world. He played guitar and sang,

Anthony was on guitar, Andy on bass, and I on drums. They wanted to play certain tunes.

These were *One More Red Nightmare* and *Red* by King Crimson (Tony does John Wetton justice), *Peaches and Regalia* by Zappa, and to my surprise, *Vanity, Vanity*, a Fred Frith tune that he did long ago with The Muffins. So, not long after, Andy called a lunch with us in Tempe, AZ, not far away and suggested doing a band. Names were tough, so we came up with SW@G, short for Sears, West and Garones.

We got through some rehearsals at my friend John Davidson's Mesa house, (it was close to all) and then Andy, citing valid job related day job time constraints as he traveled a lot, decided he could not afford the time, so the band idea sadly petered out.

Here's a funny. I was in a thrift store in line and actually about to pay for a couple of Dixie Dregs vinyls that Andy is on, when Andy called me. I said, you won't believe what I am doing at the moment...that was funny. Andy has since joined a rejuvenated Dixie Dregs, and Anthony, who had been hosting his "Make Weird Music" house concerts with the likes of Mike Keneally, and Mike Manring and his MWM website built his own video studio. Tony has moved out of the area and does other music projects back east, I think.

2015—Father and Son Band #2 and Lobotomatic

I heard through the grapevine that the great bassist Alan Davey, was thinking about moving to Arizona. Alan was in Hawkwind for many years. We had appeared on Spirits Burning CDs together, but had never met. Still haven't. I wrote to Alan suggesting that we get together if this occurred, and he informed me that he was doing work with a group called Lobotomatic, a heavy rock band in Tucson, AZ. This is Larry Bennett and his son Uriah. Both excellent guitarists and vocalists. Alan mentioned they were considering bringing in a drummer, and why don't I contact them directly? Alan mentioned that maybe we could play a doomfest in Tucson or something.

The potential for gigs always gets my attention. So I contacted them. They had already done one record with Alan, called War Lover that had e-drums on it and wanted organic drums involved on a new record. It turned out that they had tunes for most of a new album already recorded, and would I like to play on the new record? They sent me some of tunes.

Good greasy stuff. This was back to the heavy Black Sabbath type stuff that I loved as a kid, and said sure. Certainly unlike what I had been doing. I suggested that they come up to my studio, and actually be there when I record, in order to ensure that I was adding what they wanted to their music. The record is called Intergalactic Bastard. Musically this was not hard, but I have not played that heavily in a long time, and I think I lost weight doing this one. I hauled out the second bass drum and larger toms, all downtuned. Used a 30" Stagg ride cymbal. We ended up doing two one-day sessions a couple of weeks apart, and I turned in twenty-six takes total in the two days.

Paul Davidson from Mindset X guested and played GREAT bass on a tune, *Voodoo Queen*. Alan, who had played bass on—and produced—*War Lover* was going to do the same on this. A few tunes in, he told the boys that he had no time to produce. A little later, he was not in love with the mixes Larry and Uriah had done, and pulled out completely.

So, with this added hitch in the gitalong, Larry and Uriah went back and re-recorded all the bass parts themselves. Intergalactic Bastard is now complete, and released. This thing sounds great, with a very heavy early 70s vibe.

An outtake from this record is included on this book's CD.

Superior, Arizona

As of this writing, July 2018, after moving here in 2016, I am still getting used to this small-town-living thing. I am not used to seeing five, six or more people I know every time I go to the local market, bar or coffee shop. Have not met Mr. Haney yet, but he is here some-fuckin-where , I'm sure.

Deb and I both help with art and music related events here. We currently have two wonderful art galleries and a new comic book store. Our downtown is just a few blocks long, and a ten-minute walk from either of our houses, tops. The Arizona 60 highway cuts the town just about in half, and we are on the historic side of town, where Main Street is.

We have several annual festivals here, and every 2nd Friday we have street food, many shops stay open late, and we have live music in the park. A guitarist pal, Vince Almejo, brings an entire backline, with drums and a sound system for folks to use every 2nd Friday. This event would not be possible without Vince.

So, this is fun, and I get to jam with a variety of folks once a month. My friend and neighbor, Steve Holmquist, is the Music in the Park steward. Our town does not really have much of a live music mentality. That, I hope, will change. We have a local film company here, called Fishgate Productions. The director also runs the Kay Art Gallery on Main Street. My wife and I help them with local films from time to time. To date, we have helped on three films, two of which are noted in my discography for music. Since I don't know squat about video editing, having them around is a huge help. They have fancy Apple computers, video editing software, and know what they are doing. They have helped me out in video-land quite a few times. That stuff is way beyond my pay grade.

My wife and I also happen to be fans of Renaissance Festivals. We attended the huge one in Maryland for many years, and our next door neighbors in Baltimore (where we lived from 2002-2010) are performers there. The Arizona one is not far away from us—fifteen miles or so.

Not long after we beached in the desert in late 2010, I sent the Arizona Renaissance Festival an email, offering my services managing stages, and doing sound engineering work. Our British friends The Mediaeval Baebes had played there. Their sometimes guitarist and Hurdy Gurdy Player is Kavus Torabi, who also plays in the groups Guapo, Gong, Chrome Hoof, and Knifeworld. He also plays on and releases Karda Estra CDs.

The fest got back to me when they started to ramp up for the 2011 season and brought me in to meet with management, and the owner. They hired me on the spot, and wanted me to help run the Feast Hall shows there. They also hired Deb as a "Ticket Wench" (great job title) to help run the greet tower at the Feast Hall.

For me, this gig involves a sound system, a green room, staging and maintaining props, and wireless lav mics. Great food as well. It's a hilarious comedy show with music and dance entertainment brought in for each course of the feast. This is theatre, and was new to me from the production viewpoint. Not anymore. I am a fast learn. Turns out to be one of the most fun gigs ever. I have worked with mostly the same team of about twenty-five actors and musicians now for the last eight years. Folks are on time, know their stuff and are in tune.

What a luxury.

It's a treat to do the same show each day in the same environment and with the same folks. I enjoy this gig a lot, and look forward to the call each year. Anyway, you simply cannot beat this scene for people watching. Lasting friendships have formed as well.

Arizona Recording

Not long after getting the studio running with Josh Medina, the floodgates seemed to open for remote collaboration projects. Live opportunities for the type of stuff I want to do are non-existent. After leaving a somewhat plausible live music scene back east, folks from all over started asking me to record drum trax for their stuff. Top among them is producer/muso Don Falcone, who is the cousin of Ernie Falcone the guitarist who was in Mars Everywhere, a band on the Random Radar label back in the 1970s.

Don runs his own collective, Spirits Burning, which has had over the years an impressive list of collaborators including Daevid Allen, folks from Blue Oyster Cult, Camper Van Beethoven, Michael Moorcock, Cyrille Verdeaux, Robert Berry, Judge Smith, Bridget Wishart, Alan Davey and many others. I have played on several of these CDs and vinyls, and the gorgeous Clearlight Impressionist Symphony, which he produced. I am on call for whatever he wants. Karda Estra has also been productive with four CDs.

Karda Estra

After we had been in Arizona for a few years, my wife hipped me to KE, music I did not know, by playing a CD of theirs called Weird Tales, in the car. The music was gorgeous, ethereal, without drums and like nothing I'd heard before.

Some KE music would not be out of place in a 1930s or 40s movie soundtrack. I loved it. So, I wrote to Richard Wileman— the composer in England—and suggested, "hey, why don't we do something someday," if he was up for drums invading his heretofore drum-less music. He was about to bag Karda Estra, but agreed to try something. "Something" wound up as our first record called Strange Relations. I am VERY pleased with this one. A towering first project.

Richard and I ended up working together on several more CDs: Future Sounds, Time and Stars and Infernal Spheres. When I am in England visiting family in Somerset, we arrange to meet. All of our work together has been done remotely, or, if you will, not together. We have never actually played together. When I see him, I keep threatening to leg cuff him to me and bring him back to Arizona with me.

Hell, I may still...

During 2016 I think it was, I met a fellow named Ken Coffman, a muso that is also a publisher, (...of this book) and runs Stairway Press. Ken was relocating from Washington State to Gold Canyon, Arizona, and was looking to cause a little muso action.

He does this often, even putting on a Neal Morse Band show at the lovely Mesa Arts Center. My fave music venue out here.

He connected me with an excellent CA based keyboard player named Jonathan Sindelman (Keith Emerson Band-Alan White Band-The Magic Band) and arranged for a recording session at my original studio Garage Mahal in Apache Junction with Jon, Spencer Campbell, a great bassist, and Jerry Donato on saxophone. Later on, he made possible another session with Jon, but this time with two bassists, the well known California-based Michael Manring, and local ace bassist Mahlon Hawk.

Funny thing is, I have known Manring since he was in the Washington, DC area in the early 80s with a cool fusion band called Natural Bridge. We have been running into each other backstage at festivals for donkey's years.

It took Ken to pull it together for me to actually PLAY with Mike Manring. Mike and I joked about that and may play together again if the stars align.

During 2017, a (part time) neighbor named Tor S. Forest, and artist and perpetual wanderer that enjoys classical music hands me a CD and says "I met this guy in Bisbee AZ, and the music is definitely more up your alley than mine."

This was T.S. Henry Webb's CD called Obvious Necessity #2: Signal Flow. I had never heard of these people. A week or so later, I played this disc in the car and thought "how can I NOT know these people?"

Research showed that T.S. (aka Tom Webb) was in The Flock, a band I loved back in 1970. John Mayall did some of their liner notes and this band gave up violinist Jerry Goodman to the Mahavishnu Orchestra. I found out that TS lives in southern Arizona next to Bisbee. I wrote to him to tell him how much I liked this CD. He got right back in touch with me.

We have played together a few times, and a CD of T.S.'s music called "As If In A Dream" is in the works, with violinist Jerry Goodman on board, a very good bassist from Tucson, Evan Dain, Scottsdale-based Guy Filipelli on guitar, Art Jiron on conga/bongos and myself on drums. T.S. Plays keyboards, flute, and composed all the music.

We visited T.S. in this well known hipster town Bisbee not too long ago. Sort of like a Grateful Dead concert exploded and the audience landed there. Land of manbuns, dreads, beards, tats and tie dye. Nice vibe though, and several actual live music venues, which is something we totally lack here in our town of Superior.

In closing, I will say that as much as I appear to piss and moan about some things, I am basically happy out here in the desert and very fortunate to be where I am in life. I have a great family, a studio with everything I ever wanted in one place; plenty of drums, guitars, bass, amps, keyboards, even brass instruments including a mellophone, a nice sound system, good German microphones, and very important, ample floor space.

Music will always be there. It's a cake walk compared to writing from memory.

Gimme a gig.
—Jaco Pastorius.

Nice talking to you, and I really hope you enjoyed this book.

Please visit my website at www.paulsears.net

Later...

Discography, Filmography, Notes, CD Music, Info and Links

1. Sane Day—1972 45 RPM privately pressed—Vinyl USA.
Susie, b/w *Sane Day*, private and never released. Recorded by the great engineer, Ted Bodnar in Washington, DC at his studio on K Street.

2. Sane Day—Live at Fort Reno 1972 released in 2004—CD USA. I think this was recorded by my friend Nick Brown on cassette. I remember it was threatening rain, and so we were in the large gazebo near the stage.

3. Tinsel'd Sin Live at Fort Reno 1973 released in 2004—CD USA. I think this was recorded on reel tape by old friend Tom Robinson, and two guys named Ken and Dag.

4. Manna Mirage—1978 The Muffins—LP+CD USA
Recorded at The Muffins Rockville, Maryland house. This took us ages as we were also arranging The Adventures of Captain Boomerang. While good, I wish we had more live playing time before recording that piece.

5. Gravity 1979—by Fred Frith—Vinyl, Cassette, CD Several labels. Fred visited The Muffins, and brought tunes and ideas. Wish we had a little more rehearsal time. Recorded at Catch-a-Buzz studios in MD, and completed by Fred in Sweden and Switzerland. The Muffins appear on this one, along with the great Swedish band, Samla Mammas Manna.

6. Air Fiction 1979— The Muffins—Vinyl USA. Live and studio sessions, and featured an all black faux leather cover long before Spinal Tap. Never re-released. I like it a lot more now than when it was released.

7. Dancing in the Street b/w What a Dilemma—45 RPM—USA. Great single release from Fred Friths's Gravity album

8.<185> —The Muffins with Fred Frith, 1981. LP—CD USA Only record by The Muffins that was made right after doing a tour. The band had never been tighter, before, or since. Insanely tight. Recorded at Track Recorders, an excellent multitrack analogue studio, then located in Silver Spring, MD. All done and ready for mastering in four or five days. Fred Frith's first project outside his own work, I believe. It remains my fave of all our work.

9. Things Are More Like They Are Now Than They Ever were Before With Tom Scott & Steve Feigenbaum—LP—USA. A cool record that I played a little on. Has never been released other than the original vinyl press

> 9. **Painting by Numbers**—by Mike Bass, with The Muffins-LP 1979—USA. This was released on vinyl only and was never re-released. Mike called this ensemble his moderately sized orchestra. Some of the music was played live on a WGTB radio show called Take One. Be

great to see this unreleased live recording out someday.

11. Cheap at 1/2 Price—Fred Frith album, Vinyl, Cassette,—
CD USA, Switzerland. Cool record of mostly short songs, with
vocals. Fred surprisingly recycled a drum track of mine from the
Gravity sessions.

12. DISCONCERTO Chainsaw Jazz 1993—CD—USA.
My last analog to digital recording, a really fun, but short-lived
band. Some live stuff, If I can get my hands on masters, and
everyone agrees, may come out someday. Who knows? Thanks
Steve Feigenbaum for releasing Disconcerto on Cuneiform.

13. Open City—The Muffins—LP, CD—USA.
Great collection of live and outtakes from mine, and other
archives. 100% Organized by Steve Feigenbaum/Cuneiform.
Original vinyl press by CBS in Holland is our best quality vinyl
pressing in my opinion.

14. Unsettled Scores—w/ The Muffins, various artists, CD
1994 USA. This is Cuneiform bands playing each others'
material, and no doubt was influential regarding The Muffins
reformation a few years later. A great double CD.

15. Loveletter #1—The Muffins—2001, CD—USA, JP.
The Muffins first post reunion release, and contains live material
from USA and Italy. Some of it is from rehearsals for our first
reunion show at the 9353 studio in DC in July of 1998. Shout
out to Jon Gibson for the ADAT transfer. Some great post
reunion performances. This was also licensed to Marquee in
Japan for the Asian market. A great label.

16. Bandwidth—The Muffins—May 2002, CD—USA. First
new CD back on Cuneiform since reformation. My first guitar
recording, too. Tom Scott and I produced this one, with input

Paul Sears

from Dave and Billy. Pairs well with #15.

17. Double Negative—2004 The Muffins—CD—USA. This one was truly a bitch to record. For me. Compositions are complex and dense. Basic tracks done at my Baltimore studio, with lots of dubs done by Tom and Dave. This and the next one, are our last recordings with Carl Merson, as we built DAWs and took over recording ourselves. These two are the last ones where multi-track DAT was used. Our first recording with Sun Ra Arkestra's Marshall Allen, and Knoel Scott, who came down from Philly to Charm City, my Baltimore studio. I added guitar as well to this one. Our longest disc clocking in at over 78 minutes. We spent a few hours just improvising with Marshall and Knoel after finishing their parts for Double Neg, and had enough material from the improvs to add parts to and assemble another CD. I added both guitar and trombone to this next one…

18. Loveletter #2—2005 The Muffins—CD—USA. This entire disc is based entirely on improvisations with Marshall Allen, and Knoel Scott done on the same day they recorded their parts for Double Neg. Our only recording made entirely from improvisations that were then sculpted, for lack of a better term. We selected parts we liked, and added parts to them at Tom's Mountain studio in the Blue Ridge mountains in VA. Pairs well with #17. Huge thanks to Bill Milkowski for the review of this in Jazz Times.

19. CROSSTALK—Thee Maximalists—2009 ReR—USA. Download only. This recording is comprised entirely of live shows by Thee Maximalists at Orion Sound Studios, and beautifully recorded by Mike Potter. It features Marshall Allen on alto sax and EVI, Louisa Morgan on vocals and harmonica, Elliott Levin on sax, flute and words, plus Dave Newhouse on keys/woodwinds, Keith Macksoud on bass and myself on drums.

ReR USA is gone, and so we have pulled it off the Internet. We are considering a physical release.

20. Palindrome—2010 The Muffins—CD—FR. This is our first record done entirely at Tom's studio in the beautiful Blue Ridge mountains near Madison, VA. Guests include Doug Elliott on trombone and Elaine Di Falco on vocals. This one is on the French label, Musea.

21. Mother Tongue—2012 The Muffins—CD—USA. This is the last proper record by The Muffins, and was also done at Tom's studio in the mountains. Some of the tunes are based on improvisations, and includes a live one recorded at the Progday festival in North Carolina, where we headlined that year. On this one, we all worked on the compositions. All parts recorded before I relocated to Arizona in 2010.

22. Healthy Music in Large Doses—2013 Spirits Burning CD—Clearlight—GB. This marks the beginning of my long relationship with Spirits Burning, and its producer Don Falcone, and his large network of artists. He has a sometimes vexing, but kinda cool, habit of not telling me exactly who else is on a recording I am playing on until it's complete, or near complete. He also graciously grants me BMI songwriting credits on some tunes. On one of these with BMI, I was mixed up with an Italian muso also named Paul Sears. BMI fixed that quickly. I played on two tracks on this disc. One track with the great Steve York on bass, Ken Magnusson on Mellotron and Cyrille Verdeaux on piano. Another track I am on includes my Pennsylvania based pal Cyndee Lee Rule on violin, and Cyrille Verdeaux again on piano.

23. Impressionist Symphony—2014 Clearlight—CD—UK. This is the prettiest record I have ever played on, by a longshot. Cyrille Verdeaux just oozes gorgeous music, just spinning out tune after graceful tune, with his almost signature approach to melody. I had played live with Clearlight at Progday back in 2003, but this was going to be a whole new team. I was thrilled when he and Don Falcone, who was involved with, and ended up producing this gem, asked me if I wanted in. Steve Hillage, Didier Malherbe, and Tim Blake, all had played with Clearlight, (and Gong) in the past, and were also in on this recording. A couple of the tunes had drums on them already, so I got to do five. Cyrille happened to be planning a trip from Brazil to visit his daughter in San Francisco, which is near where Don Falcone is. Cyrille suggested that he actually come to my studio in Arizona on the way to California for a few days to supervise/conduct my drum takes. This he did, and it worked out really well, as we got all the takes, maybe three for each of the five tunes, done in less than two days. Since he was there calling the shots and even playing some percussion, this approach probably saved a lot of going back and forth with different takes. He wanted to put bass on a couple of tracks, and was okay with my suggesting Linda Cushma, with whom I have played and is a great bassist and stickist. There is one track on here, Degas De La Marine, that Cyrille did not want drums on. He told me that the piano tempo varied way too much for anyone to play along with it. I disagreed. So we left it that I would put drums on it myself after he left, and send it in anyway, and if he liked it, fine. If not, fine. I learned the minor tempo variations, and tried to treat the tune like we were playing live. I sent the drum tracks in. Happily, he liked them and they are on the tune on that CD. I am quite proud of this one, and Don Falcone did excellent work on the production end. I went up to Don's studio near San Francisco to be there for the final mix and wrap party hosted by pal Brad Owen in Santa Clara in 2013.

24. Starhawk—Spirits Burning 2015—CD—GB. Another SB project, again utilizing Don Falcone's considerable network of musos. This one is based on the sci-fi story Starhawk, by Mack Maloney, and the CD comes with an eight-page comic book. I play on three tracks on this one with vocalists Robert Berry, (played with Keith Emerson and Carl Palmer in 3) on vocals, Judge Smith, (Van Der Graaf Generator) Bridget Wishart, (Hawkwind) and bassists Steve York, (played with too many to mention) Bill Kopecky, and Alan Davey (Hawkwind). Nik Turner, (sax with Hawkwind) John Ellis (guitar with Peter Gabriel, The Vibrators) and again my pal Cyndee Lee Rule on violin are along for the ride, along with many others.

25. Blue Dogs—MANNA MIRAGE 2015—CD—USA. This is a cool CD by my brother and ex-Muffin, Dave Newhouse. Some of it is music from the aborted big band CD the Muffins were going to do. I played on one track. Billy Swann plays bass, and Mark Stanley, who played with The Muffins at our last gig does some great guitar. Cousin to #31.

26. Strange Relations—2015 Karda Estra—CD—GB. In my opinion, this is top of the heap as far as my recorded sound goes. Richard Wileman, the KE chief finally agreed to "try something" with me, as he does not customarily work with drummers. Strange Relations is quite the apt title, as not many who know our work would have ever imagined we two would end up working together. I conned and goaded him into it via email, truthfully. I was familiar with some of his work, and just love his writing and arrangements. For this one, he sent me some piano sketches. I learned and recorded these and sent them back. He then wrote and played additional guitar, bass, and keyboard parts, and added parts for other players including cor anglais, trumpet, oboe, clarinet, saxophone, and vocals. He also plays a contraption called a Rastrophone. He also asked for some solo drum parts, and wrote music AROUND my drums. Kavus Torabi (Gong, Knifeworld, Guapo) plays guitar on a track, and this record is on his record label/imprimatur called Believers Roast. I had no idea of what he was going to do, past the original drums/piano sketches, and I was absolutely astounded when he sent completed tracks back to me. Like opening Christmas presents.

Richard Wileman sez, "This album nearly fried my brains. I'd never done anything that was such a balancing act between composing and improvisation. When I was doing it, it reminded me a little of what I'd read about Talk Talk and the recording process of their last two albums. It was intense and there's nothing else like the more angular tracks in the rest of my discography really. Well, maybe the follow up tunes we collaborated on to a degree...I'm very pleased with the way it turned out. You can quote that for your book."

27. Future Sounds—Karda Estra 2016—CD—GB. This is a self-released EP on CD, and on here I played on one tune, Niall, which is named for my late son. Amy Fry plays clarinet, and Richard plays all other instruments. Besides his usual guitar, bass and keys, he plays glockenspiel, accordion, bouzouki, and of course, can't live without it, his trusty old Rastrophone.

28. Time and Stars—Karda Estra 2016—CD—GB. This is a full-length CD that includes the music on Future Sounds, and more. Here Richard adds to his arsenal with dulcimer, melodica and kalimba.

29. Elevenses—Daevid Allen Weird Quartet 2016—LP/CD—USA. This was a surprise. Daevid, Michael Clare (bass), Don Falcone (keys, synth, organ) and Trey Sabatelli (drums with The Tubes) had started, and then stopped making a second Weird Biscuit Teatime record some years ago. Trey was not available when the project was rejuvenated, so I got the call if I wanted in. Mind you, I had declined a New York Gong tour with Daevid way back in 1979. Nevertheless, we remained friends over the years, but I was frankly surprised when asked if I wanted to do this. Don and Daevid had done many records together already, and I am a huge Daevid fan, so I said okay. I had already met and seen Mike Clare, the bassist on this play with Daevid's GREAT group University of Errors. What I did not know was how ill Daevid was at this time. Few did, I guess. So, I recorded drums for about half the album, seven tunes. Sadly, Daevid passed away shortly after this was complete. No one knew this would be his last proper full album. He passed away in March of 2015. I miss him.

29. Empty Full Circulation—Jack Dupon 2016—CD/LP— FR. Jack Dupon is a great band from, get this, the village of Bongheat, France. Yup, it's a real place. I first met them when they were doing some shows in the U.S., and they played the Local 506 Chapel Hill, North Carolina preshow just ahead of Progday 2010. They played the RIO in France in 2011, when I was Guest Emeritus at that festival. Great, high energy Zappa-ish humor and great players. Lovely guys, and we are pals, and they sent me a tune to play on for this record, called *Burst Balloon*.

30. Superior State of Mind—Steve Holmquist 2016—(Paul produced) CD—USA. Steve is a great singer/songwriter, storyteller, neighbor and friend. Also a huge help when we moved from Apache Junction, AZ, to Superior, AZ. He really wanted to make a CD. Okay. He wanted to do this guitar/sing thing live in the studio. My only advice was "be prepared, know what you want to do, and have times." Plus, do not put new strings on the guitar the day we record. (they need time to stretch, or they won't stay in tune) Rarely have I worked with anyone as well prepared as he was. He had already played this music at gigs dozens of times, and so he had it all down. When he arrived, I asked what the time was. About an hour, he said. We came in at 57:57, which is goddamned close. Of the thirteen tunes he did, eight or nine are first takes. A nearly clam-free session. He knows his music. From sit down and start to ready to duplicate master we were at about total six hours in the studio. Whole enchilada in less than a day. I am still amazed.

31. Man or Muffin 4S'd—Sears, Scott, Swann and Stanley 2017—CD—USA. This record grew out of the aborted big band CD The Muffins were going to do. Dave Newhouse ended up pulling his tunes and recorded another disc called Manna/Mirage, on which I appear on a tune. Tom Scott wanted to press on with that project, and so he, myself, Billy Swann, and guitarist Mark Stanley recorded a bunch more of Tom's music and this disc is the result. The toughest remote project ever. Took me ages to learn, and then record my drum tracks.

32. Intergalactic Bastard—Lobotomatic 2017—CD—USA. Actually done and mastered mid-2018. Done recording a year ago. Out now on Bandcamp. Think early Back Sabbath.

33. Loon Attic—Nick Prol & The Proletarians 2017—CD— USA. Really cool song-oriented CD by this great Tucson muso. Lots of guests. I am on two tracks. Nick also did the cover and cartoons for this book.

34. Infernal Spheres—Karda Estra 2017—CD—GB. Another record featuring Richard Wileman's gorgeous compositions. I play on two tracks.

35. The Roadmap In Your Heart—Spirits Burning 2017— single—GB. Here is Gonzo Multimedia's first ever vinyl product. And it's a 45 RPM, no less. On this, I am on a track with Judy Dyble, Mike Howlett, Cyrille Verdeaux, Daevid Allen, Don Falcone and Jonathan Segel.

36. An Alien Heat—Spirits Burning with Michael Moorcock/ Al Bouchard 2018—CD—GB. On this one I appear on a track with Michael Moorcock, the well known Sci-fi author, and from Blue Oyster Cult and Blue Coupe, Al Bouchard.

37. As If in a Dream—TS Henry Webb—2018 project in

process. Includes Evan Dain on bass, Guy Filipelli on guitar and the great Jerry Goodman on violin.

Fun Best-Of Releases—Including Vintage LPs

Best of Ralph with Fred Frith 1982—LP—USA
Buy or Die, Ralph Records 1980—Sampler with great cover by Gary Panter—recordings from Fred Frith with The Muffins
Frank Johnson's Favorites 1981 with Fred Frith—LP—USA
Best of Clearlight (1975-2013) 2014—CD—GB
SPACE ROCK Interstellar Travelers Guide (With Daevid Allen Weird Quartet)

On Film

The Muffins Live at Orion—DVD—USA
NEARfest 2005—Rising to the Surface—DVD—USA

Romantic Warriors Progressive Music Saga—DVD—USA[4]
Romantic Warriors II RIO—DVD—USA
Romantic Warriors III Canterbury Tales—DVD—USA

The Advocate—Produced by Fishgate Productions. Paul produced music and has a cameo (Local Arizona film)

Rattlesnake Ranch, same as above, sans cameo

Paul Played with, and / or Appeared on Recordings

The Muffins: Off and on for over thirty-five years with the same personnel.

---

[4] Some of the Romantic Warriors series appears on PBS television in the USA.

Michael Manring: World renowned bassist, and old friend. We finally got to play together in my studio in Arizona during 2015. Visit him at: http://www.manthing.com

Jonathan Sindelman: Keys (Alan White Band, Keith Emerson Band, The Magic Band, The Steppes) Amazing keyboard player. We have done a few recording sessions at my Garage Mahal studio in AZ. Visit him at: https://sindelmanmusic.com

Nick Prol & The Proletarians: I am on one CD of Nick's, and hope to do more with him. He is also a wonderful artist, and did the art for this book.

Harvey Bainbridge: Keys (Hawkwind, Cyndee Lee Rule)
He was touring with Cyndee Lee Rule and stayed with us in Baltimore mid 2000s. I played with them at Orion Sound Studios in Baltimore and Harvey surprised me with an unplanned reggae groove. I cannot play reggae.

Braille Party: Great bass, guitar, drums trio
I played one show with this cool trio at DC Space back in the early 1980s.

Insect Surfers: This long standing surf rock band is based in LA, but Dave Arson, boss insect, is from the DC area. Insect Surfers started there. We were neighbors for awhile, and have been friends since the early 1980s. We would have dinner together once a week for awhile. I was even Insect for a Day once. We played together a few times. Dave also has a cool Iggy Pop tribute group called The Raw Power Rangers in LA. Visit them at: https://www.insectsurfers.com

Spirits Burning: (Don Falcone, Steve York and many others)
This is a long time going project by muso/producer Don Falcone. I have played on several of his records. He also

produced the Clearlight Impressionist Symphony disc I am on.

Robert Berry:, vocals, bass, 3 (with Keith Emerson and Carl Palmer), Spirits Burning
Robert is a great player and singer. We are on the Spirits Burning Starhawk disc together.

William Kopecky: Bass (Far Corner, Kopecky, Telescope Road) Tremendous bassist, and friend. We appear together on the above mentioned Starhawk disc and we played a festival jam with Mike Keneally and pals at Progday many years ago.

Spencer Campbell: Bass (Toy Matinee, Sheryl Crow, Kevin Gilbert). Great bassist, and did a whole day session with Jon Sindelman at my Garage Mahal studio in AZ, that was arranged by pal Ken Coffman.

Don Preston and Bunk Gardner: Don on keys, Bunk on woodwinds, (Frank Zappa, Mothers of Invention). Hosted them at our home in Baltimore when they were touring the Don And Bunk Show. Played with them some at the house, and played with them at their last gig of the April 2010 tour at Orion Sound Studios in Baltimore. Here's the skinny...

Don Preston: keyboards, vocals, iPod touch and gong
Bunk Gardner: saxophone, flute and vocals
Special guest: Paul Sears: drums and vocals

Setlist: Announcements and Introduction, *King Kong*, technical troubles and song intro, *The Eric Dolphy Memorial Barbecue*, Medley: *You Didn't Try to Call Me/Toads Of The Short Forest/The Idiot Bastard Son*, Pound for a Brown story, *Pound For a Brown* then *Free Energy*, Uncle Meat story, *Uncle Meat*, *Absolutely Free*, keyboard tuning, *Mother People*, Zappa's taste in music, *Go Cry on Somebody Else's Shoulder*, Don recites Carlin's "Modern Man",

Q&A session, *Hey Joe*, *Flower Punk/Bunk*, *Trouble Every Day*, *Who Are the Brain Police*, *Neon Meate Dream of a Octafish*, food freakout, *Evelyn*, a *Modified Dog*, *Help I'm a Rock*, *It Can't Happen Here*, *I'm the Slime*, *The Eternal Question*, encore: *Wowie Zowie*.

A highlight for me was (don't laugh) singing on *It Can't Happen Here*, *Who Are the Brain Police* and *Help I'm a Rock*—song faves from when I was a teen.

Fred Frith, John Greaves, Peter Blegvad: (Henry Cow, Slapp Happy and others)

I played on Fred's Gravity album with The Muffins, and one of my drum tracks from that record was reused on his next one, Cheap at Half the Price. Fred also played on and produced The Muffins 3rd LP called <185> in 1980. A little later, John Greaves and Peter Blegvad came over to the states from England. Peter may have even moved to NYC, or was about to by then. I forget. Fred, John, Peter, and The Muffins rehearsed (not nearly enough.) some great Blegvad/Greaves compositions at our house Rockville, Maryland. John Paige set up a gig near Georgetown University at Trinity Theatre that included all three of them, The Muffins, Mars Everywhere, and a German performance artist named Heinz that utilized a chair and a black and white TV in his act. Mike Zentner may have played violin with him, but I forget.

Steve Hillage: Guitar (Khan, Clearlight, Gong and more)
Great guitarist. Been a fan since the 1970s Khan days. He returned to the Clearlight fold and played on the Clearlight Impressionist Symphony record that I am on.

Daevid Allen: Guitar, vocals (Soft Machine, Gong, University of Errors, Daevid Allen Weird Quartet)

I had been a fan of his for most of my adult life, and played with him in NY in 1979 when I was asked to play in New York Gong, which I had to pass up because of practical considerations. Much later I was asked to play on a new Weird Biscuit Teatime CD, which became Daevid Allen Weird Quartet's ELEVENSES LP and CD. This is sadly, his last proper full album.

Tim Blake: Synths (Gong, Hawkwind, Clearlight)
He is also on the Clearlight Impressionist Symphony CD.

Didier Malherbe: Woodwinds, others (Gong, Clearlight)
He appears with me on the same Clearlight record as Steve Hillage.

Pepe Gonzalez: Bassist (Zapata, Magick Theatre)
Dear friend, and first bassist I was ever in a band with back in the late 1960s. We played together again in Magick Theatre in the mid 1970s. He is today a force in the Washington, DC jazz scene, and also teaches.

Thee Maximalists: This is the all improvising group Keith Macksoud (bass) and I started back in 2003. It did the proverbial snowball, and has since included many people, including Dave Newhouse. He came up with our motto: "All of the fun, and none of the work."

Jack Dupon: Great French band that I had seen a few times in France, and the U.S. I appear on an LP/CD of theirs called Empty Full Circulation. Would love to play live with them someday.

Karda Estra: Brainchild of Swindon, England-based multi-instrumentalist and composer Richard Wileman. We have done several CDs together. I hope to do more work with him, and perhaps help cause a Karda Estra festival appearance someday, somewhere, somehow.

Kavus Torabi: Guitar, Hurdy Gurdy (Karda Estra, Gong, Knifeworld, Guapo, Mediaeval Baebes) This is one busy dude. Great guitarist, and good friend. A few of the Karda Estra CDs are via his imprimatur, on his Believers Roast label in England. He also plays on KE CDs. Have yet to play with him live, but perhaps someday that will happen.

Present: The "dark and wonderful Present" as Chad Hutchinson called them at NEARfest. Lead by Belgian guitarist/composer Roger Trigaux. I was invited to play the TUBE, which was actually an old bomb shell at an Orion Sound Studios show in 2005 on the tune Promenade *Au Fond D'un Canal*. "Don't play the tube like a pussy" fearless leader Roger Trigaux told me. I tried to not do that.

Linda Cushma: Bass, Stick, vocals (Oxygene8, Clearlight)
I played with this great gal who is a fine bassist, singer, and stickist in her band Oxygene 8 with Francesco D'Angelo. Sadly the band broke up. She did, however, appear on the Clearlight Impressionist Symphony CD with me. Hope to work with her again someday.

Lobotomatic: So far I have done one truly heavy rock album with these guys, called Intergalactic Bastard. Just released in 2018 as of this writing. A follow up is being planned as I write.

Alan Davey: Bass (Hawkwind, Psychedelic Warlords, Spirits Burning, Lobotomatic) I have appeared on Spirits Burning CDs with Alan. Great bassist. He replaced Lemmy Kilminster in Hawkwind when Lemmy went off to start Motorhead.

Cyndee Lee Rule: Violin Great violinist. Good friend. She has gigged twice with Thee Maximalists and I was fortunate to do one great show with her and Harvey Bainbridge, ex keys guy in Hawkwind. She has also played with Daevid Allen, and Steve Jolliffe.

The Red Masque: Great avant-progressive band in the Philadelphia area. I guested together with David Kerman, also on drums, at a New Jersey Proghouse show of theirs back in 2006. Singer and co-founder Lynnette Shelley is a well known artist, and also designed and maintains my www.paulsears.net website. They arrange many concerts for themselves and others in the Philadelphia area. Lynnette also works with another band there in the Philadelphia area called Green Cathedral.

Elvis Death: Great band fronted by my vocalist friend Dan Neimann. I played with them briefly during the 1990s, but never got to do a gig.

9353: I played with several versions of this band starting in 1995 until 2007. They were unlike any other band in the Washington, DC area back in the 1980s when they started. This was when the DC hardcore punk scene was ramping up big time, and 9353 were a whole different animal, and musically a refreshing change from that. Song-oriented. I was a 9353 fan, and used to see them all the time in DC. My pal Bernie Wandel was their bassist for awhile. I had played with he and guitarist Phil Duarte in their band Guilt Combo. 9353 were practically the house band at the original old 9:30 club when it was at 930 F Street NW, hence the name. I think they were the only band ever to play every night for a whole week at DC Space.

Jay Tausig: Guitar (Spirits Burning, Hawkwind alums, etc.) Great guitarist/muso. He has done quite a lot of stuff. I am on a Spirits Burning track with him on the Starhawk disc.

Bernie Wandel: Bass (Henry Rollins, 9353, Guilt Combo)

Great bassist, and friend from my Washington, DC days. I played with him and guitarist Phil Duarte in their band Guilt Combo, which was then a trio. Hope to play with Bernie again someday. He was also in 9353, but before I was. He is on the 9353 Insult to Injury/Magically Delicious CD.

Henry Kaiser: Guitar Quite well known guitarist. Has made a zillion records. I was honored to work with him back in 1980, and even do a couple of gigs. Hard to keep up with, as he has always been a busy guy.

John Ellis: Guitar (Peter Gabriel, Vibrators, Stranglers)
Great guitarist. He and I appear together on the Spirits Burning Starhawk disc.

David Byers: Guitar, vocals (The Enzymes, Static Disruptors, Human Rights) Lovely guy, and I met him when he was a kid. Recorded some jazz standards with him back in the late 1990s that were never released.

Bill Laswell: Bass, producer (has worked with too many to mention) I used to play with him occasionally in NYC before he became the monster producer he is now. We were to be in New York Gong together, but that did not pan out.

Dave Kerman: Drums (Present, Red Masque, Thinking Plague, 5UUs) A dear friend. Great drummer and ex label boss. We both sat in with The Red Masque at the NJ Proghouse in 2006.

Paul Whitehead: (Borg Symphony) He painted early Genesis, and Van Der Graaf Generator covers. I got to play with him at Progday in NC, back in 2003, doing an improvised Borg Symphony set. A real character.

Yanni Papadopoulos: Guitar (Stinking Lizaveta, Thee

Maximalists) Great Philadelphia guitarist, and pal. He did two shows with Thee Maximalists, including our first ever show.

Yochk'o Seffer: Piano, saxophones (Magma, Zao, Neffesh Music) Great sax and keyboard player that was with Magma early on, and later had his own groups, Zao, and Neffesh Music. We played together at the Zu Festival in NYC in 1978.

Steve Stills: Guitar CSN, CSNY, many others.
Got to jam with him once, back in the early 1980s in a small Washington, DC nightclub.

Cyrille Verdeaux's Clearlight: I was honored to both play live with Clearlight at Progday 2003 in North Carolina, and then record the Impressionist Symphony disc with Cyrille and a new Clearlight in 2014.

Marshall Allen and Knoel Scott, Saxophones, EVI (Sun Ra Arkestra) Both of them appear on The Muffins Double Negative, and Loveletter #2 CDs. I have been lucky enough play a couple of shows with Marshall when he guested with Thee Maximalists, and he appeared on our Crosstalk recording.

Elliott Levin: Saxes, flute, poetry (Cecil Taylor, New Ghost, Thee Maximalists); he's done many shows with Thee Maximalists and is a long time staple in the Philadelphia jazz scene.

Mike Keneally: Guitar, keyboards (Frank Zappa, Steve Vai, Mike Keneally Band, Joe Satriani and Dethklok); I have been lucky enough to be asked to jam with him at gigs, both in Baltimore, and Progday in North Carolina.

Bryan Beller: Bass (The Aristocrats, Dweezil Zappa, Mike Keneally, Steve Vai and Joe Satriani) Same as Mike Keneally.

Paul Sears

Glenn Phillips: Guitar (Hampton Grease Band and Glenn Phillips Band) Was part of the Progday jam with Mike Keneally.

MORGLBL: Great rock trio from France. Dear friends. Got to play some Hendrix with them at a gig in Baltimore years ago.

Andy West: Bass (Dixie Dregs, Crazy Backwards Alphabet, T. Lavitz) Got play with him for some hot hours in Arizona with in a band that never made it to the runway, SW@G. Andy on bass, Tony Garone on guitar/vocals, and Anthony Garone on guitar.

Doug Walker: Keys (Yeti Band, Alien Planetscapes)
Great keys and flute player that was a staple in the space rock scene for many years. Billy Swann, Dave Newhouse, and I did a gig with him opening for Mars Everywhere at American University in Washington, DC, I think, in 1979 or 80.

Jimmy Cavanaugh: Bass (Danny Gatton, Dream Kitchen, Sleepy La Beef, Jumpin Jupiter) Great player, and old friend that lived with me for awhile. I got to do a show with Dream Kitchen at the Lone Star club in NYC back in the 1990s.

T.S. Henry Webb: Keys, woodwinds, vocals (The Flock and others). Great keyboard and flautist. We have recorded and played live. We are doing a recording in 2018 called As If in a Dream.

Jerry Goodman: Violin (The Flock, Original Mahavishnu Orchestra). He is on the above recording with TS, and me.

Al Bouchard: Multi instruments (Blue Oyster Cult, Blue Coupe) I appear on track with him on the Alien Heat disc by Spirits Burning and Michael Moorcock.

Michael Moorcock: (Sci-Fi writer & singer, An Alien Heat,

Spirits Burning). Same as above.

Judy Dyble: Autoharp, vocals, piano, recorder (Giles, Giles & Fripp and Fairport Convention) Out of the blue, I got to be on a 45 vinyl with this great gal, *The Roadmap In Your Heart*. See discography.

Mike Howlett: Bass (Gong, Strontium 90, Spirits Burning and many others).

Cloud Over Jupiter: Great band, run by guitarist and bassist Jerry King. I have recorded a few tracks during 2018 for an upcoming COJ CD.

Randy George: Bass, This great bassist and composer, best known for his work with Neal Morse, lives about a half-hour from me here in Arizona. We have done a smidgen of playing, and I hope we get to do some serious work together someday!

Marion Brown: Saxophones, Guitar (Sun Ra, John Coltrane, Archie Shepp). The Muffins were honored to play a show with him in NYC on Broadway at Symphony Space.

About the Cover and the Cartoon Artist

NICK PROL IS a Tucson, Arizona-based cartoonist and the eponymous leader of noise-makers in "Nick Prol & The Proletarians."

When not making crude drawings while being held at gunpoint or composing music for deaf children, Nick can be found offering cheap taxidermy lessons underneath your nearest overpass.

Want some art? He can be found on Instagram as "spuzzwick".

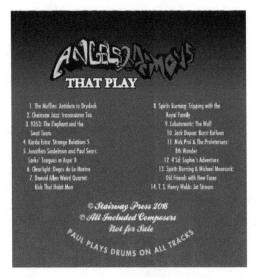

About the Included Music

INCLUDED FOR YOUR listening pleasure, I present a sampler CD that features music from some of the recordings I played on.

Track Listing for Angels and Demons that Play Music CD

Paul Plays drums on all tracks.

1. The Muffins—*Antidote to Drydock*
2. Chainsaw Jazz—*Iranasaurus Tex*
3. 9353—*The Elephant and the Swat Team*
4. Karda Estra—*Strange Relations 5*
5. Jonathan Sindelman/Paul Sears—*Larks' Tongues in Aspic II*
6. Clearlight—*Degas De La Marine*
7. Daevid Allen Weird Quartet—*Kick That Habit Man*
8. Spirits Burning—*Tripping With the Royal Family*
9. Lobotomatic—*The Wolf*
10. Jack Dupon—*Burst Balloon*

11. Nick Prol & The Proletarians—*8th Wonder*
12. 4S'd—*Sophie's Adventure*
13. Spirits Burning & Michael Moorcock—*Old Friends with New Faces*
14. T.S. Henry Webb—*Jet Stream*

Books purchased directly from Stairway Press with have the CD attached inside the back cover. For books purchased elsewhere, carefully tear out the last page and send it to Stairway Press (see address on the last page or the front of this book) along with USD $10 to cover printing and shipping. This $10 is a not-for-profit contribution. All profits (if there are any) will be donated to Seattle Music Partners.

http://www.seattlemusicpartners.org/donate.html

Special thanks to those who graciously gave me permission to use this music.

Cleopatra Records for allowing the use of *Kick That Habit Man* from the Daevid Allen Weird Quartet record titled Elevenses.

Cyrille Verdeaux for the use of the *Degas De La Marine* track from the Clearlight Impressionist Symphony CD.

Cuneiform Records for The Muffins track, *Antidote to Drydock* (Newhouse) on that label from the <185> recording, and for the Chainsaw Jazz track *Iranasaurus Tex* (Smoot) from the Disconcerto CD. Thanks to Mark Smoot and Dave Newhouse as well.

Robert Fripp for permission to use the heretofore unreleased *Larks Tongues in Aspic Part II* (Fripp) cover recorded by Jonathan Sindelman on keyboards and myself on drums. (Exclusive!)

Don Falcone for permission to use the Spirits Burning tracks from both the Starhawk (*Tripping with the Royal Family*) and An Alien Heat (Old Friends with New Faces) CDS. Al Bouchard from Blue Oyster Cult appears on this track. Alan Davey and Judge Smith appear on Tripping.

Richard Wileman for permission to use the Karda Estra track from the Strange Relations, (Wileman-Sears). *Strange Relations 5*.

Tom Scott for permission to use the 4S'd track *Sophie's Adventure* from the Man or Muffin CD

Jack Dupon for permission to use a track I played on, *Burst Balloon*, from the Jack Dupon Empty Full Circulation record.

Lobotomatic for permission to use *The Wolf*, (Bennett-Bennett) which is an outtake from the Intergalactic Bastard recording. (Exclusive!)

Dave Newhouse/The Muffins for permission to use *Antidote to Drydock* from the <185> CD.

Bruce Hellington of 9353 for the rare unreleased instrumental mix of *The Elephant and the Swat Team*. This track may or may not surface on a future 9353 release. Writ by Hellington-Hwang. Susan Hwang—keyboards, Bruce Hellington—guitars, Paul Sears—drums, Vance Bockis—bass, Darryl Willis—lead guitar, Doc Night—saxes. (Exclusive!)

Nick Prol for permission to use a track *8ᵗʰ Wonder* from the Nick Prol & The Proletarians Loon Attic CD.

T.S. Henry Webb For the use of a first pass mix of *Jet Stream*, a track from a current work in progress called As If in a Dream. Jerry Goodman plays violin on this, Evan Dain on bass, Guy Filipelli on guitar and Art Jiron on congas/bongos. (Exclusive!)

Internet Links

Cuneiform Records Bandcamp:
https://cuneiformrecords.bandcamp.com
and http://cuneiformrecords.com

Jon Sindelman: https://sindelmanmusic.com

Mike Heath: Michael maintains two blogs: *The San Francisco Nobody Sings* thesfnobodysings.blogspot.com, and *The Groover's Grotto*, at the website of fantasy novelist Tad Williams https://www.tadwilliams.com

Lobotomatic: https://lobotomatic.com

Dave Newhouse: http://www.mannamirage.com

Ted White:
https://fcnp.com/2016/12/29/press-pass-conduit
http://www.isfdb.org/cgi-bin/ea.cgi?1431
His reviews of progressive rock and jazz recordings can be found at:
http://www.societyartrock.org/dr-progresso/85-dr-progresso/81-dr-p-reviews.html

Chester Hawkins: http://www.chesterhawkins.org

Tommy Linthicum Tribute: http://www.tommylinthicum.com

Nick Prol: proletarians.bandcamp.com or email at:
spuzzwick@gmail.com

Karda Estra: http://www.kardaestra.co.uk

Tom Scott: http://www.4sd.biz/catalog.html

Spirits Burning:
http://home.earthlink.net/~falcone/sbmain.html

Robert Fripp and King Crimson: https://www.dgmlive.com

Jack Dupon: http://jackdupon.net

E. Doctor Smith: www.edoctorsmith.com

Jerry Donato: http://jerrydonato.com/

Publisher's Note

THOSE OF US who know and love Paul have certainly noticed his ever-present habit of uttering the rapid-fire phrase, "Right, right, right." This would not be an honest memoir without that staccato phrase ringing in our ears. So, here it is.

Say it and imagine Paul's characteristic mutterance.

Right, right, right!

Paul Sears

If the CD was not included in this book, carefully cut out this page and send it—along with USD $10.00—to the address below.

Stairway Press
1000 West Apache Trail, Suite 126
Apache Junction, AZ 85120

For questions: email Ken@StairwayPress.com

CPSIA information can be obtained
at www.ICGtesting.com
Printed in the USA
JSHW020338050122
21803JS00002B/136